The Grammar Dictionary

by

Dr. George Stern

To Deborah—together through thick and thin ...

The Grammar Dictionary

First published in 2000 by R.I.C. Publications
Republished 2001

American English version published in 2001 by R.I.C. Publications
Published in the United States and Canada by Didax Inc. – *info@didaxinc.com*
Distributed in Japan and Korea by Tuttle Publishing/Tuttle ELT – *tuttle@gol.com*

Copyright Dr George Stern 2000

R.I.C. Publications, PO Box 332, Greenwood WA 6924

"The most impressive of human abilities is that of language."

— John D Barrow (astronomer), *Impossibility*.

"Grasping grammatical theory provides an intellectual pleasure that is rare in the social sciences."

— Steven Pinker (cognitive scientist), *The Language Instinct*.

"[There is] this continuous tension between the pure theories of syntax and the messy facts of language acquisition."

— Vivian J Cook (linguist), *Chomsky's Universal Grammar*.

"Language seems to "evolve" ... at a rate which is orders of magnitude faster than genetic evolution."

— Richard Dawkins (zoologist), *The Selfish Gene*.

"What we know about language today is only a fragment of what there is to be found out."

— MAK Halliday (linguist), *Terms in Systemic Linguistics*.

"I think that extreme precision of definition is not worthwhile, and sometimes it is not possible: in fact mostly it is not possible."

— Richard Feynman (theoretical physicist), *The Meaning of It All*.

"There is a thimbleful of knowledge [about language] that has been attained in careful experimental work and rigorous data-processing ..."

— Noam Chomsky (linguist), *Language and Mind*.

"The beginning of wisdom, as the Chinese say, is calling things by their right names."

— Edward O Wilson (zoologist), *The Diversity of Life*.

Introduction

This dictionary is for students and for general readers alike—anyone who might be interested in knowing what is meant by "noun", "verb", "subject" or "predicate" and the like. It is intended to offer accessible information on language and grammar. I mention language and grammar together, because they are intimately bound together: grammar is the organizing principle of language, and language makes sense because it is grammatically organized.

We can see the organizing (some call it "structuring") role of grammar from the two sentences: "Jack looked for Jill" and "Jill looked for Jack." These sentences have the same words, but they give us different senses because they are differently organized. And the string of words "For looked Jill Jack" makes no sense at all because it is not organized at all.

The plan of the book is to deal with the most common grammar terms in some 250 self-contained entries. Each term is defined and explained in the simplest, clearest language possible, without compromising scholarly integrity. The latter condition means that there are a few entries that are harder than others to understand. Overall, though, the explanations, taken together with the illustrative examples, should make the entries accessible to the careful reader.

The illustrative examples come from over a hundred real-life texts that range from newspaper headlines and magazine articles to literary and scientific books. The texts are at the heart of the *Dictionary*, because they serve to illustrate the points of grammar. They also serve two other purposes.

One is to get away from the sort of trivial examples that most grammar texts use as illustrations—"The fox chased the hare." The other is to show that the grammar features actually exist: real people in the real world use them.

To give an example. I often hear discussions over whether you can use conjunctions (words such as *and*, *but*, *because*) at the start of sentences. Some say yes; others say no. You can adduce all sorts of reasons on either side of the argument—just as you can reason over whether the world should be flat or round. But the discussion stops when you look at the real world and at real texts. If they show things one way or the other, that authenticates them. By the way, if you are interested in the *and-but-because* question, look up the entry LANGUAGE MYTH.

In writing a work such as this, there are two problems. One problem is what to call the various grammar features that the book deals with. There are some half dozen competing grammar systems, each with differing terms for the same grammar features. So, for example, one grammarian's "*–ing*" form is another grammarian's "present participle" or "gerund."

As Sidney Greenbaum wrote despairingly, "There is no standard terminology for grammar" (1988:42). Or John Lyons: "There is unfortunately no generally accepted set of notational conventions [in grammar]" (1981:47).

The solution to this problem adopted in the present work is twofold: first, to use the terms most current among modern grammarians; second, to cross-reference the entries so that, if you don't catch any given term under one entry, you will be led to another. I have also, in brackets under many entries, given the alternative name or names for the entry term.

Still on the subject of terminology: I have found, both in teaching grammar and in writing this book, that for some quite significant grammar features there are no extant terms at all. The great Otto Jespersen (1860–1943) found it necessary to invent "a few new technical terms" (I counted thirty or so); Noam Chomsky (1928–) has invented scores. I was tempted to coin a dozen but—this is the good news—restricted myself to two essential ones (see EXTRA and COMPLETION).

The other problem, which is somewhat related to the first, is which slant to use for the grammar explanations: traditional grammar, transformational generative grammar, systemic functional grammar, tagmemics, structuralist grammar, or what? The solution I have adopted is to try for a synthesis. But where the synthesis breaks down, I simply flag the differences among the differing grammar systems—see, for example, PHRASE.

I have also devoted separate entries to terms derived from different grammar systems. So, for example, we have SYNTAGM AND PARADIGM from structuralist grammar, ACTOR, BENEFICIARY, GOAL from functional grammar, PROJECTION from universal grammar, and so on.

But for most entries, neither a synthesis nor a separation is necessary. For most concepts, there is agreement among grammarians across the board. For example, there is little or no disagreement, even among scholars of divergent views, about how to define MODAL VERB or UNMARKED INFINITIVE or TAG QUESTION. Hence the body of this work incorporates expert consensus and is, therefore, uncontroversial.

To those who may disagree with my treatment of any term, I extend an invitation to take up the issue by writing to me care of the publisher. Nothing will make me happier than to learn something new or to be shown the error of my ways.

George Stern, 2000.

Acknowledgments

I am most grateful to Dr Wayne Beswick—severe critic and good friend—who trawled through several versions of this work and saved it from many errors and infelicities. Any errors that remain are my own.

World Library Inc. (Irvine CA, 1994) has kindly permitted the use of quotations from *Library of the Future*, Compact Disc, of their editions of the following works.

Henry Adams, *The Education of Henry Adams*
Louisa May Alcott, *Little Women*
Jane Austen, *Pride and Prejudice*
Jane Austen, *Sense and Sensibility*
The Bible, *Authorized Version*
William Blake, "Auguries of Innocence"
James Boswell, *The Life of Samuel Johnson*
Lord Byron, *Don Juan*
Charlotte Brontë, *Jane Eyre*
Emily Brontë, *Wuthering Heights*
Robert Browning, "Song"
Thomas Bulfinch, *The Age of Chivalry*
Lewis Carroll, *Alice in Wonderland*
Lewis Carroll, *Sylvie and Bruno*
Lewis Carroll, *Through the Looking-Glass*
Geoffrey Chaucer, *Canterbury Tales*
Wilkie Collins, *Moonstone*
Joseph Conrad, *The Heart of Darkness*
Joseph Conrad, *Lord Jim*
Stephen Crane, "The Blue Hotel"
Charles Darwin, *The Origin of Species*
Charles Dickens, *David Copperfield*
Charles Dickens, *Great Expectations*
Charles Dickens, *Hard Times*
Charles Dickens, *Oliver Twist*
Charles Dickens, *A Tale of Two Cities*
Emily Dickinson, *Poems*
Arthur Conan Doyle, "Black Peter"
Arthur Conan Doyle, "The Blanched Soldier"
Arthur Conan Doyle, "The Crooked Man"
Theodore Dreiser, *Sister Carrie*
John Dryden, *All for Love*
Nathaniel Hawthorne, *House of the Seven Gables*
Nathaniel Hawthorne, "The Ambitious Guest"
Washington Irving, *Alhambra*
Washington Irving, "The Country Church"
Henry James, *Daisy Miller*
Henry James, *Washington Square*
James Joyce, *Portrait of the Artist as a Young Man*
Charles Lamb, *Essays of Elia*

DH Lawrence, *Sons and Lovers*
Jack London, *The Call of the Wild*
John Stuart Mill, *On Liberty*
LM Montgomery, *Anne of Green Gables*
Thomas Paine, *The Age of Reason*
Edgar Allen Poe, "The Angel of the Odd"
Alexander Pope, *The Rape of the Lock*
Ezra Pound, "Dance Figure"
Anna Sewell, *Black Beauty*
William Shakespeare, *Hamlet*
William Shakespeare, *Macbeth*
William Shakespeare, *Othello*
William Shakespeare, "Sonnet 16"
William Shakespeare, *Venus and Adonis*
George Bernard Shaw, *Man and Superman*
George Bernard Shaw, *Pygmalion*
Mary Shelley, *Frankenstein*
Percy Bysshe Shelley, "To a Skylark"
Richard Sheridan, *School for Scandal*
Adam Smith, *The Wealth of Nations*
Edmund Spenser, *The Faerie Queen*
John Steinbeck, *Pearl*
Robert Louis Stevenson, *El Dorado*
Robert Louis Stevenson, *Kidnapped*
Robert Louis Stevenson, *The New Arabian Nights*
Robert Louis Stevenson, *Treasure Island*
Alfred, Lord Tennyson, "Break, Break, Break"
Mark Twain, *The Adventures of Huckleberry Finn*
Mark Twain, *The Adventures of Tom Sawyer*
Mark Twain, *Innocents Abroad*
Mark Twain, *Life on the Mississippi*
Lew Wallace, *Ben Hur*
Edith Wharton, *Ethan Frome*
Oscar Wilde, *The Importance of Being Earnest*
Oscar Wilde, *Lady Windermere's Fan*
Oscar Wilde, *The Picture of Dorian Gray*
Oscar Wilde, *A Woman of No Importance*
Mary Wollstonecraft, *Vindication of the Rights of Woman*

I also gratefully acknowledge the generosity and kindness of the authors, publishers and copyright holders who have allowed me to use citations from the following books.

Jean Aitchison. 1994. *Words in the Mind: An Introduction to the Mental Lexicon.* Oxford: Blackwell.

Jean Aitchison. 1997. *The Language Web: The Power and Problem of Words.* Cambridge: CUP.

Francis Crick. 1994. *The Astonishing Hypothesis: The Scientific Search for the Soul.* London: Touchstone Books.

Paul Davies. 1994. *The Last Three Minutes: Conjectures about the Ultimate Fate of the Universe.* London: Weidenfeld and Nicolson.

Richard Dawkins. 1989. *The Selfish Gene.* Third edition. Oxford: OUP.

Daniel C Dennett. 1995. *Darwin's Dangerous Idea: Evolution and the Meanings of Life.* London: Allen Lane, The Penguin Press.

Jared Diamond. 1991. *The Rise and Fall of the Third Chimpanzee.* London: Vintage.

Fred Hoyle and Chandra Wickramasinghe. 1996 [1993]. *Our Place in the Cosmos: The Unfinished Revolution.* London: Phoenix.

Caroline Jones. 1992. *The Search for Meaning: Conversations with Caroline Jones.* Sydney: The Australian Broadcasting Corporation and Collins Dove.

Caroline Jones. 1995. *The Search for Meaning Collection.* Sydney: The Australian Broadcasting Corporation and Harper Collins.

Richard Leakey and Roger Lewin. 1993. *Origins Reconsidered: in Search of What Makes Us Human.* London: Abacus.

Melina Marchetta. 1992. *Looking for Alibrandi.* Melbourne: Penguin Australia.

Celia M Millward. 1988. *A Biography of the English Language.* New York: Harcourt Brace Jovanovich.

Bill Moyers. 1989. *Bill Moyers: A World of Ideas.* Edited by Betty Sue Flowers. New York: Doubleday. (Copyright 1989 by Public Affairs Television Inc. Used by permission of Doubleday, a division of Bantam Doubleday Dell Publishing Group Inc.)

Laurie Oakes. 1998–99. *The Bulletin* columns. Sydney: Australian Consolidated Press.

George Orwell. 1968. *Collected Essays, Journalism and Letters.* In four volumes, edited by Sonia Orwell and Ian Angus. Harmondsworth: Penguin.

George Orwell. 1986 [1933]. *Down and Out in Paris and London.* London: Penguin.

Parliamentary Debates: House of Representatives Hansard. 1998. Canberra: Commonwealth Government Printer.

Patricia Shaw. 1994. *Valley of Lagoons.* Sydney: Reader's Digest.

Ric Throssell. 1998. *Jackpot.* Canberra: Ginninderra Press.

The publishers of the following periodicals have kindly made texts from their publications available for citation.

The Economist. 1998–99. London: The Economist Newspaper Limited.

New Scientist. 1997–99. London: New Science Publications.

Presidents & Prime Ministers. 1999. Glen Ellyn, IL: EQES.

TIME. 1996–99. New York: Time Inc.

The ABC Cricket Book. 1998–99. Sydney: The Australian Broadcasting Corporation.

National Geographic. 1999. Washington: National Geographic Society.

I have also used a number of short quotations culled from a variety of sources, including the following:

Australian Chess Forum. 1998. Canberra: Australian Chess Forum.

BBC. 1998. *The World Today.*

Inside Edge. 1998. Sydney: Australian Consolidated Press.

The Oxford Dictionary of Quotations. 1974 [1953]. Second edition. London: OUP.

The Oxford English Dictionary. 1992. Compact disc, second edition. Oxford: OUP.

New in Chess. 1999. Alkmaar: Interchess BV.

From these and additional sources, I have cited texts from the following authors and personalities.

Walter Bagehot	Princess Diana	John F Kennedy
GP Baker and PMS Hacker	Henry Fielding	John Lyons
Wayne Beswick	John Fisher	John Ruskin
Leonard Bloomfield	Mahatma Gandhi	Edward Sapir
Robert Burchfield	Sidney Greenbaum	Ferdinand de Saussure
Earl of Chesterfield	MAK Halliday	Boris Spassky
Noam Chomsky	Patrick Henry	James Watson
Winston Churchill	Robert Herrick	Mark Waugh
Bill Clinton	R Jakobson and M Halle	Guy West
David Crystal	Otto Jespersen	William Whewell
René Descartes	Samuel Johnson	

For a critical note (see LANGUAGE MYTH) I have quoted from the following.

Edward Down. 1991. *Mastering Grammar.* Melbourne: Longman Cheshire.

Adapted texts come from two sources:

George Coote. 1994. *The Serious Joke Book.* Norman Park, Qld: Gap Publications.
Fred Metcalf (editor). 1993. *The Penguin Dictionary of Jokes.* London: Penguin.

Note: This edition uses American spelling.

List of entries

A

a or *an*
abbreviation
absolute construction
accidence
accusative—see case
acronym—see abbreviation
active—see voice
actor, beneficiary, goal
adjective
adjective subclasses
adjective clause
adjective phrase
adjunct
adverb
adverb subclasses
adverb clause
adverb phrase
affix
agreement of antecedent and pronoun
agreement of subject and verb
alliteration—see figure of speech
alternative question—see question types
ambiguity
anaphor—see reference
And at the start of a sentence—see language myth
anomalous finite
antecedent and pro-form
antithesis—see figure of speech
antonomasia—see figure of speech
apostrophe—see figure of speech
apposition
article
aspect—see tense and aspect
assonance—see figure of speech
attribute
attributive and predicative
auxiliary verb

B

base form—see root and stem
Because at the start of a sentence—see language myth
beneficiary—see actor, beneficiary, goal

blend—see abbreviation
But at the start of a sentence—see language myth

C

case
cataphor—see reference
chain and choice—see syntagm and paradigm
chiasmus—see figure of speech
circumstance—see participant, process, circumstance
clause
clause complex
clause types
clauses, their interrelationships
cleft sentence—see sentence types
cliché—see figure of speech
clipping—see abbreviation
closed class—see open and closed classes
cohesion
common gender—see gender
comparative—see degrees of comparison
complement—see completion
completion
complex sentence—see sentence types
compound
compound sentence—see sentence types
compound-complex sentence—see sentence types
conditional
conjoined clause—see clause types
conjunction
conjunction subclasses
content word and function word
context
continuous aspect—see tense and aspect
contraction—see abbreviation
coordinate clause—see clause types
copula—see transitivity
count noun and noncount noun

D

dative—see case
degrees of comparison
demonstrative—see determiner
dependent clause—see clause types
determiner

nominative—see case

nonfinite clause

nonstandard—see standard and nonstandard English

noun

noun subclasses

noun clause

noun phrase

null element

number

O

object

objective—see case

onomatopoeia—see figure of speech

open and closed classes

oxymoron—see figure of speech

P

paradigm—see syntagm and paradigm

paradox—see figure of speech

parallelism—see figure of speech

parse

participant, process, circumstance

participle

participle phrase

particle

parts of speech—see word classes

passive—see voice

past participle—see participle

past participle phrase—see participle phrase

past tense—see tense and aspect

patient—see actor, beneficiary, goal

perfect aspect—see tense and aspect

person

personification—see figure of speech

phrasal verb

phrase

phrase in modern grammar

phrase in traditional grammar

platitude—see figure of speech

plural—see number

positive—see degrees of comparison and mood

possessive—see case

prefix—see affix

preposition

preposition at the end of a sentence—see language myth

preposition phrase

present participle—see participle

present participle phrase—see participle phrase

present tense—see tense and aspect

process—see participant, process, circumstance

pro-form—see antecedent and pro-form

progressive aspect—see tense and aspect

projection

pronoun

pronoun subclasses

pun—see figure of speech

Q

quantifier—see determiner

question tag—see anomalous finite

question types

R

reference

register

relative clause—see adjective clause

relative pronoun

rheme—see theme and rheme

root and stem

S

sarcasm—see figure of speech

sentence

sentence parts

sentence types

simile—see figure of speech

simple aspect—see tense and aspect

simple sentence—see sentence types

singular—see number

split infinitive—see infinitive

standard and nonstandard English

stem—see root and stem

strong verb—see irregular verb

subject—see sentence parts

subjective—see case

subjunctive

subordinate clause—see clause types

suffix—see affix
superlative—see degrees of comparison
synecdoche—see figure of speech
syntagm and paradigm
syntax

T

tag question—see question types
tenor—see context
tense and aspect
text grammar
theme and rheme
transition word—see extra
transitivity
turn-taking

V

verb
verb phrase
verbal
very true—see language myth
vocative
voice

W

weak verb—see irregular verb
wh-question—see question types
word classes
word formation—see affix

Y

yes-no question—see question types

Z

zero—see null element
zeugma—see figure of speech

A* or *AN—two forms of the indefinite article (see ARTICLE). You use *an* before an initial vowel sound (usually spelled *a–, e–, i–, o–* or *u–*), and *a* before an initial consonant sound. Here are some examples.

VOWEL SOUND	CONSONANT SOUND
an apple	a game
an evening	a song
an idea	a poem
an order	a flower
an underpass	a letter

There are three initial letters that are problematic: "o," "u" and "h." Before these letters you use *an* if the word begins with a vowel sound, and you use *a* if the word begins with a consonant sound.

1. A word beginning with "o":

- takes *an* if the letter "o" is pronounced like a vowel ("o"):

an only child	an odd number

- takes *a* if the letter "o" is pronounced like a consonant ("wuh"):

a one-day wonder	a once-in-a-lifetime chance

2. A word beginning with "u":

- takes *an* if the letter "u" is pronounced like a vowel ("uh"):

an urn	an usher	an urge	an uncle

- takes *a* if the letter "u" is pronounced like a consonant ("yoo"):

a university	a union	a utopia	a unit

3. A word beginning with "h":

- takes *an* if the letter "h" is silent (unpronounced):

an hour	an honor	an honest person

- takes *a* if the letter "h" is audible (pronounced):

a human	a hot bath	a history book

There is some discussion about whether the words *historic* and *historical* take *a* or *an*. Some writers prefer the former; some the latter. You can feel free to use either but, in modern usage, *a* is more usual.

This is no fable, but <u>an historical</u> event I tell.
(Geoffrey Chaucer, *Canterbury Tales*. 14th century.)

We find them to have been as rational and shrewd to detect <u>an historic</u> anomaly as ourselves.
(Charles Lamb, *Essays of Elia*. 19th century.)

Johnson was engaged in preparing <u>an historical</u> account of the British Parliament.
(James Boswell, *The Life of Samuel Johnson*. 18th century.)

It was <u>an historic</u> moment.
(John Steinbeck, *Pearl*. 20th century.)

We have been in <u>a historical</u> section of country all day.
(Mark Twain, *Innocents Abroad*. 19th century.)

Adams became almost <u>a historical</u> monument in London.
(Henry Adams, *The Education of Henry Adams*. 19th century.)

The farm brought to mind Washington's Mount Vernon: a handsome setting linked to <u>a historical</u> figure.
(*National Geographic*, June 1999.)

Enrico Fermi co-invented and designed the first man-made nuclear reactor, starting it up in <u>a historic</u> secret experiment at the University of Chicago on Dec. 2, 1942.
(*TIME*, March 29, 1999.)

President Clinton is presently in the Middle East where he is about to make <u>a historic</u> visit to Gaza.
(BBC. *The World Today*, December 14, 1998.)

The same discussion goes on over the word *hotel*. Here too, *an* is old-fashioned; *a* is modern.

At the sea she stayed her month at <u>an hotel</u>.
(Henry James, *Washington Square*. 19th century.)

He perceived a man sleeping on the floor in the costume of <u>an hotel</u> under-servant.
(Robert Louis Stevenson, *The New Arabian Nights*. 19th century.)

"Good heavens, mamma!" cried Miss Rachel, "is this <u>an hotel</u>? Are there thieves in the house?"
(Wilkie Collins, *Moonstone*. 19th century.)

We all got into a coach, which took us to a beautiful large house, larger than this and finer, called <u>an hotel</u>.
(Charlotte Brontë, *Jane Eyre*. 19th century.)

I had supposed that establishment to be <u>a hotel</u> kept by Mr. Barnard.
(Charles Dickens, *Great Expectations*. 19th century.)

"I keep <u>a hotel</u>," he shouted.
(Stephen Crane, "The Blue Hotel." 19th century.)

"Blankets are for <u>a hotel</u>," said one of the men.
(Jack London, *Call of the Wild*. 20th century.)

I just wish I were a rich American and could spend my summer at <u>a hotel</u>.
(LM Montgomery, *Anne of Green Gables*. 20th century.)

The partners in the world's largest management consultancy have created something that feels like a cross between <u>a hotel</u> and a luxurious club. The reception desk looks like <u>a hotel</u> foyer.
(*The Economist*, September 13, 1999.)

ABBREVIATION—from the Latin for "brief" or "shortened." A shortened or incomplete form of a written or spoken word or words. There are various types of abbreviations, and they go under different names. But you can also call all or any of the following by the generic name "abbreviation."

1. **Initialism**—a word that is formed by initial letters that are individually pronounced.

BBC	(bee-bee-see) [British Broadcasting Corporation]
WHO	(double-you-aitch-oh) [World Health Organisation]

2. **Acronym**—a word formed by initial letters that are pronounced together as a word.

Qantas	[Queensland and Northern Territory Aerial Services Ltd]
radar	[radio detection and ranging]

3. **Clipping**—(also called "reduction") a word with a part missing from the beginning, the end or both.

phone	[telephone]
fax	[facsimile]
flu	[influenza]

4. **Contraction**—a word written with a part missing from the middle.

Mr. [mister]	dept [department]

5. **Elision**—a word or a combination of words with an apostrophe to mark the missing letter or letters.

goin' [going]	I've [I have]

6. **Blend**—a fusion of two words, shortened and combined into one.

motel [motor + hotel]	brunch [breakfast + lunch]
smog [smoke + fog]	Internet [international + network]

ABSOLUTE CONSTRUCTION—a language form (underlined) that features a verb ending in *–ing*, with the *–ing* form having a subject (bold) different from that of the rest of the sentence.

ABSOLUTE CONSTRUCTION		REST OF THE SENTENCE	
Our team	having won,	**we all**	celebrated.
SUBJECT	*–ING* FORM	SUBJECT	VERB

Our team is the subject of the absolute construction; *we all* is the subject of the rest of the sentence.

Here are two textual examples.

ABSOLUTE CONSTRUCTION		REST OF THE SENTENCE	
The agreement being ratified,		**Elidure** took the crown	
SUBJECT	*–ING* FORM	SUBJECT	VERB
The marriage being solemnized,		**the Trojans** took to the sea.	
SUBJECT	*–ING* FORM	SUBJECT	VERB

(Thomas Bulfinch, *The Age of Chivalry*.)

The absolute construction is similar to that of a present participle phrase. ("Present participle" is another name for an *–ing* form.) The difference between an absolute construction and a present participle phrase is that the former does, and the latter does not, have a separate subject.

ABSOLUTE CONSTRUCTION		REST OF THE SENTENCE	
The children	being tired,	**the whole family** went home.	
SUBJECT	–ING FORM	SUBJECT	VERB

PARTICIPLE PHRASE	REST OF THE SENTENCE		
Being tired	**the whole family** went home.		
–ING FORM	SUBJECT	VERB	

See PARTICIPLE PHRASE.

ACCIDENCE—a term used in traditional grammar for variations in word forms. For example, the variation from singular to plural in nouns (*nose—noses*); from plural to singular in verbs (*see—sees*); from present to past in verbs (*walk—walked*); and so on. In modern grammar, such changes are seen as belonging to morphology. See MORPHOLOGY.

The word "accidence" is related to "accident," suggesting that some word changes (*mouse—mice*, not *mouses*) seem to happen just like that, as if by accident.

ACCUSATIVE—See CASE.

ACRONYM—See ABBREVIATION.

ACTIVE—See VOICE.

ACTOR, BENEFICIARY, GOAL—terms in functional grammar.

1. **What are "actor," "beneficiary," "goal"?**

   They are grammar terms for the roles that nouns (or noun equivalents such as pronouns) can play in a sentence.

   • THE ACTOR is the agent (the doer) of the process expressed by the verb.

   • THE BENEFICIARY is the receiver of the process expressed by the verb.

   • THE GOAL (also called "patient") is the done-to of the process expressed by the verb.

Chris	**sent**	Kim	a letter.
ACTOR	PROCESS	BENEFICIARY	GOAL

In the example above, *Chris* is the actor (the doer of the sending); *Kim*, the beneficiary (the receiver of what is sent); *a letter*, the goal (the thing that the sending is done to).

The three roles—actor, beneficiary, goal—are jointly referred to as "participants" (or "arguments") of the sentence. They relate to the process of the sentence, expressed by a verb. So, in the boxed example above, the verb *sent* expresses the process of the sentence; and *Chris*, *Kim* and *a letter* are the participants that relate to the process.

The three terms (actor, beneficiary, goal) remain invariant—unchanged—wherever in the sentence the words *Chris*, *Kim* and *a letter* occur.

Chris	**sent**	Kim	a letter.
ACTOR	PROCESS	BENEFICIARY	GOAL

Kim	**was sent**	a letter	by Chris.
BENEFICIARY	PROCESS	GOAL	ACTOR

A letter	**was sent**	to Kim	by Chris.
GOAL	PROCESS	BENEFICIARY	ACTOR

In the following text, there is one process (expressed by a verb in bold) on each line. Each process is accompanied by one or more participants.

Mrs. Dashwood	**gave**	her	an answer
ACTOR	PROCESS	BENEFICIARY	GOAL

which	**marked**	her contempt,	
	PROCESS	GOAL	

and	**left**	the room.	
	PROCESS	GOAL	

A letter	**was delivered**	to her	from the post,
GOAL	PROCESS	BENEFICIARY	

which	**contained**	a proposal particularly well timed.	
	PROCESS	GOAL	

(Jane Austen, *Sense and Sensibility*.)

2. Syntactic and functional terms.

In a syntactic analysis of the first example sentence in part 1 above, we would use the following grammar terms.

Chris	**sent**	Kim	a letter.
SUBJECT	VERB	INDIRECT OBJECT	DIRECT OBJECT

If we put *Kim* or *a letter* in front of the verb, *Kim* or *a letter* becomes the "subject."

Kim	was sent a letter by Chris.
SUBJECT	VERB

A letter	was sent to Kim by Chris.
SUBJECT	VERB

In the functional analysis, we called *Chris* the "actor," *Kim* the "beneficiary," *a letter* the "goal"—wherever in the sentence the words *Chris*, *Kim* and *a letter* stood. See part 1 above.

What is the reason for the variation of terms in a syntactic analysis and for the invariance of terms in a functional analysis?

It is that a syntactic analysis takes account of the grammar relationships of the words in a sentence. If you change the order of the words, the grammar labels also change.

But a functional analysis takes account of the logical relationships of the words in a sentence—*Chris* is always the doer and, therefore, the "actor" of the process; *Kim* is always the recipient and, therefore, the "beneficiary" of the process; *a letter* is always the done-to and, therefore, the "goal" of the process. In a functional analysis it makes no difference where the words stand in the sentence.

So the two sets of terms reflect different kinds of analyses: one looks at the invariant functional roles of the participants; the other looks at the variant grammar relationships of the words.

3. A note on terminology.

The functional terms discussed above come from Halliday, 1994. In earlier works, Halliday sometimes used "patient" for "goal", but in 1994 he settled on the term "goal." His example sentence is *The lion caught the tourist*, and he comments:

> The doing ... was directed at, or extended to, the tourist. The term Goal implies directed at; another term that has been used for this function is Patient, meaning one that suffers or undergoes the process. We will keep the familiar term Goal in the present analysis, although neither of the two really hits the mark ... (109–110).

I agree with Halliday that neither "patient" nor "goal" is particularly apt. Nor, in my view, are "actor" and "beneficiary." Take the sentence:

The police officer	**handed**	the innocent man	an arrest warrant.
ACTOR	PROCESS	BENEFICIARY	GOAL (OR PATIENT)

I don't know that the police officer would appreciate being called an "actor," or that the innocent man would consider himself to be the "beneficiary" of the arrest warrant, or that the arrest warrant is properly described as a "patient" or a "goal." The trouble is that the words in quotation marks have connotations outside, as well as inside, the field of grammar.

I would prefer the more neutral terms:

- AGENT   for "actor"
- RECIPIENT   for "beneficiary"
- TARGET   for "patient" or "goal."

But the terms bequeathed to us by Halliday in 1994 will probably stay in use.

ADJECTIVE—from the Latin for "putting near." One of the word classes. Adjectives are usually near nouns or pronouns.

1. How do you identify adjectives?

(a) Adjectives are words that modify (that is, enhance or change) the meaning of a noun or of a noun equivalent such as a pronoun. If we take the noun *trees*, for example, we can modify the noun with any of a variety of adjectives (underlined):

> tall trees   American trees   interesting trees   gnarled trees

(b) We can also identify adjectives from the fact that they can be scaled on degrees of comparison with –*er* (or *more*) and –*est* (or *most*).

DEGREES OF COMPARISON FOR ADJECTIVES

POSITIVE	COMPARATIVE	SUPERLATIVE
fine	finer	finest
big	bigger	biggest
lovely	lovelier	loveliest
popular	more popular	most popular

There are a few irregular comparatives and superlatives: *good*, *better*, *best* (not: *good*, *gooder*, *goodest*). See IRREGULAR ADJECTIVE.

The above two features—(a) and (b)—are enough to identify adjectives: any word that has both these features is an adjective. But adjectives have two more features as well.

(c) An adjective is any word that fits into the blank space in the following sentence frame. (This method works for most, but perhaps not all, adjectives.)

They are very _____. [shy distant helpful obliging kind ...]
           ADJECTIVE

(d) Adjectives come from various sources.

- Some adjectives derive from members of other word classes with the help of suffixes (underlined).

NOUN	ADJECTIVE	VERB	ADJECTIVE
fame	fam*ous*	create	creat*ive*
friend	friend*ly*	read	read*able*
thought	thought*ful*	digest	digest*ible*
fear	fear*less*	permit	permiss*ive*

- You can even derive adjectives from other adjectives with the suffix *–ish*.

ADJECTIVE	ADJECTIVE
big	bigg*ish*
cheap	cheap*ish*

- But many adjectives are not derived—they are original.

hot	cold	bright	dim	red	blue

All of the above features—from (a) to (d)—define what adjectives are.

2. What do adjectives modify?

Adjectives (underlined) modify nouns and noun equivalents (bold).

Piaget grew up near Lake Neuchatel in a <u>quiet</u> **region** of <u>French</u> **Switzerland**.
                                       ADJECTIVE NOUN   ADJECTIVE NOUN

He found the secrets of <u>human</u> **learning**.
                    ADJECTIVE GERUND

Though **he** may not be as <u>famous</u> as Freud, his **contribution** to psychology may be <u>more lasting</u>.
  PRONOUN   ADJECTIVE   NOUN   ADJECTIVE

Disciples of Piaget have a tolerance for children's <u>primitive</u> **laws of physics**.
                                          ADJECTIVE NOUN PHRASE

Whether this has led to deeper understanding remains, like everything about Piaget, <u>controversial</u>.
           NOUN CLAUSE   ADJECTIVE

(*Time*, March 29, 1999.)

Here is another text, with the adjectives underlined and the words that they modify in bold.

> The revolution in <u>mathematical</u> **logic** early in the 20th century opened up a <u>delicious</u> **prospect**: a <u>rigorous</u> **science** of meanings. Just as the <u>atomic</u> **theory** in physics had begun to break matter down into its <u>constituent</u> **parts** and show how they fit together to produce all the effects in nature, logic held out the promise of accounting for all <u>meaningful</u> **texts and utterances**—from philosophy and <u>geometrical</u> **proofs** to history and legislation—by breaking them into their <u>logical</u> **atoms** and showing how those parts fit together in an <u>ideal</u> **language** to compose all the meanings there could be. (*TIME*, March 29, 1999.)

3. Where do adjectives stand in a sentence?

Adjectives can stand in either of two positions.

(a) They can stand before the words that they modify, in which case they are called "premodifiers" or "attributive adjectives."

> It's so exciting receiving tablecloths and <u>crocheted</u> **doilies**.
> "You can't catch <u>old</u> **age** by sleeping with your grandmother."
> Sister gave us a <u>funny</u> **look**. But I'm past the <u>caring</u> **stage**.
> (Melina Marchetta, *Looking for Alibrandi*.)

(b) They can stand after the words that they modify, in which case they are called "postmodifiers" or "predicative adjectives."

> **I** am not <u>sure</u> why I put up with it.
> **Seraphina** is <u>skinny</u> yet <u>voluptuous</u>.
> **Sister Gregory** is <u>famous</u> for nostril-flaring.
> The **car** is <u>black</u> and <u>red</u>. (Melina Marchetta, *Looking for Alibrandi*.)

ADJECTIVE SUBCLASSES—there are three subclasses of adjectives, one of them with two subdivisions.

1. COMMON ADJECTIVES: little, sharp

2. PROPER ADJECTIVES: Churchillian, Machiavellian

3. VERBAL ADJECTIVES
   - (a) Present Participles: interesting, boring
   - (b) Past Participles: interested, bored

We look at each of these below.

1. What are common adjectives?

Common adjectives (also called "descriptive adjectives") are everyday descriptive words (underlined).

<u>small</u> wonder	<u>fine</u> food	<u>red</u> flowers
<u>comfortable</u> chairs	<u>childish</u> behavior	

All the adjectives listed under the entry ADJECTIVE (part 1 (d)) are common adjectives.

2. What are proper adjectives?

Proper adjectives (underlined) are those that derive from proper nouns and that are usually spelled with initial capital letters.

<u>British</u> people	<u>American</u> music	<u>Australian</u> wool
a <u>Machiavellian</u> plot	a <u>Churchillian</u> speech	

3. What are verbal adjectives?

Verbal adjectives are participle verbs (see PARTICIPLE) used as adjectives. There are two kinds of participles: present participles and past participles—and both can function as adjectives.

(a) Present participles (underlined) always end with the suffix *–ing* and, as verbal adjectives, they modify nouns (bold).

> We aren't different enough to make the life-<u>defining</u> **difference** that people cherish.
>   PRESENT PARTICIPLE   NOUN
>
> There is an <u>underlying</u> **agreement** between them.
>   PRESENT PARTICIPLE   NOUN
>
> The information-<u>encoding</u> **properties** of real language are practically limitless.
>   PRESENT PARTICIPLE   NOUN
>
> Was language necessary for this great <u>civilizing</u> **advance**?
>   PRESENT PARTICIPLE   NOUN
>
> (Daniel C Dennett, *Darwin's Dangerous Idea*.)

(b) Past participles (underlined) typically end with the suffix *–en* or *–ed* or *–t* and, as verbal adjectives, they modify nouns (bold).

> The difference is due to two <u>intermeshed</u> **factors**.
>   PAST PARTICIPLE   NOUN
>
> Olfaction is another, highly emotionally <u>charged</u> **language**.
>   PAST PARTICIPLE   NOUN
>
> <u>Controlled</u> **experiments** could yield the answers.
> PAST PARTICIPLE   NOUN
>
> Weaver birds can weave audaciously <u>engineered</u> hanging **nests**.
>   PAST PARTICIPLE   NOUN
>
> (Daniel C Dennett, *Darwin's Dangerous Idea*.)

ADJECTIVE CLAUSE—(also called "relative clause") a clause that does the job of an adjective: that is, it modifies a noun (bold) or a noun equivalent such as a pronoun. Typically, an adjective clause (underlined) starts with a relative pronoun such as *who, whom, which, that, whose*.

> Some **people** <u>who depend on the Copper River</u> are beginning to worry that the next big spill will be a break in the pipeline.
> The town shelters some 7,500 **residents**, <u>most of whom, directly or indirectly, are economically dependent on bottom fish, crabs and salmon</u>.
> The **ecosystem** <u>that is there today</u> is not the **ecosystem** <u>that was there before the spill</u>, and that is due both to the effects of the spill and to natural **change**, <u>which is happening all the time</u>.
> (*National Geographic*, March 1999.)

See CLAUSE.

ADJECTIVE PHRASE—a term with different meanings in (1) traditional grammar and in (2) modern grammar.

1. In traditional grammar, an adjective phrase is a phrase that modifies a noun. (A phrase is a string of words that does not have a finite verb—see PHRASE.) In the examples below, the adjective phrases are underlined; the nouns that they modify, in bold.

> **Government and media**, <u>two bumptious and vainglorious institutions</u>, are not the best places to look for **judgments** <u>on anybody's personal life</u>.
> (*TIME*, January 4, 1999.)

> After twice failing to win a fellowship at the University of Cambridge's **Trinity College**, <u>a lodestar at the time for mathematicians from around the world</u>, Turing received a fellowship from King's College, Cambridge. King's provided <u>a remarkably free and tolerant **environment**</u> <u>for Turing</u>.
> (*TIME*, April 29, 1999.)

2. **In modern grammar,** an adjective phrase is either:

   (a)   an adjective (underlined)

   > War is a <u>dirty</u> **business**, and the war on drugs involves plenty of filth, including damage to <u>civil</u> **liberties**, not to mention <u>outright</u> **violence**.
   > (*The Economist*, January 2, 1999.)

   or

   (b)   a string of words (underlined) that has an adjective as its head word (bold underlined) and that modifies a noun—

   > If these were **<u>novel</u>** <u>or</u> **<u>incidental</u>** **mistakes**, **the war** might be <u>more **understandable**</u>. But modern drug policy has from the start involved fear and unreason.
   > (*The Economist*, January 2, 1999.)

   The difference between the traditional and the modern concepts of "adjective phrase" is as follows.

   - An "adjective phrase" in the traditional sense is a string of words that may, but need not, contain an adjective—it is enough that the phrase as a whole modifies a noun (or a noun equivalent).

   - An "adjective phrase" in the modern sense is either an adjective, or a string of words that has an adjective as its head (see HEAD) and that modifies a noun (or a noun equivalent).

See PHRASE.

ADJUNCT—a word that is related to the word "adjoining" or "joining." This suggests that adjuncts join other language units.

The grammar term "adjunct" is used in two different senses in (1) functional grammar and in (2) other grammars.

1. **Adjunct in functional grammar**

   An adjunct is any word or string of words that adjoins and modifies (that is, enhances or changes the meaning of) another word or string of words. In the example below, the adjuncts are underlined.

   > <u>Usually</u> I eat a <u>big</u> breakfast <u>early in the morning</u>.

   - *Usually* is a sentence adjunct: it modifies the whole of the rest of the sentence, *I eat a big breakfast*.

- *Big* is an adjectival adjunct: it modifies the noun *breakfast.*
- *Early in the morning* is an adverbial adjunct: it modifies the verb *eat.*

2. Adjunct in other grammars

An adjunct (also called a "sentence adverb") is an adverb that modifies a sentence as a whole and that is not part either of the subject or of the predicate. This use of the term is much the same as that for *usually* in part 1 above. The adjunct has two characteristics:

(a) it is usually separated from the rest of the sentence with a comma or commas
(b) it can appear in various positions in the sentence—the beginning, the middle or the end.

We see both characteristics in the following examples.

> She is, <u>luckily</u>, too poor to be an object of prey to anybody.
> (Jane Austen, *Pride and Prejudice.*)
> [Or: <u>Luckily</u>, she is too poor to be an object of prey to anybody.]
> [Or: She is too poor, <u>luckily</u>, to be an object of prey to anybody.]
> [Or: She is too poor to be an object of prey to anybody, <u>luckily</u>.]

> <u>Hopefully</u>, this book will prove of interest to anyone concerned with words.
> (Jean Aitchison, *Words in the Mind: an Introduction to the Mental Lexicon.*)
> [Or: This book, <u>hopefully</u>, will prove of interest to anyone concerned with words.]
> [Or: This book will, <u>hopefully</u>, prove of interest to anyone concerned with words.]

In the examples on the previous page, the adjuncts (or "sentence adverbs") *luckily* and *hopefully* do not modify the verbs *is* and *will prove*: they modify the whole of the rest of the sentences in which they occur. *Hopefully* in the second example does not mean *in a hopeful manner*: it means *I hope that*.

Adjuncts are one subclass of what I call "extras."

See EXTRA.

ADVERB—from the Latin for "near a verb." One of the word classes.

1. How do you identify adverbs?

(a) Adverbs are words that modify any of the following language items (bold).

• A VERB:	I **worked** <u>steadily</u>.
	VERB ADV
• AN ADJECTIVE:	I have a <u>very</u> **big** appetite.
	ADV ADJ
• A DETERMINER:	I waited for <u>almost</u> **two** hours.
	ADV DET
• A CONJUNCTION:	I will do it <u>only</u> **if** you agree.
	ADV CONJ

- A PREPOSITION: The lamp is <u>just</u> **above** the table.

                                            ADV   PREP

- ANOTHER ADVERB: I worked <u>really</u> **steadily**.

                                            ADV   ADV

- A PHRASE: They arrived <u>precisely</u> **at midnight**.

                                            ADV   PHRASE

- A CLAUSE: They took <u>only</u> **what they needed**.

                                            ADV   CLAUSE

- A SENTENCE: <u>Luckily</u>, **nothing came of it**.

                                          ADV   SENTENCE

In short, an adverb is a broad-gauge modifier—it modifies anything and everything except nouns and pronouns. Nouns and pronouns are modified by adjectives.

Here is a text, with the adverbs underlined and the words that they modify in bold.

> Igor Stravinsky (1882–1971) was rooted in the nationalistic school that drew inspiration from Russia's <u>beautifully</u> **expressive** folk music. The orchestration that Stravinsky brought to his **was** <u>clearly</u>
>
   ADVERB   ADJECTIVE   VERB   ADVERB
>
> **derived** from Rimsky-Korsakov. But the primitive, <u>offbeat</u> **rhythmic** drive he added **was** <u>entirely</u>
>
   VERB   ADVERB   ADJECTIVE   VERB   ADVERB
>
> his own. Stravinsky's <u>audaciously</u> **innovative** works confirmed his status as the leading composer
>
                           ADVERB   ADJECTIVE
>
> of the day. He experimented with <u>virtually</u> **every** technique of 20th century music. In the end, his own
>
                                       ADVERB   DETERMINER
>
> musical voice <u>always</u> **prevailed**. In his long career, there **was** <u>scarcely</u> a musical form that Stravinsky
>
                    ADVERB   VERB   VERB   ADVERB
>
> did not turn his hand to. He <u>regularly</u> **produced** symphonies, concertos, oratorios and an <u>almost</u>
>
                              ADVERB   VERB   ADVERB
>
> **bewildering** variety of choral works.
>
   ADJECTIVE
>
> (*TIME*, June 14, 1999.)

(b) Many adverbs can be scaled on degrees of comparison with –*er* (or *more*) and –*est* (or *most*).

DEGREES OF COMPARISON FOR ADVERBS		
POSITIVE	COMPARATIVE	SUPERLATIVE
soon	sooner	soonest
beautifully	more beautifully	most beautifully

(c) An adverb is any word that fits into the blank space in the following sentence frame.

What they do they do _____.   [well   easily   always   there ...]
ADVERB

(d) Adverbs come from two sources.

- Many adverbs derive from adjectives with the addition of the suffix (ending) –*ly*.

ADJECTIVE	ADVERB
quick	quickly
hesitant	hesitantly
interesting	interestingly

But don't be fooled by the *–ly* suffix: there are also some adjectives (underlined)—words that modify nouns (bold)—that have the same suffix.

The <u>early</u> **bird** gets its worm.
ADJECTIVE NOUN

They made a <u>costly</u> **mistake**.
ADJECTIVE NOUN

- Other adverbs start off as adverbs and don't have a *–ly* suffix.

A multinational with low research and development spending **buys** <u>abroad</u>.
VERB ADVERB

(*The Economist, 18* June 1999.)

Globules of petroleum <u>still</u> **lurk** <u>here</u> and <u>there</u> under a carpet of
ADVERB VERB ADVERB ADVERB

gravel and rocks. (*National Geographic*, March 1999.)

All of the above features—from (a) to (d)—define what adverbs are.

2. Where do adverbs stand in a sentence?

Adverbs can stand in any of three positions.

(a) They can stand before the words they modify, in which case they are called "premodifiers" or "attributive modifiers."

Mary Leakey <u>quickly</u> **set** new standards in the study of African prehistory.
ADVERB VERB

(*TIME*, April 10, 1999.)

The favored techniques include counting to 10 while <u>slowly</u> **exhaling**.
ADVERB VERB

(*TIME*, May 6, 1999.)

(b) They can stand after the words they modify, in which case they are called "postmodifiers" or "predicative modifiers."

Pollution is poison, and poison **kills** <u>slowly</u>.
VERB ADVERB

(*Presidents & Prime Ministers*, May 23, 1999.)

The ice **is moving** <u>pretty</u> <u>quickly</u>. (*New Scientist*, April 17, 1999.)
VERB ADVERB ADVERB

In the last example sentence above, the adverb *pretty* modifies the adverb *quickly*, which modifies the compound verb *is moving*.

(c) They can stand in the middle of the string of words they modify, in which case they are called "central modifiers."

People **can** <u>clearly</u> **weigh** the pros and cons of animal experimentation.
VERB ADVERB VERB

To committed supporters of animal rights, such experiments **can** <u>never</u>
VERB ADVERB

be justified. (*New Scientist*, May 22, 1999.)
VERB

Can weigh and *can be* in the text above are compound verbs. The adverbs *clearly* and *never* stand in the middle of these verbs.

3. Where do sentence adverbs ("adjuncts") stand?

Adjuncts, which modify whole sentences, can stand pretty much anywhere—at the beginning of the sentence, in the middle, or at the end.

> <u>Unfortunately</u>, I made no enquiries of any kind till after I had been actually married four or five months.
> (Oscar Wilde, *A Woman of No Importance*.)
> <u>Unfortunately</u> the habits of crustaceans are very imperfectly known.
> (Charles Darwin, *The Descent of Man*.)
> I <u>unfortunately</u> fell asleep in less than twenty seconds.
> (Edgar Allan Poe, "The Angel of the Odd.")
> It was, <u>unfortunately</u>, a morbid trait.
> (Nathaniel Hawthorne, *House of the Seven Gables*.)
> Our people are a bad lot, ma'am; but that is no news, <u>unfortunately</u>.
> (Charles Dickens, *Hard Times*.)

ADVERB SUBCLASSES—there are three main subclasses of adverbs.

1. COMMON ADVERBS (including adjuncts): We walked <u>slowly</u>.
2. INTERROGATIVE ADVERBS: <u>How</u> do you do?
3. CONJUNCTIVE ADVERBS
   (also called "transition words"): I think, <u>therefore</u> I am (René Descartes).

We look at each of these below.

1. What are common adverbs?

Common adverbs (underlined) tell you where, when, how, or to what extent something occurs. Some grammars subdivide common adverbs into adverbs of "place," "time," "manner," "extent," "frequency," and so on.

All of the underlined words below are common adverbs.

> The blooms are <u>here</u> <u>today</u> but, <u>sadly</u>, <u>often</u> gone <u>quite</u> <u>quickly</u> by <u>tomorrow</u>.
>   PLACE TIME   MANNER FREQUENCY   MANNER MANNER   TIME

2. What are interrogative adverbs?

Interrogative adverbs (INT ADVERB) ask questions about the where, when, how (and so on) of an occurrence. The replies to questions headed by interrogative adverbs are common adverbs, adverb phrases or adverb clauses.

QUESTIONS WITH INTERROGATIVE ADVERBS	ANSWERS WITH ADVERBS, ADVERB PHRASES OR ADVERB CLAUSES
<u>Where</u> are you? INT ADVERB	(I am <u>here</u>.) ADVERB
<u>When</u> did you begin? INT ADVERB	(I began <u>some time ago</u>.) ADVERB PHRASE
<u>Why</u> do you call it sad? INT ADVERB	(I call it sad <u>because it makes me feel sad</u>.) ADVERB CLAUSE
<u>How</u> are you getting along? INT ADVERB	(I am getting along <u>well</u>.) ADVERB

(Lewis Carroll, *Alice in Wonderland*.)

3. What are conjunctive adverbs?

Conjunctive adverbs (also called "transition words") act partly as adverbs and partly as conjunctions. There are some dozen of these words, including *however* and *therefore*. I deal with conjunctive adverbs in some detail under EXTRA. Here are two textual examples.

> If he wanted the money he wanted it, and it was nobody's business to ask why. He <u>therefore</u> made his demand with the awkwardness of a proud man.
> She laughed with him, as if she liked his audacity. <u>Nevertheless</u> he sat still a moment, straining his eyes down the long hill.
> (Edith Wharton, *Ethan Frome*.)

Each of the words *therefore* and *nevertheless* in the examples above has two roles:

(a) the adverbial function of modifying the sentence in which it occurs (see EXTRA).

(b) the conjunctive function of linking the sentence in which it occurs with the sentence before (see CONJUNCTION).

It is because of this dual role that these words are called "conjunctive adverbs."

ADVERB CLAUSE—a clause (underlined) that does the job of an adverb: it modifies a verb (bold).

> I **am justified** in availing myself of the usual privilege of a dedication, <u>when I mention that there has been a long and uninterrupted friendship between us</u>.
> She **might have** sometimes **introduced** her unwelcome topic with more success, <u>if she could have diversified her conversation</u>.
> A scholar who is a blockhead, **must be** the worst of all blockheads, <u>because he is without excuse</u>.
> Knowledge is certainly an object which every man **would wish** to attain, <u>although, perhaps, he may not take the trouble necessary for attaining it</u>. (James Boswell, *The Life of Samuel Johnson*.)

Adverb clauses start with adverbial conjunctions (not to be confused with "conjunctive adverbs"—see EXTRA). The adverbial conjunctions in the texts above are *when*, *if*, *because*, *although*.

It is a defining characteristic of adverb clauses that they can stand before or after their companion clauses. In each of the four example sentences above, the adverb clause follows the main clause. The following examples show that an adverb clause (headed by the same conjunction—*when*, *if*, *because* or *although*) can also stand before its companion clause.

> <u>When the Duke of Marlborough was one day reconnoitring the army in Flanders</u>, a heavy rain **came** on.
> <u>If the biographer writes from personal knowledge,</u> there is danger lest his interest **overpower** his fidelity.
> <u>Because he thought it right to collect many words which had fallen into disuse</u>, it **has been imagined** that all of these have been woven into

his own compositions.

Although he committed to writing many particulars of the progress of his mind and fortunes, he never **had** persevering diligence enough to form them into a regular composition.
(James Boswell, *The Life of Samuel Johnson*.)

ADVERB PHRASE—a term with different meanings in (1) traditional grammar and in (2) modern grammar.

1. **In traditional grammar,** an adverb phrase is a phrase that modifies a verb—as does a single-word adverb (see ADVERB). A phrase, in traditional grammar, is a string of words that does not have a finite verb (see PHRASE). In the example text below, the adverb phrases are underlined; the verbs that they modify, in bold.

To see a World in a Grain of Sand	God Appears and God **is** Light
And Heaven in a Wild Flower,	To those poor Souls who **dwell** in Night,
Hold Infinity in the palm of your hand	But does a Human Form **Display**
And Eternity in an hour.	To those who Dwell in Realms of day.
(William Blake, from "Auguries of Innocence.")	

2. **In modern grammar,** an adverb phrase is either:

   (a) an adverb

quickly	suddenly	luckily	soon	tomorrow

   or

   (b) a string of words (underlined) with an adverb (bold) as its head word. See HEAD.

   Some of the first electronic computers were devised **specifically** for use by physicists working on the development of atomic weapons.
   (*The Economist*, July 2, 1999.)

   In Britain, experiments involving primates are very **tightly** controlled.
   (*New Scientist*, May 22, 1999.)

The difference between the traditional and the modern concepts of "adverb phrase" is as follows.

• An "adverb phrase" in the traditional sense is a string of words that may, but need not, contain an adverb—it is enough that the phrase as a whole modifies a verb.

• An "adverb phrase" in the modern sense is either an adverb, or a string of words that has an adverb as its head (see HEAD) and that modifies a verb.

See PHRASE.

AFFIX—an incomplete word-part (also called a "bound morpheme") that attaches ("fixes") either to the beginning or to the end of another word. Example: *disbelieving*.

1. What positions can affixes take?

Affixes can attach to the beginnings of words (*dis–*), in which case they are called "prefixes;" or they can attach to the ends of words (*–ing*), in which case they are called "suffixes." The terms "prefixes" and "suffixes" relate only to the positions of affixes; they don't tell us their functions.

2. What are the functions of affixes?

Most affixes help us to derive—

(a)   words of one meaning from words of another meaning (*unlock* from *lock*; *impossible* from *possible*)

(b)   words of one word class from words of another word class (the verb *entangle* from the noun *tangle*; the adjective *helpless* from the noun *help*).

Affixes of type (a) and (b) are called "derivational affixes." Derivational affixes may be prefixes or suffixes.

A third function of affixes is to change—

(c)   words of one grammar form into words of another grammar form (the singular *dog* into the plural *dogs*; the positive *fine* into the comparative *finer*).

Affixes of type (c) are called "inflections" or "inflectional suffixes." All inflections are suffixes.

See MORPHEME.

We look at types (a) to (c) below.

(a)   Derivational prefixes change the meanings of words. The main derivational prefixes are the following.

a–	(not, without)	amoral, aseptic, atheist
a–	(in a state of)	asleep, awake, ablaze
a–	(in, at, on)	abed, ashore, afield
ante–	(before)	antenatal, antechamber, antedated
anti–	(against)	antiwar, antiseptic, antidemocratic
be–	(verb)	bestir, besprinkle, besmear
bi–	(two, dual)	bicycle, bifocal, bicameral
bio–	(life)	biography, biology, biomass
by–	(secondary)	bypath, by-laws, bypass
circum–	(around)	circumnavigate, circumpolar, circumscribe
co–	(together)	co-author, cooperate, cohabitation
contra–, counter–	(against)	contradict, counterweight, counterargument
de–	(from, away)	deplane, defrost, detoxify
dis–	(apart, not)	dislocate, disorderly, dismember
e–, ex–	(from, out of)	evade, exhale, exclude
en–, em–	(make) (verb)	enrage, enable, empower

for–	(not)	forget, forbid, forswear
fore–	(in advance)	forecast, foretell, forerunner
giga–	(a billion)	gigabyte, gigahertz, gigawatt
hyper–	(more than)	hypersensitive, hyperventilate, hyperinflation
il–, in–, im–, ir–	(not)	illogical, inordinate, immeasurable, irreparable
in–	(in)	inland, inlet, insight
inter–	(among, between)	interact, interchange, interrelationship
macro–	(large)	macroeconomics, macrocosm, macronutrient
mal–	(badly)	maladjusted, malfunction, malediction
mega–	(a million, many)	megabucks, megabyte, megalomania
micro–	(small)	microeconomics, microscope, microcosm
milli–	(a thousand, a thousandth)	millipede, millimeter, milligram
mini–	(small)	minibus, minibudget, minicab
mis–	(bad, badly)	misdeed, mismanage, mislead
mono–	(single)	monorail, monomania, monochrome
neo–	(new)	neolithic, neonate, neologism
non–	(not)	nonresident, nonconformist, nonflammable
omni–	(all)	omniscient, omnipresent, omnivorous
out–	(exceed) (verb)	outdistance, outdo, outshine
post–	(after)	postwar, postgraduate, postoperative
pre–	(before)	preheat, prewar, prefabricate
pro–	(forward)	progress, propel, proceed
pro–	(in favor of)	pro-democratic, pro-peace, pro-American
re–	(again)	reborn, return, recall
semi–	(half)	semitrailer, semiliterate, semicircle
sub–	(under, less than)	submarine, subzero, substandard
super–, supra–	(over, beyond)	supernatural, supranational, supramolecular
syn–, sym–	(together)	synchronic, symphony, sympathetic
trans–	(across)	transport, trans-Pacific, transcontinental
tri–	(triple)	triplane, trilateral, tripartite
uni–	(single)	unilateral, unicycle, uniform
un–	(not, reverse)	untruth, undo, unkind
with–	(from, against)	withdraw, withhold, withstand

(b) Derivational suffixes change the word class of words. Here are the main derivational suffixes.

–able, –ible	(adjective)	comfortable, lovable, convertible
–acy	(noun)	democracy, theocracy, literacy
–age, –edge	(noun)	dotage, mileage, knowledge
–al	(noun)	denial, revival, survival
–al	(adjective)	regional, personal, historical
–an	(noun or adjective)	Asian, European, American
–ant, –ent	(adjective)	reliant, ignorant, reticent
–ary	(noun or adjective)	revolutionary, military, ordinary
–ate	(verb)	renovate, resonate, elevate
–craft	(noun)	handicraft, priestcraft, witchcraft
–dom	(noun)	wisdom, kingdom, freedom
–en	(verb)	lengthen, shorten, widen
–er, –or	(actor noun)	boxer, driver, actor
–ern	(adjective)	eastern, western, northern
–ess	(feminine noun)	princess, duchess, abbess
–fold	(adjective or adverb)	twofold, tenfold, manifold
–ful	(adjective)	wonderful, truthful, tearful
–hood	(noun)	childhood, manhood, womanhood
–ian	(noun)	historian, electrician, barbarian
–ic	(adjective)	historic, electric, barbaric
–ify	(verb)	electrify, glorify, purify
–ion, –tion	(noun)	solution, promotion, expectation
–ise, –ize	(verb)	advertise, theorize, apologize
–ish	(adjective)	youngish, thirtyish, childish
–ish	(noun or adjective)	British, Spanish, Turkish
–ism	(noun)	materialism, idealism, hedonism
–ist	(noun)	materialist, idealist, hedonist
–ity	(noun)	oddity, nobility, spirituality
–ive	(adjective)	intensive, extensive, attractive
–less	(adjective)	aimless, shameless, hopeless
–like	(adjective)	childlike, godlike, catlike
–ly	(adjective)	friendly, neighborly, womanly
–ly	(adverb)	definitely, surely, certainly
–ment	(noun)	development, judgment, adjournment
–most	(adjective)	foremost, hindmost, uppermost
–nce	(noun)	reliance, ignorance, reticence
–ness	(noun)	goodness, happiness, holiness
–ous	(adjective)	obvious, glorious, joyous
–ship	(noun)	leadership, friendship, lectureship
–some	(adjective)	winsome, burdensome, troublesome
–t	(noun)	height, weight, sight
–th	(noun)	health, wealth, width
–ure	(noun)	closure, failure, departure
–ward	(adjective or adverb)	homeward, westward, forward
–y	(adjective)	hilly, busy, bushy

The process of deriving a word of one class from a word of another class with an affix is called "word formation." We can see word formation in action, using the foregoing affixes, in the following examples.

VERB	⇨	ADJECTIVE	NOUN	⇨	VERB	ADJECTIVE	⇨	VERB
reason		reasonable	revolution		revolutionize	fine		refine
read		readable	computer		computerize	glad		gladden

ADJECTIVE	⇨	ADVERB	NOUN	⇨	ADJECTIVE	VERB	⇨	NOUN
true		truly	mountain		mountainous	lead		leader
smart		smartly	guilt		guilty	intend		intention

(c) Inflections change the grammar of words. For example, the addition of the inflection –*s* to a noun changes it from singular to plural: *person—persons*. There are eight regular inflections (also called "inflectional suffixes").

1. PLURAL –*S* WITH NOUNS: gardens   trees   flowers
   [But note irregular plurals such as: children   geese   mice]

2. POSSESSIVE (OR "GENITIVE")
   –*'S* OR –*S'* WITH NOUNS: student's   students' Daphne's

3. THIRD PERSON SINGULAR
   –*S* WITH VERBS: carries   skips   plays

4. PAST TENSE –*ED* WITH VERBS: carried   skipped   played
   [But note irregular verbs such as: went   ran   swam]

5. PAST PARTICIPLE –*EN* WITH
   VERBS: eaten   taken   shaken
   [But note verbs such as: put   cut   hit]

6. PRESENT PARTICIPLE –*ING*
   WITH VERBS: working   resting playing

7. COMPARATIVE –*ER* WITH
   ADJECTIVES AND ADVERBS: smaller   slower   wiser

8. SUPERLATIVE –*EST* WITH
   ADJECTIVES AND ADVERBS: smallest   slowest wisest

The word "inflection" comes from the Latin for "bending." Inflections "bend" the grammar of words to which they attach. For more information on the uses of inflections see:

IRREGULAR NOUN	IRREGULAR VERB	—*ING* FORM
FORMS OF THE VERB	FINITE AND NONFINITE	CASE
PARTICIPLE	DEGREES OF COMPARISON	

The following passage illustrates how prevalent affixes are. The roots of multipart words are underlined (see ROOT AND STEM); the affixes are separated from the roots and from each other with hyphens.

It is the great multi-<u>pli</u>-ca-tion of the pro-<u>duc</u>-tion-s of all the <u>differ</u>-ent <u>art</u>-s, in con-<u>sequen</u>-ce of the di-<u>vis</u>-ion of labor, which oc-<u>cas</u>-ion-s, in a well-<u>govern</u>-ed <u>socie</u>-ty, that <u>univers</u>-al <u>opul</u>-ence which ex-<u>tend</u>-s to the <u>low</u>-est <u>rank</u>-s of the people. (Adam Smith, *The Wealth of Nations*.)

AGREEMENT OF ANTECEDENT AND PRONOUN—the notion that, if you use a singular noun first (that is, as the antecedent), you follow it with a singular pronoun or determiner; and if you use a plural noun first, you follow it with a plural pronoun or determiner. (The antecedents are in bold.)

> **An animal** protects <u>its</u> young.
> SINGULAR   SINGULAR
>
> **Animals** protect <u>their</u> young.
> PLURAL   PLURAL
>
> If **anybody** that belonged to the band told the secrets, <u>he</u> must
> SINGULAR   SINGULAR
>
> have <u>his</u> throat cut.
> SINGULAR
>
> (Mark Twain, *Huckleberry Finn*.)

The question nowadays is whether, in the interests of gender equity, we should use something other than *he*, *him*, *his* after a singular antecedent.

One solution that many writers adopt is to use *he* and *she* (and similar pairs) in tandem.

> This will call for customer relationship marketing: getting so close to the **customer** that you can almost predict when <u>he or she</u> is going to want to buy a new car. (*The Economist*, May 28, 1999.)
> Pocket-sized smart cards might soon be able to store all of a **person's** physical data needed to verify <u>his or her</u> identity.
> (*The Economist*, May 7, 1999.)
> As a graduate student, you're best if you work for a young **person** who's later going to be important, because <u>he or she</u> will have relatively new ideas. (James Watson in *TIME*, March 23, 1999.)
> He casts a spell, making each **listener** believe he was speaking only to <u>him or her</u>. (*TIME*, April 10, 1999.)

Another solution is to throw grammatical caution to the winds and to use the plural *they* after a singular antecedent: *Everybody can do what <u>they</u> like!*

This is not as new as some people might think. *The Oxford English Dictionary* (*OED*) says that *they* has been "often used in reference to a singular noun made universal by *every*, *any*, *no*, etc., or applicable to one of either sex (= 'he or she')." Among other citations, dating from the sixteenth century on, the *OED* gives the following.

> He never forsaketh any **creature** unless <u>they</u> forsake themselves.
> (John Fisher, *The Ways of Perfect Religion*. 1535.)
> **Everybody** fell a-laughing, as how could <u>they</u> help it?
> (Henry Fielding, *Tom Jones*. 1749.)
> If **a person** is born a gloomy temper, <u>they</u> cannot help it.
> (Earl of Chesterfield, *Letters*. 1759.)
> **Nobody** can deprive us of the Church, if <u>they</u> would.
> (William Whewell, *Life*. 1835.)
> **Nobody** fancies for a moment that <u>they</u> are reading about anything beyond the pale of ordinary propriety.
> (Walter Bagehot, *Literary Studies*. 1858.)
> **Nobody** does anything well that <u>they</u> cannot help doing.
> (John Ruskin, *Crown of Wild Olives*. 1856.)

What goes for *they* goes also for *their*, *theirs* and *them* alongside *every*, *any* and the like. "In [allowing] cases like these," Otto Jespersen wrote, "English commonsense has triumphed over grammatical nonsense" (1933:212).

AGREEMENT OF SUBJECT AND VERB—the notion that a subject and a verb have to agree in number: if the subject is singular, the verb has to be singular too; if the subject is plural, the verb has to be plural too.

SINGULAR WITH SINGULAR	PLURAL WITH PLURAL
The <u>child</u> <u>is</u> happy.	The <u>children</u> <u>are</u> happy.
SUBJECT VERB	SUBJECT VERB

But more complicated cases arise too. We consider these below, under eight headings.

1. A plural-looking subject that is singular.

This is a word that ends in the letter *–s* but that is actually singular. Such a word therefore agrees with a singular verb.

The <u>news</u> <u>is</u> good.
<u>Mathematics</u> <u>is</u> an interesting subject and so <u>is</u> <u>physics</u>. So <u>is</u> <u>acoustics</u> and so <u>is</u> <u>economics</u>.

2. A singular-looking subject that is plural.

This is an adjective used as a noun, usually preceded by the word *the*.

<u>The good</u> <u>are</u> rewarded and <u>the wicked</u> <u>are</u> punished.

3. A Latin plural ending with the letter *–a*.

Many English words that end in *–a* come from Latin plural forms which, in Latin, have their singular forms ending in *–um*.

SINGULAR	PLURAL
agendum	agenda
datum	data
medium	media

With *agenda*, a singular verb is now common; with the other *–a* words, plural verbs are common.

The <u>agenda</u> <u>is</u> ready. The <u>media</u> <u>have</u> reported the event, and the <u>data</u> <u>have</u> confirmed it.
What <u>is</u> your <u>agenda</u> for industrial growth in your country in the next five years?
(*Presidents & Prime Ministers*, January–February 1999.)
The <u>media</u> <u>have</u> concentrated on just a few aspects of the web.
(*The Economist*, July 2, 1999.)
Biological <u>data</u> <u>are</u> flooding in at an unprecedented rate.
(*The Economist*, July 2, 1999.)

4. A subject with *and*.

(a) Such a subject takes a plural verb if the subject refers to two or more people or things.

<u>My brother and sister</u> <u>are</u> here.

(b) The subject takes a singular verb if the two parts of the subject refer to one person or thing.

> The chief cook and bottle-washer is in the kitchen.

(c) In arithmetic, for two numbers joined with *and*, *plus* or *times*, you can use either a singular or a plural verb.

WITH A SINGULAR VERB	WITH A PLURAL VERB
One and one is two.	One and one are two.
Two plus two is four.	Two plus two are four.
Two times two is four.	Two times two are four.

5. **A subject with *either, or, neither, nor*.**

There are two cases.

(a) If both parts of the subject are singular, use a singular verb.

> Neither Jack nor Jill is up the hill.
> Tia or Adam was here.
> Either of my friends is ready to help me.
> Neither of my parents likes noise.

(b) If one part of the subject is singular, and the other is plural, the verb is singular or plural depending on which part of the subject it is nearer to.

He or they are arriving soon.	[*They* is nearer to the verb, so the verb is plural—*are*.]
Is he or they arriving soon?	[*He* is nearer to the verb, so the verb is singular—*is*.]

6. **A collective subject.**

This is a word that looks singular but that means a collection of things or people. Examples: *the class*, *the staff*, *the team*, *the band*.

Whether you use such words with singular or with plural verbs depends on the meaning of the sentence. If, in the sentence, you are talking about the collection as a whole, you use a singular verb. If you are talking about the individual members of the collection, you can use either a singular or a plural verb.

The team has just arrived.	[The team as a whole.]
The team is now putting on their uniforms.	[The team as a group.]
The team are now putting on their uniforms.	[The team as individuals.]

And some real texts.

> The congregation was composed of the neighboring people of rank.
> (Irving Washington, "The Country Church.")
> The congregation were sitting in the well of the church.
> (George Orwell, *Down and Out in Paris and London*.)

> So far, the team has found three different ways in which the butterflies increase the visibility of their blue flashes.
> (*New Scientist*, June 26, 1999.)
> The team are also investigating a range of other species.
> (*New Scientist*, June 26, 1999.)

> One group has taken to the air.
> (*New Scientist*, June 12, 1999.)
> The only group who clearly backed animal research were those who had worn a fur coat or taken part in a blood sport.
> (*New Scientist*, May 22, 1999.)

The <u>crowd</u> <u>is</u> younger.
(*National Geographic*, April 1999.)
The <u>crowd</u> of 5,000 <u>have</u> gathered to catch a glimpse of the latest heartthrob.
(*TIME*, May 24, 1999.)

One more point. In sport, when we are talking of a team, we often use the name of the country to stand for the team. In that case, you can use a singular or a plural verb in the predicate. A plural verb is more usual.

It is not good for the game if <u>the enemy</u> <u>are</u> weak. <u>England</u> <u>are</u> not weak at the moment, but neither are they strong … <u>Australia</u> <u>were</u> in a bad way in the eighties. (*The ABC Cricket Book*, 1998–99 Season.)

7. A subject consisting of a hendiadys.

A hendiadys (pronounced "hen-DYE-adis"—from the Greek for "one thing from two") is a pair of words joined with *and*, acting as one and usually attracting a singular verb. So we say <u>*rock and roll* *is*</u> … (not *are* …).

He saw that my <u>bread and butter</u> <u>was</u> gone.
(Charles Dickens, *Great Expectations*.)
The <u>hue and cry</u> <u>was</u> raised all about.
(Edmund Spenser, *The Faerie Queen*.)

8. A subject with *of* in the middle.

Below are two examples of this kind of subject.

SINGULAR *OF* PLURAL	PLURAL *OF* SINGULAR
<u>A bag of coins</u> …	<u>Buckets of water</u> …
SINGULAR PLURAL	PLURAL SINGULAR

The problem is: does the verb agree with the word before or the word after *of*?

We look at the answer in several parts.

(a) In general, the verb agrees with the word before *of*.

SINGULAR *OF* PLURAL	PLURAL *OF* SINGULAR
<u>A bag of coins</u> <u>is</u> …	<u>Buckets of water</u> <u>are</u> …

So *is* agrees with *bag* (not with *coins*), and *are* agrees with *buckets* (not with *water*).

(b) When the word before *of* is a collective (*number*, *bunch*, *crowd*, *crew*, *team* and so on), things get more complicated. In these cases, use a singular verb to focus on the collection as a whole; a plural verb to focus on the individuals in the collection.

The <u>number of patients</u> <u>is</u> growing bigger.   [Focus on the number—not the patients.]
A <u>number of patients</u> <u>are</u> coughing.   [Focus on the patients—not the number.]

(c) When the sentences are not so clear-cut as in the above two examples, you can use either a singular or a plural verb. The sentences will then have slightly different meanings.

A <u>group of students</u> <u>was</u> waiting.   [The group as a whole.]
A <u>group of students</u> <u>were</u> waiting.   [The students as individuals.]

A <u>squad of cadets</u> <u>was</u> marching along.   [The squad as a whole.]
A <u>squad of cadets</u> <u>were</u> marching along.   [The cadets as individuals.]

(d) The case of *none of them* or *none*. Which of the following sentences is right?

<u>None</u> of them <u>is</u> ready.   <u>None</u> of them <u>are</u> ready.

You will hear—and read—both kinds of sentences: *none is*, and *none are*. The difference between them is one of formality. The word *none* derives from two Anglo-Saxon words (*ne an*) that mean "not one." In strict grammar, therefore, *none* should go with a singular verb.

<u>None</u> of them <u>is</u> ready.   [= <u>Not one</u> of them <u>is</u> ready.]

But at an informal level—in casual conversation—most people would use *are* instead of *is*.

<u>None</u> of them <u>are</u> ready.

So whether you use *is* or *are* will depend on whether you want to sound formal or casual.

NONE WITH A SINGULAR VERB.

There <u>was</u> <u>none</u> of the men of the house there within.
(*Genesis* 39:11.)
There <u>is</u> <u>none</u> that I can smile at half so much.
(Charles Dickens, *David Copperfield*.)
<u>None</u> <u>has</u> suffered so little from the ravages of time.
(Irving Washington, *Alhambra*.)
<u>None</u> <u>was</u> so excited as Anne Shirley.
(LM Montgomery, *Anne of Green Gables*.)
There <u>is</u> <u>none</u> like thee among the dancers.
(Ezra Pound, "Dance Figure.")
<u>None of them</u> <u>was</u> quick enough to see her go.
(Joseph Conrad, *Lord Jim*.)
<u>None of those fields</u> <u>seems</u> to be suffering unduly.
(*The Economist*, July 2, 1999.)

NONE WITH A PLURAL VERB.

<u>None of the rest</u> <u>are</u> so much as spoken of.
(Thomas Paine, *The Age of Reason*.)
This is an objection which <u>none of my critics</u> <u>have</u> urged against me.
(John Dryden, *All for Love*.)
Barclay's remarks were subdued and abrupt so that <u>none of them</u> <u>were</u> audible to the listeners.
(Arthur Conan Doyle, "The Crooked Man.")

(e) The case of *a lot of them* and *a couple of them*. The words *lot* and *couple* are both singular. They should, therefore, in strict grammar go with singular verbs. But here strict grammar simply gets blown away by the winds of usage and we always use a plural verb with either of these subjects.

> A lot of my friends <u>are</u> here.
> A couple of my friends <u>are</u> here.

9. **The mysterious case of a singular subject with the verb *were*.**

   (a)   Usually, when you have a singular subject, you use the verb *was* in the predicate; and when you have a plural subject, you use *were* in the predicate.

   > <u>She</u> <u>was</u> here yesterday.
   > <u>We</u> <u>were</u> talking about football.

   (b)   But sometimes you hear—or see—sentences such as the following.

   > I wish <u>he</u> <u>were</u> here.
   > Suppose <u>I</u> <u>were</u> to tell you a secret.

   (c)   What is the explanation?

   It is that the use of *were* in such cases is about something imaginary—something that is not the case now or that may or may not be the case in the future.

I wish he <u>were</u> here.	[= He is not here now.]
Suppose I <u>were</u> to tell you a secret.	[= I might or might not tell you a secret in the future.]

   The grammar name for this use of *were* about something imaginary is "subjunctive."

See SUBJUNCTIVE.

ALLITERATION—See FIGURE OF SPEECH.

ALTERNATIVE QUESTION—See QUESTION TYPES.

AMBIGUITY—double meaning; language that can be taken in more than one sense. The term comes from the Latin for "driving in two directions."

> When the cat is under the chair, don't kick it.
> [This could mean, "Don't kick the cat" or "Don't kick the chair."]

Sometimes ambiguity is deliberate; sometimes accidental.

1. **Examples of accidental ambiguity.**

   > Hamas looks forward to heightened confrontation.
   > (Magazine headline.)
   > [Does this mean that they expect it will come or that they hope it will come?]
   >
   > Delinquents facing up to life.
   > (Newspaper headline.)
   > [What—the challenge of life or a life sentence?]
   >
   > I like understanding people.
   > [I like to understand them or I like people who are understanding?]

2. Many jokes, particularly blue jokes, are based on deliberate ambiguity.

Such ambiguity is called *double entendre*—a French expression that means "double understanding."

> What do you call somebody who dies from an overdose of sex pills? A stiff.
>
> What do you call people who hijack a truckload of sex pills? Hardened criminals.

ANAPHOR—See REFERENCE.

***AND* AT THE START OF A SENTENCE**—See LANGUAGE MYTH.

ANOMALOUS FINITE—(also called "auxiliary") any of a set of twenty-four finite verbs that are in some way anomalous. "Anomalous" means "deviating from the rule."

In what way are these verbs deviant? In that they are the only verbs in modern English that can be followed by the word *not* (or with the abbreviation *–n't*).

> I <u>am not</u> tired.   I <u>haven't</u> worked hard.   I <u>don't</u> want to go to sleep.

The twenty-four anomalous finites (or "auxiliaries") are the following:

am	can	must
is	could	ought
are	shall	need
was	should	dare
were	will	used (in the sense of "was in the habit")
have	would	**do**
has	may	**does**
had	might	**did**.

The verbs *do*, *does* and *did* are in bold because, with all normal verbs in English, you add one of these three anomalous finites if you want to use *not* (or *–n't*).

> He <u>doesn't snore</u>.   [Not: He <u>snoresn't</u>.]
> They <u>do not swim</u>.   [Not: They <u>swim not</u>.]
> They <u>didn't do</u> what I said.   [Not: They <u>didn't</u> what I said.]

What else characterizes the anomalous finites?

Six of the anomalous finites can form their negatives in either of two ways:

(a) without the anomalous *do*, *does*, *did*; or
(b) with the anomalous *do*, *does*, *did*.

The six are: *have*, *has*, *had*, *need*, *dare*, *used*.

WITHOUT THE ANOMALOUS *DO*, *DOES*, *DID*	WITH THE ANOMALOUS *DO*, *DOES*, *DID*
I <u>haven't</u> any answers.	I <u>don't have</u> any answers.
She <u>hasn't</u> the time.	She <u>doesn't have</u> the time.
I <u>hadn't</u> the patience.	I <u>didn't have</u> the patience.
They <u>needn't</u> help me.	They <u>don't need</u> to help me.
I <u>dare not</u> go there.	I <u>don't dare</u> go there.
I <u>used not</u> to do it.	I <u>didn't use</u> to do it.

The anomalous finites have eight uses.

1. TO FORM THE NEGATIVE: <u>We weren't</u> worried.
2. TO FORM THE INTERROGATIVE: <u>Were they</u> worried?
3. TO FORM THE NEGATIVE-INTERROGATIVE: <u>Weren't they</u> worried?
4. TO ASK A POSITIVE TAG QUESTION: They were worried, <u>weren't they</u>?
5. TO ASK A NEGATIVE TAG QUESTION: They weren't worried, <u>were they</u>?
6. TO INVERT A SENTENCE WITH AN ADVERB OF FREQUENCY: <u>Never have I</u> seen such a sight.
7. WITH *DO, DOES* OR *DID*, TO EMPHASIZE A NORMAL VERB: <u>I do hope</u> you are well.
8. TO SUBSTITUTE FOR A LEXICAL VERB: She knew the answer and <u>so did I</u>.

We look at each of these in greater detail below through a range of textual examples.

1. **To form the negative with *not* or *–n't*.**

   <u>I'm not</u> teasing you.
   (Mark Twain, *Tom Sawyer*.)
   It will be our fault if we <u>are not</u> there to receive him.
   (Arthur Conan Doyle, "Black Peter.")
   He <u>isn't</u> so spry as he once was.
   (LM Montgomery, *Anne of Green Gables*.)

   There are two ways with any of the six verbs *have, has, had, need, dare, used*.

   He <u>hasn't</u> anything.
   [Or: He <u>doesn't have</u> anything.]
   (Theodore Dresiser, *Sister Carrie*.)
   I <u>didn't use</u> to listen to anyone, and preferred to go my own way.
   (Boris Spassky, quoted in *New in Chess*, 1991/1.)
   [Or: I <u>used not</u> to listen to anyone, and preferred to go my own way.]

2. **To form the interrogative: that is, a question.** In interrogatives, the anomalous finites stand before their subjects (bold).

   Then why <u>did **you**</u> buy it?
   (George Bernard Shaw, *Man and Superman*.)

   <u>Does</u> **he** prevail against his slayer?
   (George Bernard Shaw, *Man and Superman*.)

   <u>Can</u> **I** do anything to make you more comfortable?
   (Mary Shelley, *Frankenstein*.)

   There are two ways with any of the six verbs *have, has, had, need, dare, used*.

   <u>Do</u> **you**, then, have some other attachment?
   (Mary Shelley, *Frankenstein*.)
   [Or: <u>Have</u> **you**, then, some other attachment?]

3. To form the negative-interrogative: that is, a negative question. The subjects are in bold.

> <u>Can't</u> **you** make them do?
> (Louisa May Alcott, *Little Women*.)
>
> <u>Weren't</u> **you** going to stop and see me, mother?
> (DH Lawrence, *Sons and Lovers*.)
>
> Why <u>don't</u> **you** let me settle him?
> (DH Lawrence, *Sons and Lovers*.)

There are two ways with any of the six verbs *have*, *has*, *had*, *need*, *dare*, *used*.

> <u>Daren't</u> **you** jump over the creek?
> [Or: <u>Don't</u> **you** dare jump over the creek?]

4. To ask a positive tag question. This is a question to which you expect the answer "Yes." Such a question consists of a statement (not underlined) followed by a negative-interrogative question tag (underlined).

> Men persecute us dreadfully, <u>don't they</u>?
> (Oscar Wilde, *A Woman of No Importance*.)
>
> That would be all the better, <u>wouldn't it</u>?
> (Lewis Carroll, *Through the Looking-Glass*.)
>
> I may come tonight, <u>mayn't I</u>?
> (Oscar Wilde, *Lady Windermere's Fan*.)

There are two ways with any of the six verbs *have*, *has*, *had*, *need*, *dare*, *used*.

> Mrs. Daubeny has a wonderful memory, <u>doesn't she</u>?
> (Oscar Wilde, *A Woman of No Importance*.)
> [Or: Mrs. Daubeny has a wonderful memory, <u>hasn't she</u>?]

5. To ask a negative tag question. This is a question to which you expect the answer "No." Such a question consists of a negative statement (not underlined) followed by an interrogative question tag (underlined).

> It is not very nice, <u>is it</u>? (Oscar Wilde, *A Woman of No Importance*.)
> You didn't mean anything by it, now <u>did you</u>?
> (Lewis Carroll, *Sylvie and Bruno*.)
> Dreams don't often come true, <u>do they</u>?
> (LM Montgomery, *Anne of Green Gables*.)

There are two ways with any of the six verbs *have*, *has*, *had*, *need*, *dare*, *used*.

> You needn't take such an attitude, <u>need you</u>?
> [Or: You don't need to take such an attitude, <u>do you</u>?]

6. To invert a sentence with an adverb of frequency. An adverb of frequency is a word or an expression such as *frequently*, *never*, *rarely*, *often*, *hardly ever*, *scarcely*, *no sooner* and the like. If you put an adverb of frequency at the beginning of a sentence for emphasis, it makes an anomalous finite go before the subject. If you put an adverb of frequency in other positions, there is no such effect.

In the text below, we see the original word order with the adverbs of frequency (bold) at the beginning of the sentences. The verbs and the subjects are underlined. In square brackets you can see the word order as it would be with the adverbs of frequency elsewhere in the sentences.

> How **often** <u>did I wish</u> it! [How <u>I</u> **often** <u>wished</u> it!]
>
> **Never** <u>had any week passed</u> so quickly. [<u>A week had</u> **never** <u>passed</u> so quickly.]
>
> **No sooner** <u>did she perceive</u> any symptom of love in his behavior to Elinor than she considered their serious attachment as certain. [<u>She</u> **no sooner** <u>perceived</u> any symptom of love ...]
>
> **Hardly** <u>could I believe</u> the melancholy and sickly figure before me, to be the remains of the lovely, blooming, healthful girl. [<u>I</u> <u>could</u> **hardly** <u>believe</u> the melancholy and sickly figure before me ...]
>
> **Scarcely** <u>had she determined</u> it, when the figure of a man on horseback drew her eyes to the window. [<u>She had</u> **scarcely** <u>determined</u> it ...]
> (Jane Austen, *Sense and Sensibility*.)

7. **With *do, does* or *did* to emphasize a normal verb.** The texts in square brackets are the unemphatic versions.

> He <u>does love</u> me. [He <u>loves</u> me.]
> (George Bernard Shaw, *Pygmalion*.)
>
> It really <u>did seem</u> as if kind spirits had been at work there. [It really <u>seemed</u> as if ...]
> (Louisa May Alcott, *Little Women*.)
>
> I <u>do wish</u> they would put their hands down! [I <u>wish</u> they would ...]
> (Lewis Carroll, *Alice in Wonderland*.)

8. **To substitute for a lexical verb.** That is, we use an anomalous finite to save repeating a verb—even a whole clause—that we have already mentioned in a text. In the examples below, I bracket and cross out the words saved from repetition.

> He doesn't believe the same things as you <u>do</u> (~~believe~~).
> (Oscar Wilde, *A Woman of No Importance*.)
>
> "Now, will you take a little drop of something, Mr. Bumble?" asked Mrs. Mann. "I think you <u>will</u> (~~take a little drop~~)."
> (Charles Dickens, *Oliver Twist*.)
>
> Perhaps you think it doesn't make any difference to me, but it <u>does</u> (~~make a difference to me~~).
> (LM Montgomery, *Anne of Green Gables*.)

There are two ways with any of the six verbs *have, has, had, need, dare, used*.

> We used to live there and so <u>used</u> they.
> [Or: We used to live there and so <u>did</u> they.]

For additional, specialized uses of subclasses of anomalous finites SEE AUXILIARY VERB AND MODAL VERB.

ANTECEDENT AND PRO-FORM—The antecedent is the word or words referred to; the pro-form is the referring word. Example:

> <u>Jack and Jill</u> went up the hill and <u>they</u> found some water there.
> ANTECEDENT   PRO-FORM

"Antecedent" comes from the Latin for "foregoing," and it is so-called because the pro-form usually refers to a foregoing word or words. But the pro-form can also refer to something following.

> When <u>they</u> went up the hill, <u>Jack and Jill</u> found some water there.
> PRO-FORM   ANTECEDENT

"Pro" means "for," and the "pro-form" is so called because it stands for the antecedent.

Antecedents and pro-forms can be of several kinds.

ANTECEDENT (ANTE)	PRO-FORM (PRO)	
1. Noun or Noun Phrase	Pronoun or Determiner:	The <u>dog</u> wagged <u>its</u> tail. ANTE PRO
2. Noun or Noun Phrase	Adverb *there* or *then*:	They went <u>home</u> and we followed them <u>there</u>. ANTE PRO
3. Clause or Sentence	Anomalous Finite:	<u>We are well</u> and we hope you <u>are</u> too. ANTE PRO
4. Clause or Sentence	*so* or *not*:	<u>We went swimming</u> and <u>so</u> did they. ANTE PRO

We look at each of these below.

1. A noun or a noun phrase antecedent (ANTE) followed by a pronoun or a determiner pro-form (PRO).

> In the region last year, only Singapore and <u>the Philippines</u> posted positive growth rates. Although <u>our</u>
>   ANTE   PRO
>
> <u>economic growth</u> was not as strong as in the years before, <u>it</u> kept us out of a recession. <u>This year</u> will
>   ANTE   PRO   ANTE
>
> be an even more critical year for the economy. <u>It</u> will be a decisive and crucial year. We have to meet
>   PRO
>
> <u>a GNP growth target of at least 3%</u>. If <u>we</u> reach <u>that</u>, it will be full steam ahead. In support of
>   ANTE   PRO   PRO
>
> <u>our local government units,</u> <u>which</u> are our partners in countryside development, we increased <u>their</u>
>   ANTE   PRO   PRO
>
> internal revenue allotment to 103.8 billion pesos.
>
> (*Presidents & Prime Ministers*, March–April 1999.)

2. A noun or a noun phrase antecedent followed by an adverb *there* or *then* pro-form.

> Software should eventually make video surveillance possible almost anywhere, <u>at any time</u>. Street
>   ANTE
> criminals might <u>then</u> be observed and traced with ease.
>   PRO
>
> Small video cameras the size of a large wasp may some day be able to fly into <u>a room</u> and record
>   ANTE
> everything that goes on <u>there</u>.
>   PRO
>
> (*The Economist*, May 7, 1999.)

3. A clause or a sentence antecedent followed by an anomalous finite pro-form.

See ANOMALOUS FINITE.

> LADY TEAZLE: <u>I ought to have my own way in everything</u>, and what's more, I <u>will</u> too.
> ANTE   PRO
>
> LADY SNEERWELL: <u>The paragraphs were all inserted</u>?
> ANTE
>
> SNAKE: They <u>were</u>, madam.
> PRO
>
> LADY SNEERWELL: I conceive <u>you mean with respect to my neighbor, Sir Peter Teazle, and his family</u>?
> ANTE
>
> SNAKE: I <u>do</u>.
> PRO
>
> (Richard Sheridan, *School for Scandal*.)

4. A clause or a sentence antecedent with a *so* or a *not* pro-form.

> "<u>Do you know the game 'Truth'</u>?" asked Sallie.
> ANTE
>
> "I hope <u>so</u>," said Meg. (Louisa May Alcott, *Little Women*.)
> PRO
>
> "<u>Would you like cats, if you were me</u>?" cried the Mouse in a shrill, passionate voice.
> ANTE
>
> "Well, perhaps <u>not</u>," said Alice in a soothing tone.
> PRO
>
> (Lewis Carroll, *Alice in Wonderland*.)

See COHESION.

ANTITHESIS—See FIGURE OF SPEECH.

ANTONOMASIA—See FIGURE OF SPEECH.

APOSTROPHE—See FIGURE OF SPEECH.

APPOSITION—from the Latin for "positioning together." The relationship between two nouns or noun phrases, which stand side by side and which both refer to only one entity: *I rang my friend, Robin*. The noun *Robin* is in apposition to the noun phrase *my friend*—both expressions refer to one and the same person.

> For more than five years William Gaddis worked on **his first novel**, <u>The Recognitions</u>.
>
> Twenty years later, in 1975, Mr. Gaddis ventured to publish **a second novel**, <u>J.R.</u>
>
> An acquaintance recalled seeing him at a writers' conference which was attended by **Allen Ginsberg**, <u>a self-publicizing poet</u>.
>
> (*The Economist*, January 2, 1999.)

In each of the above appositional pairs, the underlined element is in apposition to the one in bold.

ARTICLE—from the Latin for "a small limb." Any one of the words *a*, *an* (both called the "indefinite article") or *the* (the "definite article").

1. How do articles function?

Articles accompany nouns, showing whether they are definite (that is, specific) or indefinite (unspecific).

In the text below, the articles are underlined; the nouns that they accompany are in bold.

> If you thought the **fate** of the **universe** was certain, think again. Last year, in a **blaze** of publicity, it was announced that the **universe** would expand forever in the **grip** of an exotic "antigravity" **force**. But now the **evidence** is in doubt.
> (*New Scientist*, July 17, 1999.)

Articles form a subclass of the word class of determiners.

- For when to use *a* or *an* in front of a word, see A OR AN.

- For more information on the word class of determiners, see DETERMINER.

2. Why are articles a special subclass of determiners?

Unlike other determiners, which can be used either adjectivally (accompanying nouns) or pronominally (standing alone), articles function only adjectivally. We can see this by comparing the two uses of the determiner *this* with the single use of the determiner *the*.

> *THIS* USED—
>
> (i) ADJECTIVALLY
>
>   This   book brought together quotations from Proust's letters.
>   DETERMINER NOUN
>
> (*The Economist*, October 1, 1999.)
>
> (ii) PRONOMINALLY
>
>   This was no big deal. (*TIME*, October 30, 1999.)
>   DETERMINER
>
> *THE* USED ADJECTIVALLY
>
> Aircraft had long before flown over the   summit.
>   DETERMINER   NOUN
>
> (*TIME*, October 30, 1999.)

Possessive determiners (*my*, *your*, *his*, *her*, …), like articles, are also used only adjectivally.

See   DETERMINER.

ASPECT—See TENSE AND ASPECT.

ASSONANCE—See FIGURE OF SPEECH.

ATTRIBUTE—a term in functional grammar. An attribute is any word or string of words that functions as the modifier of a noun. An attribute (underlined) can be:

- A WORD: big baby

- A GROUP: a <u>well-behaved</u> baby

- A PHRASE: a baby <u>with a toy</u>

- A CLAUSE: a baby <u>that doesn't cry</u>.

ATTRIBUTIVE AND PREDICATIVE—contrasting terms that relate to the positions of adjectives or adverbs relative to the words that they modify.

See MODIFIER.

1. **Attributive and predicative adjectives.**

   (a) An adjective is attributive if it stands before the noun that it modifies.

   > The <u>small</u>   <u>child</u> was in a crib.
   >   ADJECTIVE   NOUN

   (b) An adjective is predicative if it follows the noun that it modifies.

   > The <u>child</u> in the crib was <u>small</u>.
   >   NOUN   ADJECTIVE

2. **Attributive and predicative adverbs.**

   (a) An adverb is attributive if it stands before the verb that it modifies.

   > We <u>completely</u> <u>understood</u> the explanation.
   >   ADVERB   VERB

   (b) An adverb is predicative if it follows the verb that it modifies.

   > We <u>understood</u> the explanation <u>completely</u>.
   >   VERB   ADVERB

AUXILIARY VERB—(from the Latin for "helping word") any of a small subset of verbs used in such a way that the verb has no meaning but, rather, helps to perform a grammar function. Auxiliary verbs contrast with lexical verbs (also called "main verbs"), which do have meaning. The three primary auxiliary verbs are *be*, *have*, *do* and their various forms.

1. **The auxiliary functions of *be*, *have*, *do*.**

   Each sentence below has an auxiliary verb (AUX) and a lexical verb (LEX). Note that the auxiliaries have grammar functions; the lexical verbs have meanings.

   > Information could <u>be</u> <u>garnered</u> from personal letters.
   >   AUX   LEX
   >
   > [The auxiliary *be* has the grammar function of making the verb *garner* passive.]
   >
   > By 1100, English <u>had</u> <u>lost</u> many of its inflections.
   >   AUX   LEX
   >
   > [The auxiliary *had* has the grammar function of putting the verb *lose* in the past perfect tense-aspect.]
   >
   > Why <u>does</u> language <u>change</u>?
   >   AUX   LEX
   >
   > [The auxiliary *does* has the grammar function of making the sentence a question.]
   > (CM Millward, *A Biography of the English Language*.)

2. **The lexical functions of *be, have, do*.**

    Each of the same three verbs—*be, have, do*—can also be used in a lexical sense, with an identifiable meaning.

    > There <u>are</u> [exist] at least three ways to approach the analysis of speech sounds.
    > LEX
    >
    > Most native speakers <u>have</u> [possess] a fairly good intuitive understanding
    > LEX
    >
    > of the language.
    >
    > Pidgins <u>do</u> [serve] for most practical purposes.
    > LEX
    >
    > (CM Millward, *A Biography of the English Language*.)

3. **Are there any other auxiliaries?**

    In addition to the three primary auxiliary verbs discussed above, many grammarians also include the modal verbs in this category.

See MODAL VERB.

4. **How do you identify an auxiliary?**

    A good way of telling an auxiliary from a lexical verb is the omission test: if you omit the auxiliary verb, the sentence still makes sense (though it may be ungrammatical), but if you omit the lexical verb the sentence loses its meaning. You can try this out with the six example sentences above.

BASE FORM—See ROOT AND STEM.

***BECAUSE* AT THE START OF A SENTENCE**—See LANGUAGE MYTH.

BENEFICIARY—See ACTOR, BENEFICIARY, GOAL.

BLEND—See ABBREVIATION.

***BUT* AT THE START OF A SENTENCE**—See LANGUAGE MYTH.

CASE—a term that indicates the relationship of nouns, pronouns or determiners to other words in a sentence.

1. **What relationship is meant by case?**

    Case is closely related to sentence structure. We can see this in the following example sentences.

1. I saw her.	2. She saw me.

    Each of the two sentences speaks about the same two people: me and a woman (my sister, for example). But the words relating to the two people appear in different relationships to the verb (*saw*).

    - In the first sentence I am the subject of the verb, and the form used is consequently *I*; in the second, sentence, I am the object of the verb, and the form used is consequently *me*.

    - Similarly for my sister: we use *she* when the word relating to her is the subject of the verb; *her* when it is the object.

    The case name for a noun, pronoun or determiner as subject is "subjective case"; as object, "objective case."

Among most pronouns, we can clearly see the subjective–objective case difference.

SUBJECTIVE:	I	you	he	she	it	we	you	they	who
OBJECTIVE:	me	you	him	her	it	us	you	them	whom

But among nouns this is not so: subjective and objective look alike.

1. George saw Kitty.	2. Kitty saw George.

Even though there is no outward sign among nouns, as there is among pronouns (*I–me*, *she–her*), the nouns *George* and *Kitty* are still said to be either in the subjective or in the objective case, depending on the position of these words in the sentence.

The same goes for determiners. See DETERMINER.

1. This goes with that.	2. That goes with this.

The words *this* and *that* are determiners. There is no change in the form of these determiners with a change from subjective to objective case. Because there is no change, some grammarians see the above nouns and determiners (as distinct from pronouns) as having a "common case."

2. What are the cases in English?

English has three cases:

(a) SUBJECTIVE (or "nominative"): <u>We</u> saw them.

(b) OBJECTIVE (or "accusative"): They love <u>mangoes</u>.

(c) POSSESSIVE (or "genitive"): This is <u>ours</u>. That is <u>Robin's</u>.

Some grammarians add another case: the dative. But in English (unlike in Latin or German), the dative is indistinguishable from the objective ("accusative"), so I omit it as a separate case.

Below, we look at each of the three English cases.

(a) The subjective is the case used for any noun (or pronoun or determiner) used as the subject of a verb.

- <u>We</u> <u>worked</u> hard.
  SUBJECTIVE VERB

(b) The objective is the case used for any noun (or pronoun or determiner) used in either of two ways.

- As the object of a verb: They <u>saw</u> <u>us</u>.
  VERB OBJECTIVE

- As the object of a preposition: They worked <u>for</u> <u>us</u>.
  PREPOSITION OBJECTIVE

(c) The possessive is the case used to indicate possession or, more generally, "any kind of intimate relation" (Jespersen 1933:142).

- In pronouns this is expressed by *mine, yours, his, hers* ...
- In determiners this is expressed by *my, your, his, her ... Jack's, Jill's* ...

The above three cases are illustrated in the following passage. The words to which the case words relate are in bold.

<u>Jack Drew</u> **had watched** <u>Pace MacNamara's</u>   attack   **on**   one
SUBJECTIVE   VERB   POSSESSIVE   OBJECTIVE   PREPOSITION   OBJECTIVE

of   <u>the bosses</u> **outside** <u>the barracks</u> and **had seen** <u>the troopers</u>
PREPOSITION   OBJECTIVE   PREPOSITION   OBJECTIVE   VERB   OBJECTIVE

drag <u>him</u> away. <u>Jack</u>   **agreed**   **with** <u>O'Meara and Scrappy</u>, <u>the man</u>
VERB OBJECTIVE   SUBJECTIVE   VERB   PREPOSITION   OBJECTIVE   SUBJECTIVE

was foolish **to stick** <u>his nose</u> **into**   <u>someone else's</u>   <u>fight</u>.
VERB   VERB   OBJECTIVE PREPOSITION   POSSESSIVE   OBJECTIVE

(Patricia Shaw, *Valley of Lagoons*.)

CATAPHOR—See REFERENCE.

CHAIN AND CHOICE—See SYNTAGM AND PARADIGM.

CHIASMUS—See FIGURE OF SPEECH.

CIRCUMSTANCE—See PARTICIPANT, PROCESS, CIRCUMSTANCE.

CLAUSE—a unit of grammar larger than a phrase and, often, smaller than a sentence.

See GRAMMAR UNITS.

1. How do clauses relate to sentences?

Often, two or more clauses make up a sentence.

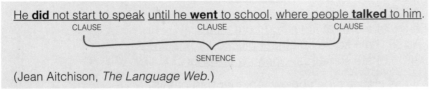

He **did** not start to speak until he **went** to school, where people **talked** to him.
       CLAUSE   CLAUSE   CLAUSE
                                 SENTENCE

(Jean Aitchison, *The Language Web*.)

But a single clause can also make up a sentence. So, for instance, the first clause in the example sentence above (*He did not start to speak*) could be a sentence on its own. The term "clause" comes from a Latin word that is related to "concluded." A clause, therefore, is a concluded (complete) sentence or sentence part.

2. What are the parts of a clause?

Typically, a clause consists of a subject (who or what the clause is about) and a predicate (what is said of the subject). Anything left over after we have split the clause into subject and predicate is an "extra." In the example sentence below (repeated from the preceding box), both of the extras are conjunctions.

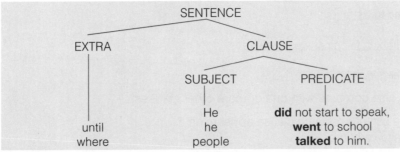

SENTENCE
EXTRA   CLAUSE
          SUBJECT   PREDICATE
          He   **did** not start to speak,
          he   **went** to school
until   people   **talked** to him.
where

See EXTRA.

3. What else characterizes clauses?

A feature of clauses is that each clause has one—and only one—finite verb. You can, therefore, tell how many clauses make up a sentence by counting the finite verbs in the sentence. The finite verbs in the last two boxes above are in bold. See FINITE AND NONFINITE.

There is, however, one kind of clause that does not have a finite verb: a clause in the imperative mood (a command). See IMPERATIVE.

> Go home!   Don't start that now!   Be good!

Some grammars recognize clauses, other than imperative clauses, that feature a range of nonfinite verbs. See NONFINITE CLAUSE. In those grammars, the type of clause discussed in this entry is called a "finite clause."

CLAUSE COMPLEX—a term in functional grammar for a sentence that consists of more than one clause. In traditional grammar a clause complex is called a "multiple sentence". See SENTENCE TYPES.

CLAUSE TYPES—different types of clauses. Below, we deal with the following types.

1. MAIN CLAUSE: <u>I ate some fruit</u>.
2. COORDINATE CLAUSE: I ate some fruit <u>and felt better</u>.
3. SUBORDINATE CLAUSE
   (a) NOUN CLAUSE: I ate <u>what I plucked from a tree</u>.
   (b) ADJECTIVE CLAUSE: I ate some fruit <u>that I plucked from a tree</u>.
   (c) ADVERB CLAUSE: I ate some fruit <u>when I was hungry</u>.

We look at each of these clause types below. Another part of this entry (part 4) deals with main clauses accompanied by multiple other clauses. Part 5 gives alternative names for the various types of clauses.

In the example sentences below, each clause appears on a separate line, with its finite verb—the characterising feature of a clause—in bold. See CLAUSE.

1. **A main clause** is one that can usually form a sentence on its own. For this reason it is also called an "independent clause." Each of the following sentences consists of a main clause only.

> <u>Language worries worth worrying about **do** exist</u>.
> MAIN CLAUSE = SENTENCE
>
> <u>Speakers therefore **need** to watch out</u>.
> MAIN CLAUSE = SENTENCE
>
> <u>The gobbledegook syndrome **is** one of these snares</u>.
> MAIN CLAUSE = SENTENCE
>
> (Jean Aitchison, *The Language Web*.)

But a main clause can also combine with one or more other clauses.

In the following example sentences, each clause appears on a separate line, with its finite verb in bold.

1. When I **was** twelve
   CLAUSE

2. I **knew**
   MAIN CLAUSE

3. that all I **wanted** to become
   CLAUSE

4. **was** a painter.
   CLAUSE

---

1. There **wasn't** a painter living in the town
   MAIN CLAUSE

2. and I **wanted** to paint.
   CLAUSE

(Judy Cassab in Caroline Jones, *The Search for Meaning*.)

Note from the above examples that each sentence has one, and only one, main clause. This is true for all sentences that consist of more than one clause.

2. **A coordinate clause** is one that is headed by a coordinating conjunction which connects it to the main clause. The coordinate clause is almost on the same level of grammatical importance as the main clause—just a mite lower, like a younger brother or sister holding an older one (the main clause) by the hand (a coordinating conjunction).

Some typical coordinating conjunctions, which join coordinate clauses to main clauses, are:

and   either   neither   either … or   so   still   not only… but also
but   or   nor   neither … nor yet   than   as well as

Any of the conjunctions above that consists of more than one word is a "conjunction group." See GROUP. (A conjunction group is also called a "compound conjunction.")

In the example sentences below, the coordinating conjunctions are in capitals and the finite verbs are in bold.

1. Dr Dorothy Rowe **is** a feature writer
   MAIN CLAUSE

2. AND **appears** regularly on radio and television.
   COORDINATE CLAUSE

---

1. My mother **could** be very loving and gentle
   MAIN CLAUSE

2. OR she **would** completely shut herself off.
   COORDINATE CLAUSE

(Caroline Jones and Dorothy Rowe in *The Search for Meaning*.)

It is often hard to tell a coordinate clause from other clauses, so here is a test. If the coordinate clause has the same subject as the main clause, it is possible to omit the subject from the coordinate clause. In the first example sentence above, we can see that the subject (*Dr Dorothy Rowe* or *she*) has been omitted from the coordinate clause. In the second example sentence above, the coordinate clause does have a separate subject (*she*), but we could omit it.

1. Dr Dorothy Rowe **is** a feature writer
   MAIN CLAUSE

2. AND (~~she~~) **appears** <u>regularly on radio and television.</u>
   COORDINATE CLAUSE

1. My mother **could** be very loving and gentle
   MAIN CLAUSE

2. OR (~~she~~) **would** <u>completely shut herself off.</u>
   COORDINATE CLAUSE

A comparative clause is a subtype of coordinate clause. A comparative clause is one that draws a comparison with something in its companion clause. Typically it is joined to its companion clause with a conjunction such as *than*, *as*, *so*.

1. Even carnelian rings **were** not SO valuable
   MAIN CLAUSE

2. AS [**is**] <u>good behavior</u>.
   COORDINATE (COMPARATIVE) CLAUSE

1. We **will** not ask for him back a minute sooner
   MAIN CLAUSE

2. THAN <u>he can be spared</u>.
   COORDINATE (COMPARATIVE) CLAUSE

(Louisa May Alcott, *Little Women*.)

Often a comparative clause is elliptical—that is, the finite verb is understood but not expressed. You can see this in the first of the two example sentences above, where the finite verb *is* (in square brackets) did not appear in the original text. This can often be the test for a comparative clause.

In any sentence that consists of a main clause and a coordinate clause, the coordinate clause always stands second. This is another test for a coordinate clause.

3. **A subordinate clause** is one that depends on a companion clause. The subordinate clause is like a child holding a parent (the other clause) by the hand (a subordinating conjunction).

   There are three subtypes of subordinate clauses.

   (a) NOUN CLAUSE: I ate <u>what I plucked from a tree</u>.
   (b) ADJECTIVE CLAUSE: I ate some fruit <u>that I plucked from a tree</u>.
   (c) ADVERB CLAUSE: I ate some fruit <u>when I was hungry</u>.

   We look at each of these below.

   (a) A noun clause relates to its companion clause as a noun—typically as the subject or as the object of a verb, or as the object of a preposition, in its companion clause. It is connected to its companion clause with a nominal conjunction (also called a "complementizer") such as:

whoever	who	which	when	how	why
whatever	whom	that	where	what	whether.

1. WHOEVER rationally **means** to be useful
   NOUN CLAUSE, SUBJECT OF *must have* IN CLAUSE 2

2. **must** have a plan of conduct.
   MAIN CLAUSE

1. I **have** repeatedly produced
   MAIN CLAUSE

2. WHAT **appeared** to me arguments drawn from matters of fact.
   NOUN CLAUSE, OBJECT OF *have produced* IN CLAUSE 1

(Mary Wollstonecraft, *Vindication of the Rights of Woman*.)

There is a test for whether a clause is a noun clause. The test is that you can always replace a noun clause with the word *something* or *someone*.

1. Whoever rationally means to be useful
   NOUN CLAUSE, SUBJECT OF *must have* IN CLAUSE 2

2. must have a plan of conduct.
   MAIN CLAUSE

   [= Someone must have a plan of conduct.]

1. I have repeatedly produced
   MAIN CLAUSE

2. what appeared to me arguments from matters of fact.
   NOUN CLAUSE, OBJECT OF *have produced* IN CLAUSE 1

   [= I have repeatedly produced something.]

A main clause that is associated with a noun clause is the only kind of main clause that cannot form a stand-alone sentence. This is because some vital part of the main clause—the subject or the object—is missing from the main clause. This makes such a main clause incomplete.

(b) An adjective clause (also called a "relative clause") relates to its companion clause as an adjective: that is, it modifies a noun (or a pronoun) in its companion clause. It is joined to its companion clause with a relative pronoun such as:

who   whom   whose   which   that   when   where.

1. I **am** a very fun lady
   MAIN CLAUSE

2. WHO **does**n't really often think of my disability.
   ADJECTIVE CLAUSE, MODIFYING *lady* IN CLAUSE 1

1. I **am** living in this body
   MAIN CLAUSE

2. THAT **moves** slowly.
   ADJECTIVE CLAUSE, MODIFYING *body* IN CLAUSE 1

(Dominique Hromek in Caroline Jones, *The Search for Meaning*.)

A test for an adjective clause is that it can often be replaced with the words *of a certain kind*.

1. I **am** a very fun lady
   MAIN CLAUSE

2. who doesn't really often think of my disability.
   ADJECTIVE CLAUSE, MODIFYING *lady* IN CLAUSE 1

   [= I am a very fun lady of a certain kind.]   cont....

1. I **am** living in this body
   MAIN CLAUSE

2. <u>that moves slowly</u>.
   ADJECTIVE CLAUSE, MODIFYING *body* IN CLAUSE 1

   [= I am living in this body <u>of a certain kind</u>.]

It is a special feature of an adjective clause that it often nests within its companion clause (underlined).

1. (a) <u>In the interval</u>
   START OF MAIN CLAUSE

2. <u>which **marked** the preparation of the meal</u>
   ADJECTIVE CLAUSE, MODIFYING *interval* IN CLAUSE 1

1. (b) <u>Carrie **found** time to study the flat.</u>
   END OF MAIN CLAUSE

1. (a) <u>Those</u>
   START OF MAIN CLAUSE

2. <u>who **have** never experienced such an influence</u>
   ADJECTIVE CLAUSE, MODIFYING *those* IN CLAUSE 1

1. (b) <u>**will** not understand.</u>
   END OF MAIN CLAUSE

1. (a) <u>A man in his situation,</u>
   START OF MAIN CLAUSE

2. <u>who **comes** upon a young, innocent soul,</u>
   ADJECTIVE CLAUSE, MODIFYING *situation* IN CLAUSE 1

1. (b) <u>**is** apt to hold aloof.</u>
   END OF MAIN CLAUSE

(Theodore Dreiser, *Sister Carrie*.)

(c) An adverb clause relates to its companion clause as an adverb: that is, it modifies a verb in the companion clause. It is joined to its companion clause with an adverbial conjunction such as:

after	if	because	when	until	whenever	although
before	as	unless	while	since	wherever	though.

1. The journey within **is** a very rough road
   MAIN CLAUSE

2. <u>BECAUSE it **is** the road of self-knowledge.</u>
   ADVERB CLAUSE, MODIFYING *is* IN CLAUSE 1

1. <u>IF it **were** not for God's continued help,</u>
   ADVERB CLAUSE, MODIFYING *wouldn't exist* IN CLAUSE 2

2. I **would**n't exist.
   MAIN CLAUSE

(Melissa Jaffer in Caroline Jones, *The Search for Meaning*.)

An adverb clause and its companion clause can always change positions with each other: you can put the adverb clause first or second. That is the test for whether a clause is an adverb clause. In the first of the two example sentences above, the adverb clause stands first; in the second, it stands last. You could just as well reverse the positions of the clauses.

The journey within is a very rough road <u>because it is the road of self-knowledge</u>.
[Because it is the road of self-knowledge, the journey within is a very rough road.]

<u>If it were not for God's continued help</u>, I wouldn't exist.
[I wouldn't exist, if it were not for God's continued help.]

4. A main clause with multiple other clauses.

Each of the example sentences in parts 2 and 3 above features one main clause plus one clause of another kind—coordinate or subordinate. But a sentence is not restricted to having two clauses.

(a)　It can have a main clause and multiple coordinate clauses that are parallel to each other.

1.　I **saw** a book
　　MAIN CLAUSE

2.　<u>AND **opened** it</u>,
　　COORDINATE CLAUSE

3.　<u>BUT I **did**n't read it</u>
　　COORDINATE CLAUSE

4.　<u>SO I **put** it away</u>.
　　COORDINATE CLAUSE

The three coordinate clauses are parallel to each other in the sense that they all relate to the main clause in the same way—each could be a lone coordinate clause relating to the main clause. (Parallel clauses are also called "stacked clauses.")

(b)　Or a sentence can have a main clause and multiple subordinate clauses that are parallel to each other.

1.　There **is** a huge gap between
　　MAIN CLAUSE

2.　<u>WHAT schools **need**</u>
　　NOUN CLAUSE, OBJECT OF *between* IN CLAUSE 1

3.　<u>and WHAT they **can** afford</u>.
　　NOUN CLAUSE, OBJECT OF *between* IN CLAUSE 1

(*TIME*, April 19, 1999.)

The two noun clauses are parallel to each other in the sense that they both relate to the main clause in the same way—as objects of the preposition *between*. (End of underlining: from here on, all the clauses are featured clauses.)

(c)　A sentence can also consist of a mix of main clause + coordinate clause(s) + subordinate clause(s).

1.　My work **is** now (1859) nearly finished;
　　MAIN CLAUSE

2.　but AS it **will** take me many more years to complete it,
　　ADVERB CLAUSE, MODIFYING *have been urged* IN CLAUSE 4

3.　and AS my health **is** far from strong,
　　ADVERB CLAUSE, MODIFYING *have been urged* IN CLAUSE 4

4.　I **have** been urged to publish this abstract.
　　COORDINATE CLAUSE

(Charles Darwin, *The Origin of Species*.)

Clauses 2 and 3 above are parallel to each other—both modify the same verb in the coordinate clause.

> 1. The foreign policy establishment **reacted** with horror,
>   MAIN CLAUSE
>
> 2. AND editors **were** aghast,
>   COORDINATE CLAUSE
>
> 3. WHEN the Senate **rejected** the treaty
>   ADVERB CLAUSE, MODIFYING *reacted* AND *were* IN CLAUSES 1 AND 2
>
> 4. WHICH **would** ban nuclear tests.
>   ADJECTIVE CLAUSE, MODIFYING *treaty* IN CLAUSE 3
>
> (*TIME*, October 25, 1999.)

5. A note on terminology.

- A main clause is also called an "independent clause," "principal clause," "matrix clause," "host clause," or "superordinate clause."
- A coordinate clause is also called a "conjoined clause."
- A subordinate clause is also called a "dependent clause" or an "embedded clause."

See SENTENCE TYPES.

CLAUSES, THEIR INTERRELATIONSHIPS—we can show the relationships of the various types of clauses to each other in diagrams. See CLAUSE TYPES. Main and coordinate clauses are shown on the same level; subordinate clauses on a lower level. Some of the examples come from the entry above.

1. Main clause alone.

> 1. Language worries worth worrying about do exist.
>   MAIN CLAUSE = SENTENCE

2. Main clause and coordinate clause.

> 1. My mother could be very loving and gentle
>   MAIN CLAUSE
>
> 2. or she would completely shut herself off.
>   COORDINATE CLAUSE

3. Main clause and subordinate clause.

(a) Main clause + noun clause.

> 2. must have a plan of conduct.
>   MAIN CLAUSE
>
> 1. Whoever rationally means to be useful
>   NOUN CLAUSE, SUBJECT OF
>   *must have* IN CLAUSE 2

(b) Main clause + adjective clause.

> 1. I am a very fun lady
>   MAIN CLAUSE
>
> 2. who doesn't really often think of my disability
>   ADJECTIVE CLAUSE, MODIFYING *lady*
>   IN CLAUSE 1

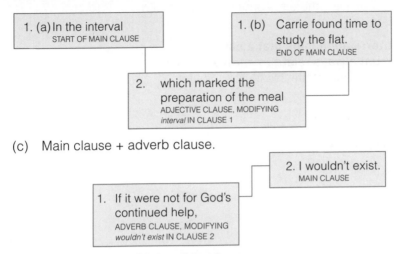

1. (a) In the interval
   START OF MAIN CLAUSE

1. (b) Carrie found time to study the flat.
   END OF MAIN CLAUSE

2. which marked the preparation of the meal
   ADJECTIVE CLAUSE, MODIFYING *interval* IN CLAUSE 1

(c)   Main clause + adverb clause.

2. I wouldn't exist.
   MAIN CLAUSE

1. If it were not for God's continued help,
   ADVERB CLAUSE, MODIFYING *wouldn't exist* IN CLAUSE 2

4. **Main clause and multiple other clauses.**

(a)   Main clause + multiple coordinate clauses that are parallel to each other.

1. I saw a book
   MAIN CLAUSE

2. and opened it,
   COORDINATE CLAUSE

3. but I didn't read it
   COORDINATE CLAUSE

4. so I put it away.
   COORDINATE CLAUSE

(b)   Main clause + multiple subordinate clauses that are parallel to each other.

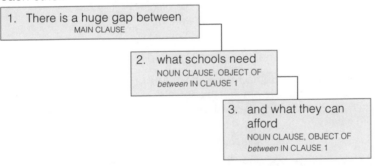

1. There is a huge gap between
   MAIN CLAUSE

2. what schools need
   NOUN CLAUSE, OBJECT OF *between* IN CLAUSE 1

3. and what they can afford
   NOUN CLAUSE, OBJECT OF *between* IN CLAUSE 1

(c)   Main clause + coordinate clause(s) + subordinate clause(s).

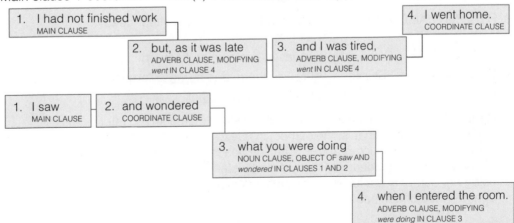

1. I had not finished work
   MAIN CLAUSE

4. I went home.
   COORDINATE CLAUSE

2. but, as it was late
   ADVERB CLAUSE, MODIFYING *went* IN CLAUSE 4

3. and I was tired,
   ADVERB CLAUSE, MODIFYING *went* IN CLAUSE 4

1. I saw
   MAIN CLAUSE

2. and wondered
   COORDINATE CLAUSE

3. what you were doing
   NOUN CLAUSE, OBJECT OF *saw* AND *wondered* IN CLAUSES 1 AND 2

4. when I entered the room.
   ADVERB CLAUSE, MODIFYING *were doing* IN CLAUSE 3

Theoretically—and often in practice—more subordinate clauses can cascade down from clause 4.

5. **It is a feature of clause interrelationships that a clause can never relate to itself—it must always relate to another clause.** All the multi-clause sentences above illustrate this feature. So, for instance, in the last example sentence:

- clause 2 coordinates with clause 1
- clause 3 modifies verbs in clauses 1 and 2
- clause 4 modifies a noun in clause 3.

CLEFT SENTENCE—See SENTENCE TYPES.

CLICHÉ—See FIGURE OF SPEECH.

CLIPPING—See ABBREVIATION.

CLOSED CLASS—See OPEN AND CLOSED CLASSES.

COHESION—from the Latin for "sticking together." A term in functional grammar that relates to the grammar of texts. Cohesion is what makes the words and sentences of a text stick together as a whole. Without cohesion, a text is disjointed and dull—as the following passage shows.

> Melissa Jaffer is one of the most accomplished actresses in Australia. Melissa Jaffer had a desire to live a life of contemplative prayer. Melissa Jaffer went into a closed order of nuns. The Servants of the Blessed Sacrament is an enclosed order of nuns. Melissa Jaffer went back into acting.

Here is the same passage with its original cohesion restored.

> Melissa Jaffer is one of the most accomplished actresses in Australia, whose desire to live a life of contemplative prayer took her into an enclosed order of nuns, the Servants of the Blessed Sacrament, and then brought her back to acting.
>
> (Caroline Jones, *The Search for Meaning Collection*.)

There are four ways of giving a text cohesion. First, an illustration of each, and then a more detailed discussion.

1. REFERENTIAL COHESION: I spoke with Joe and <u>he</u> invited me to visit <u>him</u>.
2. CONJUNCTIVE COHESION: He was at home <u>when</u> I arrived.
3. ELLIPTICAL COHESION: Kitty was there, and <u>so was</u> Margaret.
4. LEXICAL COHESION: We all <u>ate</u> a good <u>meal</u>.

1. **Referential cohesion** means using pronouns or determiners to refer to the known nouns (that is, the names) in a text. You can see how, in the restored text quoted above, Caroline Jones referred to Melissa Jaffer with pronouns (such as *her*) instead of repeatedly using her name. In the following text the instances of referential cohesion are underlined.

MELISSA JAFFER: My grandmother, mother, sister and <u>I</u> had permanent bookings at the Star Theater. <u>We</u> used to go to confession at St Ignatius' Church, then <u>we</u> would go to the Star Theater.

CAROLINE JONES: After several years, as <u>she</u> approached another renewal of <u>her</u> vows, Melissa was called to an interview with a visiting French priest.

(Caroline Jones, *The Search for Meaning.*)

See ANTECEDENT AND PRO-FORM.

2. **Conjunctive cohesion** means using conjunctions (underlined) to bind the parts of a text together.

This book should be read almost <u>as though</u> it were science fiction. <u>But</u> it is not science fiction: it is science. Cliché <u>or</u> not, "stranger <u>than</u> fiction" expresses exactly <u>how</u> I feel about the truth. One of my hopes is <u>that</u> I may have some success in astonishing others.

(Richard Dawkins, *The Selfish Gene.*)

3. **Elliptical cohesion** means using ellipsis—the omission of a word or words—and relying on the readers' minds to fill in the missing bits from what they have read (or heard) before. In the following text, the words that you can omit are crossed out.

Tina looked back and (~~she~~) saw her parents. They were very happy, and she was (~~happy~~) as well. They were strolling along, and she was (~~strolling along~~) too. Do you think they got there on time? Yes, I <u>do</u> (~~think they got there on time~~).

See ANTECEDENT AND PRO-FORM.

4. **Lexical cohesion** means using the lexicon—the words—of a text to give the text unity. There are four varieties of lexical cohesion.

 (a) REPETITION (repeating the same word or words):
 <u>Play</u>, <u>play</u>, <u>play</u>: that's all you seem to do.

 (b) SYNONYMY (using words with a similar meaning):
 I saw this <u>large</u> dog. You know, really <u>huge</u>.

 (c) ANTONYMY (using words of opposite meaning):
 Get <u>educated</u>! You can't always stay <u>ignorant</u>.

 (d) COLLOCATION (using words that go with each other):
 My <u>friend</u> did me a great <u>favor</u> last week.

5. **Following is an extract from a speech that illustrates all of the cohesive devices discussed above.** The speech was delivered by Winston Churchill in the British parliament in June 1940.

 1. I have, myself, full confidence that if all do their duty, if nothing is neglected, we shall prove ourselves once again able to defend our island home, to ride out the storm of war and to outlive the menace of tyranny—if necessary for years, if necessary alone.
 2. We shall not flag or fail.
 3. We shall go on to the end.
 4. We shall fight with growing confidence and growing strength in the air.
 5. We shall defend our island whatever the cost may be.
 6. We shall fight on the beaches, we shall fight on the landing grounds, we shall fight in the fields and in the streets, we shall fight in the hills, we shall never surrender.

 (Cited in *TIME*, April 13, 1998.)

Following are the instances of cohesive techniques in the above text. The bracketed numbers refer to the sentence numbers.

- **REFERENTIAL COHESION:**

PERSONAL PRONOUNS:	I, myself, ourselves (1); we (1–6)
INDEFINITE PRONOUN:	nothing (1)
DETERMINERS:	all, their (1); the (1+3+4+5+6); our (1+5).

- **CONJUNCTIVE COHESION:** if (1); and (1+4+6); or (2); whatever (5).

- **ELLIPTICAL COHESION** (the bracketed words are omitted from the text):

  (~~we shall prove ourselves once again able~~) to ride out the storms of war (1)

  (~~we shall prove ourselves once again able~~) to outlive the menace of tyranny (1)

  (~~we shall fight~~) in the streets (6).

- **LEXICAL COHESION:**

  (a) REPETITION:

if necessary (1)	confidence (1+4)
defend (1+5)	we shall (1–6)
growing (4)	we shall fight (6)
our island (1+5)	

  (b) SYNONYMY: ride out/outlive (1)
  flag/fail (2)
  storm/menace (1)
  go on to the end/never surrender (3+6)
  beaches/landing grounds (6)

  (c) ANTONYMY:

duty/neglected (1)	fields/streets (6)
fight/surrender (6)	

  (d) COLLOCATION: war, menace, tyranny, defend, cost, fight, landing grounds, surrender (1–6).

COMMON GENDER—See GENDER.

COMPARATIVE—See DEGREES OF COMPARISON.

COMPLEMENT—See COMPLETION.

COMPLETION—one of the parts of a sentence. Below, we consider the following kinds of completions.

COMPLETION	OBJECT	INDIRECT OBJECT:	They sent us a postcard.
		DIRECT OBJECT:	They sent us a postcard.
	COMPLEMENT:		They felt fine.

1. What is a completion?

A completion is an obligatory add-on that some verbs need to make their sense complete. If you look at the following items, you will see that the verbs (bold) need some sort of add-on.

(a) They **have taken**	We **knew**	You **should remind**
(b) They **have become**	We **were**	You **remain**

Whatever you need to add on is a "completion."

2. What kinds of completions do verbs take?

Verbs take two kinds of completions: objects and complements. Whether the completions are of one kind or the other depends on the verbs:
- transitive verbs (line (a) in the box above) take object completions
- linking verbs (line (b) in the box above) take complement completions.

See TRANSITIVITY.

We look at each of these two types of completions below.

3. What is the object of a verb?

An object (underlined) is the done-to of a verb.

> We **rewarded** <u>them</u>.
>   VERB   OBJECT

The sign of an object is that, if you change the sentence from the active voice to the passive voice, the object changes into a subject. See VOICE. (For the arrow ⇨ read "becomes.")

ACTIVE	⇨	PASSIVE
We **rewarded** <u>the children</u>.		<u>The children</u> **were rewarded** by us.
VERB OBJECT		SUBJECT VERB

The following text contains some sentences with objects (underlined). Where these occur, I show how you can change the object into a subject by passivation (square brackets). "Passivation" means changing a sentence into the passive voice. The fact that such a change is possible is proof that the underlined words in the original sentences are objects.

> Mary Leakey worked and lived at Laetoli with her staff, her dogs and selected visitors.
>
> Until his death in 1972, her husband Louis visited occasionally
>
> but **spent** <u>most of his time</u> traveling around the world, lecturing and raising funds for research projects.
> [PASSIVE: but <u>most of his time</u> **was spent** traveling around the world ...]
>
> In 1978 Mary **made** <u>what may have been her greatest find</u>.
> [PASSIVE: In 1978 <u>what may have been her greatest find</u> **was made** by Mary.]
>
> Her team **was re-exploring** <u>a site in Tanzania called Laetoli</u>,
> [PASSIVE: <u>A site in Tanzania called Laetoli</u> **was being re-explored** by her team,] cont...

when they **discovered** <u>a trail of remarkably clear ancient hominid footprints</u>
[PASSIVE: when <u>a trail of remarkably clear ancient hominid footprints</u> **was discovered** by them]

impressed and preserved in volcanic ash.

(*Time*, March 29, 1999.)

4. Are there different kinds of objects?

There are two kinds of objects—direct and indirect objects. The following sentences exemplify them.

We **gave** <u>our parents</u> <u>presents</u>.
 VERB INDIRECT OBJECT DIRECT OBJECT

Mummy **told** <u>her child</u> <u>a story</u>.
 VERB INDIRECT OBJECT DIRECT OBJECT

You can see, from the above examples, why one kind of object is called "indirect" and the other "direct":

- direct objects (*presents* and *a story*) have the action done to them
- indirect objects (*our parents* and *her child*) have the actions done for their benefit.

For a more detailed treatment of the difference between direct and indirect objects, see OBJECT.

5. What is the complement of a verb?

A complement—like an object—is an obligatory add-on to a verb. But it is not the done-to (the target) of a verb and you cannot change it into the subject of a verb by passivation. We can see the difference between an object and a complement in the following sentences. (For the arrow ⇨ read "becomes.")

ACTIVE	⇨	PASSIVE
I saw the <u>dancers</u>. OBJECT		The <u>dancers</u> were seen by me. SUBJECT
They were <u>dancers</u>. COMPLEMENT		~~The dancers were by me.~~

So a complement is an obligatory add-on to a verb, other than an object. An object can be passivated into a subject, but a complement can't.

Verbs that take complements are called "linking verbs," see TRANSITIVITY. There are only a dozen or so linking verbs in English. The main linking verbs (bold) are illustrated in the following text; the complements are underlined.

Mr. Copperfield **is** <u>dead</u>.	He **seemed** <u>surprised</u>.
I **was** <u>a posthumous child</u>.	I stand by, trying **to look** <u>unmoved</u>.
You **are** <u>a pretty sharp fellow</u>.	Their sleep **became** <u>lighter</u>.
Seagoing people **were** <u>short of money</u>.	I **felt** <u>quite uncomfortable and confused</u>.
The fowls **look** <u>terribly tall</u> to me.	I **remained** <u>hungry</u>.
(Charles Dickens, *David Copperfield*.)	

6. **What language units can act as objects and as complements?**

   (a) Objects of verbs (bold) are always nouns or noun equivalents.

   > Margaret Court **inspired** <u>a generation of Australian tennis players</u> when, in 1963, she became the first
   > VERB   OBJECT (NOUN PHRASE)
   >
   > Australian woman **to win** <u>the Wimbledon singles title</u>. She **repeated** the <u>performance</u> two years later.
   > VERB   OBJECT (NOUN PHRASE)   VERB   OBJECT (NOUN)
   >
   > (*Time*, October 25, 1999.)

   For an expanded list, see OBJECT.

   (b) There are four kinds of words (or their equivalents) that can act
        as complements (underlined) of verbs (bold).

   - NOUNS (OR NOUN EQUIVALENTS):
     This **is** my <u>garden</u>. This **is** <u>it</u>.   This **isn't** <u>that</u>.
     VERB   NOUN   VERB PRONOUN   VERB   DET
   - ADJECTIVES (INCLUDING PARTICIPLES):
     I **am** <u>happy</u>.   I **am** not <u>depressed</u>.
     VERB   ADJECTIVE   VERB   PARTICIPLE
   - ADVERBS:
     They **remained** <u>there</u>.   We **stayed** <u>afloat</u>.
     VERB   ADVERB   VERB   ADVERB
   - VERBS:
     They **asked** me <u>to sing</u>.
     VERB   VERB

   In the last example sentence above, the complement *to sing* follows
   an object—*me*. So a verb (such as *asked*) can have both an object
   and a complement.

7. **Here is a text that features both kinds of completions—objects
   and complements.** The verbs are in bold.

   > Some slaves **were rowing** <u>a Roman Galley</u> along the Mediterranean coast.
   > VERB   OBJECT
   >
   > It **was** <u>a lovely cloudless day</u>.
   > VERB   COMPLEMENT
   >
   > One slave **addressed** <u>his mate</u>: "It **is** <u>great</u> **to be** <u>out</u> on a day like this, **isn't** <u>it</u>?"
   > VERB   OBJECT   VERB COMPLEMENT VERB COMPLEMENT   VERB   COMPLEMENT
   >
   > "You **won't think** <u>that</u> tomorrow," his companion **said**. "We **are taking** <u>Antony and Cleopatra</u>
   > VERB   OBJECT   VERB   VERB   OBJECT
   >
   > <u>water-skiing</u>."
   > COMPLEMENT

8. **A note on terminology.**

   Some modern grammarians use the term "complement" for what I
   have called "completion." That leaves the problem of how to
   distinguish between what, in the entry above, I have called an
   "object" and a "complement." The problem has been solved in
   various ways.

   - Most grammarians call an object an "object"—though functional
     linguists call it a "participant complement."
   - As for the complement, grammarians grope for various terms to
     describe it: "attributive complement," "identifier complement,"

"copular complement," "subject complement," and so on.

I believe that this introduces undue complexity into the terminology. My solution is to let:

- "COMPLETION" stand generically for any obligatory add-on to a verb

- "OBJECT" stand specifically for a completion that is capable of passivation

- "COMPLEMENT" stand specifically for a completion that is not capable of passivation.

This terminology is in line with the use of the terms "object" and "complement" in traditional and in structuralist grammar. The only addition is the generic term "completion," which I use to embrace both "object" and "complement."

See SENTENCE PARTS.

COMPLEX SENTENCE—See SENTENCE TYPES.

COMPOUND—from the Latin for "putting together." Two or more words that act as a single unit. Typical examples are: *sergeant major*, which is the name of a rank; or *was jogging*, which is an action. A compound is intermediate between a word and a phrase. In functional grammar "compounds" are called "groups." See GRAMMAR UNITS.

In the examples below, the square brackets contain the one-word equivalents of the underlined compounds.

Elizabeth Lavenza [she] became the inmate of my parents' house.
    COMPOUND NOUN

She herself [Justine] wept as Elizabeth spoke.
COMPOUND PRONOUN

Her presence had seemed [seemed] a blessing to them.
    COMPOUND VERB

The road ran by the side of [beside] the lake.
    COMPOUND PREPOSITION

As soon as [when] it was light, I went up on the deck.
COMPOUND CONJUNCTION

Some new object was associated with the light-hearted [happy] gaiety of boyhood.
    COMPOUND ADJECTIVE

(Mary Shelley, *Frankenstein*.)

COMPOUND SENTENCE—See SENTENCE TYPES.

COMPOUND-COMPLEX SENTENCE—See SENTENCE TYPES.

CONDITIONAL—a sentence that consists of a condition clause and a consequence clause.

1. Examples of conditionals.

CONDITION CLAUSE	CONSEQUENCE CLAUSE
If you help me	I will help you.
If I were a bird	I would be able to fly.
If I had arrived sooner	I would have been in time.

It is also possible to rewrite the last sentence without *if*.

Had I arrived sooner	I would have been in time.

It is equally valid to put the consequence clause before the condition clause.

CONSEQUENCE CLAUSE	CONDITION CLAUSE
I will help you	if you help me.
I would be able to fly	if I were a bird.
I would have been in time	if I had arrived sooner.

And the last sentence again without *if*.

I would have been in time	had I arrived sooner.

2. What tense-aspects do you use in conditional sentences?

In the three most common types of conditional sentences you use the following tense-aspects. See TENSE AND ASPECT.

Type A: future simple + present simple.

I <u>will help</u> you	if you <u>help</u> me.
FUTURE SIMPLE	PRESENT SIMPLE

Type B: future in the past simple + past simple.

I <u>would be</u> able to fly	if I <u>were</u> a bird.
FUTURE IN THE PAST SIMPLE	PAST SIMPLE

In a condition clause of type B, the verb *to be* takes the form *were* both in the singular (*if <u>I were</u> a bird*) and in the plural (*if <u>we were</u> birds*).

Type C: future in the past perfect + past perfect.

I <u>would have been</u> in time	if I <u>had arrived</u> sooner.
FUTURE IN THE PAST PERFECT	PAST PERFECT

Conditional sentences of types B and C are subjunctive sentences. See SUBJUNCTIVE.

3. What do conditional sentences imply?

Type A implies that the condition and the consequence may or may not occur in the future. Here is the type A conditional sentence again, with the implication in square brackets.

If you help me [and I wonder whether you will], I will help you [that may well happen].

Type B implies that, because the condition does not exist in the present, the consequence also does not exist. Here is the type B conditional sentence again, with the implication in square brackets.

If I were a bird [but I'm not a bird], I would be able to fly [but I can't fly].

Type C implies that, because the condition wasn't fulfilled in the past, the consequence failed to occur in the past. Here is the type C conditional sentence again, with the implication in square brackets.

> If I had arrived sooner [but I failed to arrive sooner], I would have been in time [but I was late].

The following example sentences all come from a single text. The implications are in square brackets.

Type A (also called the "possible future"):

It will not save him from getting into trouble [and I'm not sure whether it will save him] if he is not careful [and he may or may not be careful].
If he does not say the right thing to them [and it is possible that he will] we are all done for [and that may well come about].

Type B (also called the "unreal present" or "counterfactual present"):

If they left the bank in their canoes [but they are not leaving the bank] they would get lost in the fog [but they are not lost in the fog].
If I were typical [but of course I'm not], I wouldn't be talking like this with you [but, clearly, I am talking like this with you].

[Notice, in the last sentence above, the use of *If I were*, not *If I was*.]

Type C (also called the "failed past" or "counterfactual past"):

If she had offered to come aboard [luckily she didn't offer to come aboard] I really think I would have tried to shoot her [but I didn't try to shoot her].
They would have been even more impressive [but they weren't], those heads on the stakes, if their faces had not been turned to the house [but they were turned to the house].

(Joseph Conrad, *The Heart of Darkness*.)

CONJOINED CLAUSE—another name for "coordinate clause." See CLAUSE TYPES.

CONJUNCTION—from the Latin for "joining together." One of the word classes; a word that joins a variety of language units.

1. What do conjunctions join?

Conjunctions join any of the following language units.

- ONE WORD WITH ANOTHER:

  tired **but** happy
  WORD CONJ WORD

- ONE COMPOUND WITH ANOTHER:

  Romeo Montague **and** Juliet Capulet
  COMPOUND CONJ COMPOUND

- ONE PHRASE WITH ANOTHER:

  ready to go **and** eager to start
  PHRASE CONJ PHRASE

- ONE CLAUSE WITH ANOTHER:

  I went home, **because** I felt homesick.
  CLAUSE CONJ CLAUSE

- ONE SENTENCE WITH ANOTHER:

  It was raining. **So** I took an umbrella along.
  SENTENCE CONJ SENTENCE

The following text illustrates conjunctions in action.

> CONJUNCTIONS (underlined) JOIN WORDS, COMPOUNDS OR PHRASES (bold)
>
> The debate over animal experimentation has become deadly serious. In Britain, we've seen bombings, **hunger strikes** <u>and</u> **death threats**. Yet amidst the **violence** <u>and</u> **rhetoric**, one thing is missing: no one really knows what the public think because they haven't been asked where they would draw the line on animal research.
>
> CONJUNCTIONS (underlined) JOIN CLAUSES (on separate lines)
>
> Market &Opinion Research International (MORI) asked a representative sample of British adults <u>whether</u> they supported or opposed each of a series of hypothetical experiments.
>
> Our poll reveals <u>that</u> most people seem to carefully weigh the pros and cons of each experiment before deciding <u>whether</u> or not to give their support.
>
> CONJUNCTIONS (underlined) JOIN SENTENCES (on separate lines)
>
> In a democracy, people's views do count, of course.
> <u>And</u> we suspected that a desire for better drugs and vaccines might not necessarily translate into blanket approval for all the experiments that are sanctioned at the moment.
> <u>So</u> to work out exactly where the British public draw the line, we commissioned MORI to poll people aged 15 and over.
>
> (*New Scientist*, May 22, 1999.)

2. What is the connection between conjunctions and clauses?

A major use of conjunctions is to join clauses—sentence parts. When you use conjunctions in this way, it is often (but not always) possible to choose between putting the conjoined clause (headed by the conjunction) first and putting it second. Because the beginning of the sentence is more prominent, your choice will depend on which clause you want the reader or listener to focus on.

In the example sentences below, the conjunctions are bold and underlined.

| <u>I will help you</u>
UNCONJOINED CLAUSE | **<u>if</u>** <u>you help me</u>.
CONJOINED CLAUSE | [Focus on my helping you.] |
| **<u>If</u>** <u>you help me</u>
CONJOINED CLAUSE | <u>I will help you</u>.
UNCONJOINED CLAUSE | [Focus on your helping me.] |

See MARKED AND UNMARKED CLAUSE COMPLEX.

CONJUNCTION SUBCLASSES—there are two subclasses of conjunctions. One of them has three subdivisions.

1. COORDINATING CONJUNCTIONS:
   and, but, either … or, neither … nor

2. SUBORDINATING CONJUNCTIONS
   (a) NOMINAL: whoever, whichever, that
   (b) ADJECTIVAL: who, whom, which, that
   (c) ADVERBIAL: if, unless, when, because

We look at each of these on the following page.

1. What are coordinating conjunctions?

Coordinating conjunctions (bold and underlined) are conjunctions that join small-scale units of language such as words and phrases.

We visited <u>Jan</u> **<u>and</u>** <u>Kim</u>.
 WORD   WORD

We visited <u>some of our friends</u> **<u>but</u>** <u>not all of them</u>.
 PHRASE   PHRASE

Coordinating conjunctions (or "coordinators") also join clauses. The clause headed by a coordinating conjunction (bold and underlined) is called a "coordinate clause."

<u>Wells must know the right answer</u>   **<u>for</u>** <u>he was third in grammar</u>.
 MAIN CLAUSE   COORDINATE CLAUSE

<u>It was not the chapel</u>   **<u>but</u>** <u>still you had to speak under your breath</u>.
 MAIN CLAUSE   COORDINATE CLAUSE

<u>Have you a pain</u>   **<u>or</u>** <u>what's up with you</u>?
 MAIN CLAUSE   COORDINATE CLAUSE

(James Joyce, *Portrait of the Artist as a Young Man.*)

The main coordinating conjunctions (including compound conjunctions) are:

and	either	neither	either or
but	or	nor	neither nor
so	still	not only but also	
yet	than	as well as	

2. What are subordinating conjunctions?

Subordinating conjunctions (or "subordinators") join clauses to each other. But the two clauses are not equal. One is the main clause. The other—headed by a subordinating conjunction—is the subordinate clause.

In what sense is it subordinate?

In the sense that the subordinate clause, together with its subordinating conjunction, cannot stand alone but must be joined to a companion clause. It can be joined in any one of three functions.

The featured clauses are underlined; the conjunctions are bold and underlined—

(a)   AS A NOUN CLAUSE:
 <u>What</u> <u>they don't know</u>   <u>won't hurt them</u>.
 NOUN CLAUSE, SUBJECT OF *won't hurt*   MAIN CLAUSE

(b)   AS AN ADJECTIVE CLAUSE:
 <u>You've got something</u>   **<u>that</u>** <u>I would like to borrow</u>.
 MAIN CLAUSE   ADJECTIVE CLAUSE MODIFYING *something*

(c)   AS AN ADVERB CLAUSE:
 <u>When</u> <u>they are gone</u>   <u>I feel blue</u>.
 ADVERB CLAUSE MODIFYING *feel*   MAIN CLAUSE

We now look at each of these kinds of subordinate clauses, and at the conjunctions that head them, in greater detail.

(a)   A noun clause (underlined) is joined to the main clause with a nominal conjunction (bold and underlined).

What I have written   may seem to be against Jonathan Swift.
NOUN CLAUSE   MAIN CLAUSE

(George Orwell, *Collected Essays, Journalism and Letters*, vol. 4.)

The subordinate clause *what I have written* acts as a noun because it is the subject of the verb *may seem*.

The main nominal conjunctions (also called "complementizers") are:

whoever	who	which	when	how	why
whatever	whom	that	where	what	whether

(b) An adjective clause (underlined) is joined to the main clause with an adjectival conjunction (bold and underlined).

I met an American publisher
MAIN CLAUSE

who told me about his firm's nine-month lawsuit.
ADJECTIVE CLAUSE

(George Orwell, *Collected Essays, Journalism and Letters*, vol. 4.)

The subordinate clause *who told me about his firm's nine-month lawsuit* acts as an adjective because it modifies the noun *publisher*.

The main adjectival conjunctions (also called "relative pronouns") are:

who	whom	whose	which	that	when	where

(c) An adverb clause (underlined) is joined to the main clause with an adverbial conjunction (bold and underlined).

When one was not asleep,   one usually seemed to be eating.
ADVERB CLAUSE   MAIN CLAUSE

(George Orwell, *Collected Essays, Journalism and Letters*, vol. 4.)

The subordinate clause *when one was not asleep* acts as an adverb that modifies the verb *seemed*.

The main adverbial conjunctions are:

after	if	because	when	until	whenever	although
before	as	unless	while	since	wherever	though

CONTENT WORD AND FUNCTION WORD—terms that show the division of the word classes into two groups.

1. **Content words** (also called "lexical words," or "full words") are nouns, adjectives, verbs, and adverbs. These bear the main meaning of a text.

2. **Function words** (also called "form words," or "grammatical words") are members of all the other word classes. Function words place content words within coherent structures. In the following example sentence, the content words are underlined; all the rest are function words.

I composed the text for this dictionary on a very old computer.
   VERB   NOUN   NOUN   ADVERB ADJECTIVE NOUN

If you read the content words alone, you can get some sort of meaning from the text—but not if you read the function words alone.

CONTENT WORDS	FUNCTION WORDS
Composed text dictionary very old computer.	I the for this on a.

See OPEN AND CLOSED CLASSES.

CONTEXT—(also called "context of situation") a term that means "setting" or "surrounding circumstances." Context covers the things that are outside of language, but that affect the way we use language. There are three things that have such an effect.

1. THE MODE, or medium, that we use in language—a sign, speech, writing and so on.
2. THE FIELD, or topic, that the text deals with—school, business, recreation and so on.
3. THE TENOR, or social setting, of the text—a family setting, a workplace setting and so on.

We look at each of these below.

1. **The mode,** or medium, that we use to communicate affects how the text (the message) comes across. For example, we might want to let people know in writing where an entrance is. So we put up a sign.

But, in a different context, we might convey the same message by speaking the words:

"This is where you go in."

2. **The field,** or topic, that the text deals with affects the vocabulary that we use. So, for example, if we are discussing tennis we will probably use words such as:

racket	ball	game	set	match	serve	forehand

But if we are discussing movies, the vocabulary will more likely feature words such as:

western	titles	music	rating	actors	sheriff	director

3. **The tenor,** or social setting, of the text affects the general tone of the text, including register, vocabulary, and other aspects of the text. So, for example, if the social setting is that of a parent and an infant, the parent might say cajolingly:

"Here's a banana. What's that? Banana. Ba-na-na. Yes! That's right: banana!"

But if you wanted to say the same thing to a friend, you might say—

"Please, help yourself to a banana if you like."

We can see all three contextual features—the mode, the field, the tenor—in two letters that I received. The first letter was from my daughter; the second, from the Australian Broadcasting Corporation.

LETTER FROM MY DAUGHTER

Hello. I've just come back from my trip to the nature reserve with Micki and the Nature Conservation Society. It was some trip! Only fifteen people signed up so we had a minibus, not a big bus & it was more intimate—also people tended to talk to each other more & for instance today in the morning they filled the minibus with balloons and everyone sang happy birthday to me.

LETTER FROM THE AUSTRALIAN BROADCASTING COMMISSION

Your letter of 3 March has been passed to us for our attention. We are prepared to grant you permission to reproduce material from *Conversations with Caroline Jones*. This permission is granted on the understanding that you can use up to 2,000 words for a nominal fee of $100.

We can compare and contrast the contexts of the two letters as follows.

	LETTER FROM MY DAUGHTER	LETTER FROM THE ABC
MODE:	A letter.	A letter.
FIELD:	Recount of a bus tour.	Permission to use copyright material.
TENOR:	(a) Addressed to George Stern.	(a) Addressed to George Stern.
	(b) Written by George's daughter.	(b) Written by a permissions editor.

There are two points of contextual similarity in the above texts:
(i)   both are in the same mode, namely letters
(ii)   in tenor, both are addressed to the same person.

There are two points of contextual difference in the above texts:
(i)   in tenor, one is by my daughter and the other is by an official
(ii)   in field, one is about a bus trip and the other is about copyright.

4. **Why is context important?**

Context sums up and incorporates the other five features of text grammar discussed in this dictionary—the five features listed below. As such, it is an important part of grammar. As Beswick says: "The context of situation provides the foundation for systemic-functional linguistics" (1996:86). We can see this from the fact that context often affects:

• GENRE—whether you use a visual or an auditory, a literary or a non-literary, text

• REGISTER—at what level of formality you pitch the text

• MODALITY—what language and what non-language means you

use to give the text varying degrees of expressiveness

- COHESION—whether you structure your text cohesively or use bursts of language

- TURN-TAKING—whether the text involves one or more speakers or writers.

CONTINUOUS ASPECT—See TENSE AND ASPECT.

CONTRACTION—See ABBREVIATION.

COORDINATE CLAUSE—See CLAUSE TYPES.

COPULA—See TRANSITIVITY.

COUNT NOUN AND NONCOUNT NOUN—terms for two different kinds of nouns.

1. **What are the features of count and noncount nouns?**

   (a) Count nouns are those that have both singular and plural forms: *tree–trees*, *child–children*. They are called "count nouns" because it makes sense to count them: *one tree*, *two trees* …

   (b) Noncount nouns (also called "collective nouns" or "mass nouns") have only singular forms: *milk*; *honey*. They are called noncount nouns because it isn't usual to count them: ~~*one milk*~~, ~~*two milks*~~ …

   (c) A further distinction between count and noncount nouns involves the use of the indefinite article (*a* or *an*). Count nouns in the singular take indefinite articles (*a tree*); noncount nouns don't (*timber*).

   (d) Both count and noncount nouns can take definite articles (*the*).

   The following text illustrates the above features.

> Reading **the** fine <u>print</u> of **a** MasterCard annual <u>report</u> in **a** Chinese <u>café</u> is **a** perplexing <u>experience</u>.
>   NONCOUNT   COUNT   COUNT   COUNT
>
> China, where few ordinary <u>citizens</u> have **a** credit <u>card</u>—indeed where revolving consumer <u>credit</u> is
>   COUNT   COUNT   NONCOUNT
>
> illegal—is MasterCard's second-largest <u>market</u> after America. In 1997, its <u>turnover</u> in China was an
>   COUNT   NONCOUNT
>
> astounding $73 billion. How is the <u>circle</u> squared? As in some other <u>countries</u>, <u>cardholders</u> must
>   COUNT   COUNT   COUNT
>
> deposit <u>money</u> into their <u>accounts</u>. <u>Purchases</u> are deducted from these <u>funds</u>. MasterCard's <u>success</u>
>   NONCOUNT   COUNT   COUNT   COUNT   COUNT
>
> in China is thus more **an** <u>indictment</u> of the country's dreadful <u>banks</u> than **a** capitalist <u>celebration</u> of
>   COUNT   COUNT   COUNT
>
> <u>plastic</u>.
> NONCOUNT
>
> (*The Economist*, January 2, 1999.)

Note the following points about the above text.

- Apart from the noncount nouns, there are two other nouns that are not preceded by indefinite articles—*China* and *America*. These are proper nouns. Proper nouns make up another subset of nouns that don't take indefinite articles. See NOUN SUBCLASSES.

- All the plural nouns in the above text (*citizens, countries, cardholders, accounts, purchases, funds*) are by definition count nouns, since only count nouns have plural forms.

- All the nouns that are preceded by indefinite articles (*a report, a café, an experience, a card, an indictment, a celebration*) are by definition count nouns, since only count nouns take indefinite articles. The word *billion*, though it is preceded by an indefinite article, is not a count noun: it is a determiner. See DETERMINER.

- Other singular count nouns in the text are *print, market, circle* and *success*. True, they have no indefinite articles preceding them, but they are preceded by other determiners: <u>*MasterCard's*</u> … *market*, <u>*the*</u> *circle*, <u>*MasterCard's*</u> *success*. So we learn that a singular count noun doesn't have to have an indefinite article preceding it, so long as it has some other determiner preceding it. Besides, these count nouns are capable of taking articles. We could, in appropriate contexts, say: *a market, a circle, a success*.

2. Are there nouns that can have either a count or a noncount function?

There are many nouns in the language that are usually noncount nouns, but that can also function as count nouns. What determines whether a particular noun is one or the other is (a) the context and (b) the presence or the absence of an indefinite article or a plural form.

NONCOUNT FUNCTION	COUNT FUNCTION
I like <u>coffee</u>.	I'll have **a** <u>coffee</u>, please.
<u>Business</u> is booming.	They started **a** new <u>business</u> when their old <u>businesses</u> failed.
This sweater is made of <u>wool</u>.	There are dear <u>wools</u> and there are cheap <u>wools</u>.

An example text.

The <u>task</u> in the postwar <u>years</u> was to sublimate the old <u>conflicts</u>
   COUNT   COUNT   COUNT

of <u>blood</u> and <u>steel</u> into comparatively harmless commercial <u>issues</u>, over
   COUNT   NONCOUNT   COUNT

the <u>trade</u>   <u>rules</u> for <u>fruits</u> and <u>cheeses</u>.
   COUNT   NONCOUNT COUNT   COUNT

(*Time*, Winter 1996.)

Ordinarily, *fruit* and *cheese* are noncount nouns, used in the singular without an indefinite article. In the above text, however, they are count nouns, as their plural forms show.

3. Collective nouns are a subclass of count nouns.

Examples of collective nouns are *team, band, group, government*. Like other count nouns, they take indefinite articles (*a team*), and they have both singular and plural forms (*team–teams*).

The special feature of collective nouns is that they refer to a collection of individuals. Sometimes a collective noun relates to the collection, and the noun therefore goes with a singular verb (*The team is* [singular] *flying to Perth*); sometimes it relates to the individuals, and the noun therefore goes with a plural verb (*The team are* [plural] *putting on their uniforms*).

Here are some textual examples.

So far, the team has [singular] found three different ways in which the butterflies increase the visibility of their blue flashes.
(*New Scientist*, June 26, 1999.)

The team are [plural] also investigating a range of other species, from the green Papilios of Southeast Asia to the European peacock with its glittering purple eye-spots.
(*New Scientist*, June 26, 1999.)

Dr Hubel's group has [singular] measured the electrical responses of cortical nerve cells to a range of stimuli.
(*The Economist*, April 9, 1999.)

A sound abroad in the night had grown broad, deep, and terrible, before the fated group were [plural] conscious of it.
(Nathaniel Hawthorne, "The Ambitious Guest.")

DATIVE—See CASE.

DEGREES OF COMPARISON—a feature of adjectives and adverbs: the fact that you can use these words on a threefold scale as follows.

POSITIVE	COMPARATIVE	SUPERLATIVE	
small	small*er*	small*est*	[ADJECTIVE]
friendly	friendli*er*	friendli*est*	[ADJECTIVE]
carefully	*more* carefully	*most* carefully	[ADVERB]
sweetly	*more* sweetly	*most* sweetly	[ADVERB]

Words of one syllable take the *–er* and *–est* suffixes. Words of three syllables or more take *more* and *most*.

POSITIVE	COMPARATIVE	SUPERLATIVE
great	greater	greatest
sweet	sweeter	sweetest
marvellous	more marvellous	most marvellous
influential	more influential	most influential

Some words of two syllables (often those ending in *–y*) take *–er* and *–est*; others take *more* and *most*.

POSITIVE	COMPARATIVE	SUPERLATIVE
tidy	tidier	tidiest
lovely	lovelier	loveliest
secret	more secret	most secret
boring	more boring	most boring

Example texts.

> They hope to reveal your antics to the <u>wider</u> world.
> COMPARATIVE
>
> This makes genetics experiments <u>faster</u>.
> COMPARATIVE
>
> Unlike <u>more sophisticated</u> creatures, worms are <u>easy</u> to use in a laboratory.
> COMPARATIVE   POSITIVE
>
> People watch for the <u>slightest</u> signs of ageing.
> SUPERLATIVE
>
> (*The Economist*, June 11, 1999.)
>
> Scientists believe they can make <u>more rapid</u> progress.
> COMPARATIVE
>
> The <u>strongest</u> views were held by people who had signed petitions.
> SUPERLATIVE
>
> The results provide the <u>most complete</u> picture so far of the public's views.
> SUPERLATIVE
>
> We could tell which factors correlate <u>most strongly</u> with disapproval of research involving animals.
> SUPERLATIVE
>
> (*New Scientist*, May 22, 1999.)

DEMONSTRATIVE—See DETERMINER.

DEPENDENT CLAUSE—See CLAUSE TYPES.

DETERMINER—from the Latin for "limiter." One of the word classes. Determiners (DET) include words such as those underlined below.

> I saw <u>that</u> **cat**.
> DET NOUN
>
> Three **cats** sat in <u>a</u> **row**.
> DET   NOUN   DET NOUN
>
> <u>This</u> is <u>my</u> **cat**.
> DET   DET
>
> <u>Our</u> little **cats** like to doze.
> DET   NOUN
>
> <u>Some</u> **cats** were drinking milk.
> DET   NOUN
>
> <u>What</u> <u>a</u> **cat**!
> DET DET NOUN
>
> <u>Few</u> **cats** bother to chase mice.
> NOUN DET
>
> <u>Such</u> <u>a</u> **cat**!
> DET DET NOUN

1. How do determiners function?

   (a)   In the above examples, the determiners tell you how determinate—how definite—the associated nouns (bold) are. Determiners function somewhat like adjectives: they can modify nouns.

   (b)   Determiners can also substitute for nouns. In this latter function, determiners act somewhat like pronouns.

> Look at <u>that</u>.   I have <u>a</u> <u>few</u>.   I want <u>another</u> <u>three</u>.
> DET   DET DET   DET   DET

2. Why don't we classify determiners as adjectives or as pronouns?

The reason that we don't classify determiners as adjectives is that (with a few exceptions) they lack an important characteristic of adjectives: the three degrees of comparison (*small, smaller, smallest*). And the reason that we don't classify them as pronouns is that, unlike "real" pronouns, determiners can often also function adjectivally. For these reasons, determiners are in a class of their own.

Here is a text with the determiners underlined.

> At a recent conference on interactive publishing, there was only one thing on the minds of the 300 people present. Could they actually make money on the Net? For most, that means supplementing advertising revenues with subscription revenues. That causes a problem. Most believe that, because they have paid for a PC, a second telephone line and a subscription to a service provider, everything else should be free.
>
> (*The Economist*, February 14, 1998.)

DETERMINER SUBCLASSES—there are three subclasses of determiners (A–C below), each with several subdivisions. In the examples that follow, the nouns to which the determiners relate are in bold.

A. Predeterminers

MULTIPLIERS:	double, fourfold	We want double **portions**.
FRACTIONS:	half, a third, two-fifths	I drove at half **speed**.
INTENSIFIERS:	what! such!	Such **impudence**!
QUANTIFIERS:	all, both, most	I like most **people**.

B. Central determiners

ARTICLES:	a, an, the	Get a **book** from the **shelf**.
DEMONSTRATIVES:	this, that, these, those, another, other	That **tree** is in another **garden**.
DISTRIBUTIVES:	each, every, either, neither	I have a gift for each **person**.
POSSESSIVES—		
(i) PRONOMINAL:	my, your, his, her, its, our, your, their	You can borrow my **video**.
(ii) NOMINAL:	Renata's, Adam's, people's	You can borrow Kim's **video**.
INTERROGATIVES:	what? which? whose?	Whose **book** is that?
QUANTIFIERS:	some, any, no	I have no **problem** with them.

C. Postdeterminers

CARDINAL NUMBERS:	one, two, three hundred	Two **heads** are better than one.
ORDINAL NUMBERS:	first, second, thirty-fifth	It was my first **tennis match**.
QUANTIFIERS—		
(i) SIMPLE:	few, fewer, much, more, less, least	I have few **pals**; Kim has more.
(ii) COMPOUND:	a little, a lot of, a great deal of	I have lots of **time** to spare.

The names "predeterminers" (group A), "central determiners" (group B) and "postdeterminers" (group C) reflect the fact that, if there are members of two or more of the groups occurring together, they stand in the sequence
A + B + C.

> They had twice (A) the (B) **pleasure**.
> [Not: They had the (B) twice (A) **pleasure**.]
>
> I want two-thirds (A) more (C) **pudding**.
> [Not: I want more (C) two-thirds (A) **pudding**.]
>
> All (A) those (B) four (C) **students** have passed.
> [Not: Four (C) those (B) all (A) **students** have passed.]

The muddled up order of determiners in square brackets does not work. If your native language is English, you feel this intuitively: it is not something that you have to learn.

DIRECT AND INDIRECT OBJECT—See OBJECT.

DIRECT AND REPORTED SPEECH—(also called "direct and indirect speech") two different ways of showing what somebody has said or written. Direct speech indicates the actual words used; reported speech gives an indirect account of the words.

DIRECT SPEECH:	Mark Twain said, "The report of my death was an exaggeration."
REPORTED SPEECH:	Mark Twain said that the report of his death had been an exaggeration.

There is a complex set of changes that takes place between direct and reported speech. The most obvious changes illustrated above are:

- the use of quotation marks and an initial capital letter in direct speech
- the absence of these features in reported speech.

Here is a catalog of the other changes.

1. **Changes to the introductory clause.** (For the arrow ⇨ read "becomes.")

	DIRECT SPEECH ⇨	REPORTED SPEECH
(a) STATEMENTS:	She said, "It is getting late."	She said that it was getting late. Or: She said it was getting late.
(b) QUESTIONS:	I said, "Do you really think so?"	I asked whether she really thought so.
(c) COMMANDS:	Hamlet said, "Never doubt I love."	Hamlet told Ophelia never to doubt he loved.

(a) In STATEMENTS, the word *that* in the introductory clause in reported speech is optional. You can say: *She said that it was getting late* or *She said it was getting late*.

(b) In QUESTIONS.

  (i) The introductory *whether* occurs only if there is no interrogative adverb at the start of the question. If there is an interrogative adverb (underlined), use the adverb: *"Where are you going?"* becomes *I asked them where they were going*.

  (ii) Instead of *asked*, you can also use other words with a similar meaning: *I inquired where they were going*; or *I wondered where they were going*; or *I wanted to know where they were going*.

(c) In COMMANDS, instead of *told* you could also use *asked, ordered, commanded* or other words with a similar meaning: *"Eat your spinach"* becomes *I told them to eat their spinach* or *I asked them to eat their spinach* or *I begged them to eat their spinach* or *I implored them to eat their spinach*.

2. Changes to pronouns.

The changes are a matter of common sense.

DIRECT SPEECH	⇨	REPORTED SPEECH
Jack said, "<u>I</u> went up the hill." Jill said, "<u>I</u> went too."		Jack said <u>he</u> had gone up the hill, and Jill said <u>she</u> had gone too.

3. Terms indicating nearness change into terms indicating remoteness.

DIRECT SPEECH	⇨	REPORTED SPEECH
Jack said, "I need <u>this</u> pail and <u>these</u> climbing boots, and I need them <u>here</u> and <u>now</u>."		Jack asserted that he needed <u>that</u> pail and <u>those</u> climbing boots, and that he needed them <u>there</u> and <u>then</u>.

4. Changes to time designations.

DIRECT SPEECH	⇨	REPORTED SPEECH
today		that day/the same day
tonight		that night/the same night
yesterday		the day before/the previous day
the day before yesterday		two days before/two days earlier
last night (week etc.)		the previous night (week etc.) the night (week etc.) before
tomorrow		the next day/the following day
the day after tomorrow		two days later
next week (month etc.)		the following week (month etc.)
recently/lately		in the recent past

An example.

DIRECT SPEECH	⇨	REPORTED SPEECH
He said, "<u>Last week</u> I lent you a book that I would like back <u>today</u>—not <u>next week</u>."		He said that <u>the previous week</u> he had lent me a book that he would like back <u>that day</u>—not <u>the following week</u>.

5. Changes to verb tenses (see TENSE AND ASPECT).

Whether tense changes occur in the quoted words of the reported speech depends on the tense of the verb in the introductory clause.

(a) If the verb in the introductory clause is in the present tense (*She says that ...*) or in the future tense (*He will say that ...*), the tenses of the verbs in the quoted part of the sentence (underlined) remain unchanged.

DIRECT SPEECH	⇨	REPORTED SPEECH
She says, "Things <u>were</u> bad, they <u>are</u> <u>changing</u> and they <u>will become</u> better." He will say, "I <u>did</u> it, I <u>am</u> <u>doing</u> it again and I <u>will do</u> it some more."		She says that things <u>were</u> bad, they <u>are changing</u> and they <u>will become</u> better. He will say that he <u>did</u> it, he <u>is doing</u> it again and he <u>will do</u> it some more.

(b) If the verb in the introductory clause is in the past tense (*She said that ...*) or in the future in the past tense (*He would say that ...*), the following changes occur to the tenses of the verbs (underlined) in the quoted part of the sentence.

(i) The present tense changes into the past tense.

DIRECT SPEECH	⇨	REPORTED SPEECH
She said, "I <u>know</u> what to do."		She said that she <u>knew</u> what to do.
He said, "I <u>am writing</u> a letter."		He said that he <u>was writing</u> a letter.

There is one exception to this rule. If the quoted part of the sentence expresses some universal truth, you may choose between leaving the verb in the present tense or changing it into the past tense.

DIRECT SPEECH	⇨	REPORTED SPEECH
She said, "Mars <u>is</u> a planet."		She said that Mars <u>is</u> a planet.
		Or: She said that Mars <u>was</u> a planet.

   (ii)   The past simple tense changes into the past perfect tense.

DIRECT SPEECH	⇨	REPORTED SPEECH
She said, "I <u>took</u> my vacation in June."		She said she <u>had taken</u> her vacation in June.

   (iii)   If the quoted part of the direct speech is already in the past perfect tense, it stays that way.

DIRECT SPEECH	⇨	REPORTED SPEECH
He said, "I <u>hadn't thought</u> of that."		He said he <u>had not thought</u> of that.

   (iv)   The future tense changes into the future in the past tense.

DIRECT SPEECH	⇨	REPORTED SPEECH
He said, "I <u>will be going</u> there soon."		He said that he <u>would be going</u> there soon.

   (v)   The future in the past simple tense changes into the future in the past perfect tense.

DIRECT SPEECH	⇨	REPORTED SPEECH
She said, "I <u>would know</u> him anywhere."		She said that she <u>would have known</u> him anywhere.

   (vi)   If the quoted part of the sentence is already in the future in the past perfect tense, it stays that way.

DIRECT SPEECH	⇨	REPORTED SPEECH
He said, "I <u>would have done</u> it differently."		He said that he <u>would have done</u> it differently.

6. **Changes to verb moods** (see MOOD).

   (a)   The positive and the negative indicative moods don't change: the positive remains positive; the negative remains negative.

DIRECT SPEECH	⇨	REPORTED SPEECH
She said, "I <u>am</u> happy though I <u>am not</u> rich."		She said that she <u>was</u> happy though she <u>was not</u> rich.

   (b)   The interrogative (question) mood changes into the positive mood.

DIRECT SPEECH	⇨	REPORTED SPEECH
He asked me, "<u>Do you understand</u>?"		He asked me whether <u>I understood</u>.
She said, "Where <u>are you going</u>?"		She asked me where <u>I was going</u>.

(c)   The negative-interrogative mood changes into the negative mood.

DIRECT SPEECH	⇨	REPORTED SPEECH
She said, "<u>Aren't they</u> late?"		She asked me whether <u>they were not</u> late.

(d)   The imperative mood (the mood of command) changes into the infinitive with *to*.

DIRECT SPEECH	⇨	REPORTED SPEECH
He said, "<u>Tell</u> me a story."		He asked me <u>to tell</u> him a story.
She said, "<u>Don't hurry</u>."		She told me <u>not to hurry</u>.

7. **Various changes from direct into reported speech: greetings, "thanks," "yes," "no."**

(a)   Here are the options for the most common greetings.

DIRECT SPEECH	⇨	REPORTED SPEECH
They said, "<u>Hello</u>."		They <u>greeted</u> me.
		Or: They said <u>hello</u>.
They said, "<u>Good morning</u>."		They <u>wished me a good morning</u>.
		Or: They said <u>good morning</u>.

(b)   "Thanks" or "thank you."

DIRECT SPEECH	⇨	REPORTED SPEECH
He said, "<u>Thanks</u> for the dinner."		He <u>thanked</u> us for the dinner.
		Or: He <u>said thanks</u> for the dinner.

(c)   "Yes" and "No"—here are some options.

DIRECT SPEECH	⇨	REPORTED SPEECH
She asked, "Is it late?"		She asked whether it was late.
He answered, "Yes."		He answered that it was.
		He answered in the affirmative.
		He acknowledged that it was.
		He said yes.
He said, "Did you do it?"		He asked me whether I had done it.
I said, "No."		I replied that I had not.
		I answered in the negative.
		I denied that I had.
		I said no.

8. **A sample dialogue changed from direct into reported speech, illustrating 1–7 above.**

THE DAUGHTER: I'm getting chilled to the bone. What can Freddy be doing all this time? He's been gone twenty minutes.
[⇨ The daughter said that she was getting chilled to the bone. She asked what Freddy could be doing all that time. He had been gone some twenty minutes.]

THE MOTHER: Not so long. But he ought to have got us a cab by now.
[⇨ Her mother said that it had not been so long but that he ought to have got them a cab by then.]

A BYSTANDER: He won't get no cab not until half past eleven, missus, when they come back after dropping their theater fares. cont...

[⇨ A bystander told the mother that her son would not get a cab until half past eleven, when the cabs
came back from dropping their theater fares.]

THE MOTHER: But we must have a cab. We can't stand here until half past eleven. It's too bad.
[⇨ The mother said that they had to have a cab: they could not stand there until half past eleven. And on she grumbled.]

THE BYSTANDER: Well, it ain't my fault, missus.
[⇨ Taking this personally, the bystander said that it was not his fault.]

THE DAUGHTER: If Freddy had a bit of gumption, he would have got one at the theater door.
[⇨ The daughter said that if Freddy had had a bit of gumption, he would have got a taxi at the theater door.]

THE MOTHER: What could he have done, poor boy?
[⇨ The mother wondered what the poor boy could have done.]

THE DAUGHTER: Other people got cabs. Why couldn't he?
[⇨ The daughter complained that other people had got cabs and wanted to know why Freddy couldn't.]

(George Bernard Shaw, *Pygmalion*.)

9. **Here is a sample sustained passage changed from direct into reported speech, illustrating
1–7 on the previous page.**

DIRECT SPEECH

Consider, I address you as a legislator, whether, when men contend for their freedom, it is not inconsistent and unjust to subjugate women, even though you firmly believe that you are acting in the manner best calculated to promote their happiness. Who made man the exclusive judge, if woman partake with him the gift of reason? In this style, argue tyrants of every denomination—from the weak king to the weak father of a family—they are all eager to crush reason, yet always assert that they usurp its throne only to be useful. Do you not act a similar part, when you force all women to remain imprisoned in their families, groping in the dark?

(Mary Wollstonecraft, *Vindication of the Rights of Woman*.)

REPORTED SPEECH

Mary Wollstonecraft—addressing a male legislator—asked him to consider whether, when men contended for their freedom, it was not inconsistent and unjust to subjugate women, even though men firmly believed that they were acting in the manner best calculated to promote women's happiness. She asked who it was that had made man the exclusive judge, if woman partook with him the gift of reason. In this style, Wollstonecraft claimed, argued tyrants of every denomination—from the weak king to the weak father of a family—they were all eager to crush reason, yet always asserted that they usurped its throne only to be useful. She asked the legislator whether he did not act a similar part when he forced all women to remain imprisoned in their families, groping in the dark.

DISCOURSE—See TEXT GRAMMAR.

DOUBLE ENTENDRE—See FIGURE OF SPEECH.

DOUBLE GENITIVE—(also called "double possessive") the simultaneous use of two grammar forms, either of which on its own indicates possession.

First we look at the two individual ways of indicating possession (a) and (b), then at the double genitive (c).

(a) GENITIVE WITH *of*:   The government <u>of the country</u> is in trouble.

(b) GENITIVE *–'s* or *–s'*:   The <u>country's</u> population reached 4 million.
                              The two <u>countries'</u> combined population is 10 million.

(c) In the double genitive, you combine the use of both (a) *of*, and (b) *–'s* or *–s'*.

> We met Captain Langley, a friend <u>of our master's</u>.
>
> (Anna Sewell, *Black Beauty*.)
>
> She is a niece <u>of Lord Lancaster's</u>.
>
> (Oscar Wilde, *A Woman of No Importance*.)

Which form of the genitive you use—(a), (b) or (c)—is a matter of personal preference. But sometimes the use of different forms of the genitive can result in different meanings.

> A picture of Jan ...   [A picture in which Jan appears.]
> A picture of Jan's ...   [A picture that belongs to Jan.]

The word "genitive" comes from the Latin for "relating to birth." The grammar term has only a loose connection with the original meaning of the word.

DOUBLE NEGATIVE—negating something that is already negative. In mathematics, the negation of a negative amounts to a positive ($-2 \times -3 = +6$). The same goes for English.

> I am <u>not</u> <u>unlike</u> my brother.   [I am somewhat like my brother.]
> I <u>don't</u> <u>dislike</u> my neighbors.   [I'm pretty indifferent to them.]
> I <u>didn't</u> <u>do</u> <u>nothing</u>.   [I was at least a bit active.]

The double negatives illustrated above don't mean the exact opposite of the simple negatives. So, for example, *I am not unlike my brother* doesn't mean *I am just like him*—it means *I am somewhat like him*. This gives us a clue as to when the double negative may be useful: namely, when you want to make a more subtle statement than you would get by using the positive.

> Let us take these generalisations in turn, although they are <u>not</u> <u>unrelated</u>. [They are at least somewhat related.]
>
> (Francis Crick, *The Astonishing Hypothesis*.)
>
> If no castle or abbey or hermitage were at hand, their hardy habits made it <u>not</u> <u>intolerable</u> to them to lie down supperless. [They weren't exactly happy about going to bed hungry, but they put up with it.]
>
> (Thomas Bulfinch, *The Age of Chivalry*.)

DUMMY PRONOUNS *IT* AND *THERE*—pronouns that don't refer to nouns.

Normally, pronouns are all about referring to nouns: *When the dog saw the burglar <u>it</u> barked at <u>him</u>*. The pronoun *it* refers to *the dog*; the pronoun *him* refers to *the burglar*. But there are two pronouns—*it* and *there*—that you can use without referring to nouns.

1. **The dummy pronoun *it*** (also called "prop *it*").

   You use the dummy *it* in three ways.

   (a) The dummy *it* refers to nothing at all.

   > <u>It</u> is raining.   <u>It</u> is cold.   <u>It</u> is late.   I made <u>it</u> through the day.

   (b) The dummy *it* anticipates the subject of the sentence. In this use, you can substitute the true subject (underlined) for the dummy.

   > It was good <u>to hear these assurances</u>.
   > (*National Geographic*, January, 1999.)
   > [<u>To hear these assurances</u> was good.]
   >
   > It is always hard <u>to predict the impact of new technology</u>.
   > (*The Economist*, May 7, 1999.)
   > [<u>To predict the impact of new technology</u> is always hard.]

   (c) The dummy *it* in cleft sentences. "Cleft" means "split", and you use the dummy *it* at the start of cleft sentences to bring to the front anything that you want to focus on. In the examples below, the slashes mark the clefts; the underlined words are the focus of the sentences.

   > REGULAR SENTENCE
   > I took my friend to the movies in town last night.
   > VARIATIONS—CLEFT SENTENCES WITH DUMMY *IT*
   >
   > | | | |
   > |---|---|---|
   > | It was <u>my friend</u> | / | that I took to the movies in town last night. |
   > | It was to <u>the movies</u> | / | that I took my friend in town last night. |
   > | It was in <u>town</u> | / | that I took my friend to the movies last night. |
   > | It was <u>last night</u> | / | that I took my friend to the movies in town. |
   > | It was <u>I</u> | / | who took my friend to the movies in town last night. |

2. **The dummy pronoun *there*** (also called "existential *there*").

   The dummy *there* (underlined) anticipates the true subject (bold).

   > "Waiter, <u>there</u> are **flies** in my soup." "Oh, and the chef didn't know <u>there</u> was **meat** in the restaurant."
   > ["Waiter, **flies** are in my soup." "Oh, and the chef didn't know **meat** was in the restaurant."]

   Note that the dummy pronoun *there* (meaning nothing) looks like, but is different from, the adverb *there* (meaning *in that place*).

   > <u>There</u> [= 0] were three books lying <u>there</u> [= in that place].
   > PRONOUN   ADVERB

DYSPHEMISM—See FIGURE OF SPEECH.

ELISION—See ABBREVIATION.

ELLIPTICAL SENTENCE—See SENTENCE TYPES.

EPANALEPSIS—See FIGURE OF SPEECH.

EUPHEMISM—See FIGURE OF SPEECH.

EXOPHOR—See REFERENCE.

EXTRA—from the Latin for "beyond." One of the parts of a clause or a sentence. Anything that is beyond the subject and the predicate and that is, therefore, peripheral (extra) to a clause or sentence.

There are five kinds of extras:

1. INTERJECTIONS: <u>Wow</u>, that's great! <u>Gee</u>, you're clever!
2. CONJUNCTIONS: <u>But</u> I'm innocent!   <u>And</u> who isn't?
3. NOUNS OR PRONOUN *YOU* used as forms of address:
                        <u>Joe</u>, what's up?   <u>You</u>, what's up?
4. ADVERBS that modify the
   clause as a whole: <u>Really</u>, I love you. <u>Clearly</u>, you don't.
5. TRANSITION WORDS: <u>Nevertheless</u>,   <u>Moreover</u>, I won't.
                        I can't stay.

We look at each of these below.

1. **Interjections** belong neither to the subject nor to the predicate of a clause. It is a feature of interjection extras that you can often place them in various positions in sentences. We see this in the first two examples below.

> Who told you that you might meddle with such foolishness, <u>hey</u>?
> (Mark Twain, *Huckleberry Finn*.)
>
> "<u>Hey</u>!—What is that you say?" cried the alcalde.
> (Irving Washington, *Alhambra*.)
>
> <u>Goodness</u>, I don't care!
> (LM Montgomery, *Anne of Green Gables*.)
>
> ALGERNON: <u>Well</u>, in the first place girls never marry the men they flirt with. Girls don't think it right.
> JACK: <u>Oh</u>, that is nonsense!
> (Oscar Wilde, *The Importance of Being Earnest*.)

Another feature of interjection extras, also evident in the examples above, is that you usually separate them from the rest of their sentences with commas or some other punctuation marks.

2. **Conjunctions** connect clauses to each other but are peripheral to the clauses themselves. In linguistic terminology such extras are called "conjuncts," "disjuncts," and "complementizers." In the text below, each clause starts on a new line, and the conjunctions are underlined.

> "I am so very tired of being all alone here!"
> <u>As</u> she said this
> she looked down at her hands,
> <u>and</u> was surprised to see
> <u>that</u> she had put on one of the Rabbit's little white kid-gloves
> <u>while</u> she was talking.
> (Lewis Carroll, *Alice in Wonderland*.)

3. **Nouns used as forms of address** (also called "vocatives").
   Vocative extras (like many other extras) are separated from the rest
   of their sentences with commas, and they can occur in different
   positions.

   > LADY CAROLINE: <u>John</u>, the grass is too damp for you. You had better go
   > and put on your overshoes.
   > SIR JOHN: I am quite comfortable, <u>Caroline</u>, I assure you.
   > LADY CAROLINE: You must allow me to be the best judge of that, <u>John</u>.
   > (Oscar Wilde, *A Woman of No Importance.*)

   The pronoun *you* can also act as a vocative extra.

   > The half-breed cook shouted at him, "Hey, <u>you</u>, wake up!"
   > (Jack London, *Call of the Wild.*)

   See VOCATIVE.

4. **Adverbs that modify a clause as a whole** (also called "adjuncts"
   and "sentence adverbs"). Such adverbs have a different application
   from adverbs that modify verbs. I show the difference below by
   giving an example of an adverb that acts as an extra and the same
   adverb that acts as a verb modifier. Notice that adverb extras tend
   to be separated from the rest of the sentences with commas while
   verb modifiers don't.

   > <u>Hopefully</u>, you want to be able to say that you're working on something
   >   EXTRA
   >
   > that's important now.
   > (Dr James Watson in TIME, March 23, 1999.)

   > Johnny **looked** <u>hopefully</u> at his father. (Stephen Crane, "The Blue Hotel.")
   >   VERB   VERB MODIFIER

   > <u>Actually</u>, the Beatles hailed from Liverpool. (TIME, June 14, 1999.)
   >   EXTRA
   >
   > His voice <u>actually</u> **trembled**. (Lew Wallace, *Ben Hur.*)
   >   VERB MODIFIER   VERB

   > It's a long tail, <u>certainly</u>. (Lewis Carroll, *Alice in Wonderland.*)
   >   EXTRA
   >
   > I had <u>certainly</u> **acted** imprudently. (Mary Shelley, *Frankenstein.*)
   >   VERB MODIFIER VERB

   > <u>Supposedly</u>, big-game hunting was what induced proto-human males to
   >   EXTRA
   >
   > cooperate with each other.
   > (Jared Diamond, *The Rise and Fall of the Third Chimpanzee.*)
   > Their cousins **were** <u>supposedly</u> **evolving** into more advanced creatures
   >   VERB   VERB MODIFIER   VERB
   >
   > like human beings.
   > (Phillip E Johnson, *Darwin on Trial.*)

5. **Transition words (also called "conjunctive adverbs")** act partly as
   conjunctions (joining one clause or sentence to another) and partly
   as adverbs in an adjunctive sense (see part 4 above). There are

only a dozen or so transition words in English:

however	furthermore	moreover	otherwise
nevertheless	therefore	meanwhile	similarly
consequently	indeed	accordingly	albeit.

Transition words are also characterized by:

- usually being separated off by commas
- having various positions in sentences
- being able to stand in separate sentences or in combined ("multiple") sentences.

We see all these features below.

SEPARATE SENTENCES	COMBINED ("MULTIPLE") SENTENCES
They were late. <u>However</u>, we didn't mind.	They were late; <u>however</u> we didn't mind.
They were late. We, <u>however</u>, didn't mind.	They were late; we, <u>however</u>, didn't mind.
They were late. We didn't, <u>however</u>, mind.	They were late; we didn't, <u>however</u>, mind.
They were late. We didn't mind, <u>however</u>.	They were late; we didn't mind, <u>however</u>.

The following texts illustrate the use and the possible positions of *however*.

> She had never forgotten that, if you drink much from a bottle marked "poison," it is almost certain to disagree with you sooner or later. <u>However</u>, this bottle was not marked "poison." First, <u>however</u>, she waited for a few minutes.
> (Lewis Carroll, *Alice in Wonderland*.)
>
> I am not sure, <u>however</u>, that Jane is right in taking him out of his position.
> (Oscar Wilde, *A Woman of No Importance*.)
>
> He hasn't got that far yet, and I doubt that he ever will. At least he's trying, <u>however</u>.
> (Daniel C Dennett, *Darwin's Dangerous Idea*.)

What works for *however*, works also for the other transition words.

6. **A note on terminology.**

Grammarians have a clutch of names for specific kinds of extras—"conjuncts," "disjuncts," "sentence adverbs," "complementizers," "vocatives," "transition words," and more. I use the generic term "extra" to embrace them all. The generic term points to the characteristic that all the specific kinds of extras have in common: namely, that they stand in a clause or a sentence but are extra to (not part of) the subject and the predicate.

For the role of extras in sentence structures, see SENTENCE.

FEMININE—See GENDER.

FIELD—See CONTEXT.

FIGURE OF SPEECH—the use of special effects in language, intended to make the text memorable, pleasing or surprising. Language that is rich in figures of speech is called "figurative language." Here are two texts that feature figurative language.

<u>Fully fit</u>, Gilchrist could be the <u>scourge of summer</u>.
(*The ABC Cricket Book*.)
[The repetition of the letters *f* and *s* makes the text vivid.]

Graeme Hick remains a consistent <u>butcher</u> of domestic bowling.
(*The ABC Cricket Book*, 1998–99 Season.)
[To call a cricketer a "butcher" makes the reader sit up and take notice.]

The sub-entries that follow deal with the thirty most common and useful figures of speech—along with a few useless ones to be avoided. I have grouped them into three broad classes—

A. **PHONOLOGICAL FIGURES OF SPEECH:** based on sound effects

B. **LEXICAL FIGURES OF SPEECH:** depending for their effect on the use of words

C. **SYNTACTIC FIGURES OF SPEECH:** depending for their effect on sentence structures.

A. PHONOLOGICAL	10. Pun	21. Personification
1. Alliteration	11. Double entendre	22. Apostrophe
2. Assonance	12. Irony	**C. SYNTACTIC**
3. Onomatopoeia	13. Sarcasm	23. Inversion
B. LEXICAL	14. Euphemism	24. Hyperbaton
4. Metaphor	15. Dysphemism	25. Chiasmus
5. Simile	16. Metonymy	26. Antithesis
6. Cliché	17. Synecdoche	27. Epanalepsis
7. Platitude	18. Oxymoron	28. Parallelism
8. Hyperbole	19. Paradox	29. Litotes
9. Meiosis	20. Antonomasia	30. Zeugma

A. **PHONOLOGICAL FIGURES OF SPEECH based on sound effects.**

1. **Alliteration**—(from the Latin for "with letters"), starting a series of words with the same consonant sounds: *A big black boulder*.

> Drowning in data. (Headline in *The Economist*, July 2, 1999.)
> Angus Fraser has always been a burly blessing for his captain. (*The ABC Cricket Book*.)
> The way to Bligh Reef runs northwest to the cusp of Busby Island, then bounces into the bright blue chop of Prince William Sound. (*National Geographic*, March 1999.)

Compare with 2 below.

2. **Assonance**—(from the Latin for "from sounds"), a term used in two different senses:

(a)   the same vowel sounds with different consonants—

> No play, no pay—new O'Neill deal. (Headline in *The Canberra Times*, March 4, 1999.)

(b)   different vowel sounds between the same consonants—

> Butter is better.
> He was fit even though he was fat.

3. **Onomatopoeia**—(from the Greek for "making sounds"), a figure of speech in which a word resembles the sound that the word represents.

The clucking of hens.
The bang of a hammer.
The tick-tock of a clock.
The sound of a whippoorwill.

B. LEXICAL FIGURES OF SPEECH depending for their effect on the use of words.

4. **Metaphor**—(from the Greek for "transferring"), saying that one thing is another, suggesting that you transfer the meaning of one thing to another: *My fingers are ice*.

> The gigantic Chess Palace was still <u>an architectural skeleton</u> with <u>quite a bit of flesh missing</u>: whole walls were uncompleted and it was covered in scaffolding. At Moscow airport, I saw Russian <u>faces that told stories</u>: deeply etched faces of people who have had to <u>color their lives</u> from within.
> (Guy West in *Australian Chess Forum*, December 1998.)
>
> Ricky Ponting is <u>the gun player</u> of his generation.
> (Mark Ray, *The ABC Cricket Book*.)
>
> The staging of five Test matches over·seven weeks will probably <u>kill off most of the front-line bowlers</u>. (Jim Maxwell in *The ABC Cricket Book*.)
> The infuriating <u>warble</u> of the phone <u>drilled</u> in her ear.
> (Ric Throssell, *Jackpot*.)

Compare with 5 below.

5. **Simile**—(related to the word "similar"), saying that one thing is similar to another: *My fingers are like ice*.

> Getting a smile from the Aeroflot cabin crew is <u>tougher than getting a jar of sturgeon caviar through Australian customs</u>.
> (Guy West in *Australian Chess Forum*, December 1998.)
>
> Primer's voice has a rough edge; his harmonica produces torrents of sound. It is <u>as if he is trying to force life back into the bleak streets outside</u>. "Sweet Home Chicago," he sings, not with irony but fervent belief ... Raising a good cotton crop is <u>just like a lucky man shooting dice</u>.
> (*National Geographic*, April 1999.)
>
> The first big puzzle facing researchers is why the streams run so fast while the rest of the ice <u>moves like molasses</u>.
> (*New Scientist*, April 17, 1999.)

6. **Cliché, also spelled "cliche"**—(from the French for "stencil"), a worn-out simile or metaphor: *Pure as the driven snow; thrown to the wolves*.

> Other researchers were skeptical. "They had to make so many assumptions that I felt <u>the whole thing was like a house of card</u>s," one said.
> (*New Scientist*, April 17, 1999.)

Compare with 7 below.

7. **Platitude**—(from the French for "flatness," "dullness"), an expression made dull by overuse, especially when it is pronounced as though it were new or significant. Election material is full of platitudes, often involving clichés.

We will strive for ever-better educational opportunities for our young, leading them to a better and brighter tomorrow. We will foster sunrise industries so that our graduates will be able to enter fields that yield them a greater harvest of opportunity and satisfaction ...

8. **Hyperbole**—pronounced "hy-PER-bo-lee" (from the Greek for "excess"), an exaggeration or overstatement. Hyperbole often involves metaphor (see 4 above).

They've got tons of money.
We've got loads of time.
The rain was coming down in buckets.

Compare with 9 below.

9. **Meiosis**—pronounced "my-OH-sis" (from the Greek for "less"), an understatement. Meiosis often involves metaphor (see 4 above).

"Gee, you've got a bad wound."
"Oh, it's just a little scratch."

"I hear you won a packet at the races."
"Not really. Just chickenfeed."

10. **Pun**—(nobody knows for sure where this word came from—maybe from a word that means "quibble"), a figure of speech that makes humorous use of the double meanings of words.

"I've got a hunch."
"And I thought you were just round-shouldered."

"I passed by your house last week."
"How kind of you."

Compare with 11 below.

11. **Double entendre**—(from the French for "double understanding"), something with a double meaning; similar to a pun, but used in blue jokes.

"Do you shrink from making love?"
"If I did, I'd be a midget."

Sex is bad for one—but it's fun for two.

12. **Irony**—(from the Greek for "pretend"), saying the opposite of what one actually means.

Some friends they've turned out to be!	[When they have let you down.]
Lovely weather we're having.	[When it is stormy.]
I like your short haircut.	[To someone with long hair.]

Compare with 13 below.

13. **Sarcasm**—(from the Greek for "flesh-tearing"), a biting form of irony (see 12 above).

A Moscow newspaper, commenting on a Kremlin report that President Yeltsin would be playing tennis six months after his heart surgery: "In a year he'll be speaking English, and another week after that he'll start playing the violin."
(*TIME*, January 20, 1997.)

14. **Euphemism**—pronounced "YOU-feh-mism" (from the Greek for "well-speaking"), an inoffensive word or expression substituted for one that is thought to be offensive or taboo.

To pass away.	[To die.]
Making love.	[Copulating.]
Collateral damage.	[Unintentionally killing civilians.]

Compare with 15 below.

15. **Dysphemism**—(from the Greek for "ill-speaking"), an offensive word or expression substituted for one that is neutral or normal. A dysphemism is meant to disparage or offend.

> What do you call that pile of junk—a car?
> How do you expect to think with that pea-brain of yours?

16. **Metonymy**—(from the Greek for "a change of name"), referring to something by naming something else that is associated with, or related to, that thing.

> This is Crown land.
> [It belongs to the government.]
>
> The statement came from the White House.
> [It came from the president who lives there.]
>
> The criminals appeared before the bench.
> [They appeared before a judge who sits on a bench.]

Compare with 17 below.

17. **Synecdoche**—pronounced "sin-ECK-do-kee" (from the Greek for "gathering together"), a term used in two different senses.

(a) A word that represents a part of something but is used to stand for the whole of that thing.

> They have a hundred head of cattle.
> [They really have whole cattle, not just heads.]
>
> We need all hands on deck.
> [We need people and not just their hands.]

(b) A word that represents a whole of something but is used to stand for a part of that thing.

> England played Australia for the trophy.
> [It was really teams from each country, not the whole of the countries, that played.]
>
> It's an American movie.
> [A movie from the USA rather than from the American continent as a whole.]

18. **Oxymoron**—(from the Greek for "sharp-dull"), a short, apparently self-contradictory or absurd expression.

> Somebody I know is a devout atheist.
> Another is an honest politician.
> And a third is a cheerful pessimist.

Compare with 19.

19. **Paradox**—(from the Greek for "contrary opinion"), a statement that is apparently self-contradictory or absurd. A paradox is similar to an oxymoron (see 18 above). But while an oxymoron is usually associated with a short phrase, often appearing in a joke, a paradox is likely to appear in a literary setting—often a sustained passage.

> It was the best of times, it was the worst of times, it was the age of wisdom, it was the age of foolishness, it was the epoch of belief, it was the epoch of incredulity, it was the season of light, it was the season of darkness, it was the spring of hope, it was the winter of despair, we had everything before us, we had nothing before us, we were all going direct to heaven, we were all going direct the other way.
> (Charles Dickens, *A Tale of Two Cities*. Dickens was describing the period just before the French Revolution.)

20. **Antonomasia**—(from the Greek for "substitute naming"), naming a person or a thing after another, to show that the two share some characteristic.

> Chomsky is the Einstein of linguistics.
> So-and-so is the office Don Juan.

21. **Personification**—speaking of a thing as if it were a person.

> The sun smiled happily on that day.
> The clouds frowned in the sky.

John Ruskin, the 19th century English writer and critic, disliked attributing human qualities to non-humans. He called this a "pathetic fallacy."

cowardly jackals	proud mountains	threatening floods
cruel storms	impassive cliffs	the benign moon

All of the above are pathetic fallacies. On the other hand, *a playful kitten* is all right—because kittens do play.

Compare with 22 below.

22. **Apostrophe**—(from the Greek for "turning aside"), turning aside from one's speech to address a thing as if it were a person.

> O Earth, O Earth, return!
> Arise from out the dewy grass! (William Blake, "Hear the Voice.")
>
> Fair daffodils, we weep to see
> You haste away so soon. (Robert Herrick, "To Daffodils.")

C. **SYNTACTIC FIGURES OF SPEECH depending for their effect on sentence structures.**

23. **Inversion**—(from the Latin for "turning around"), turning around the normal word order for literary effect.

> "Where is mother?" asked Meg [Meg asked].
> "She will be back soon," said Meg [Meg said].
> (Louisa May Alcott, *Little Women*.)
>
> Never have I seen [I have never seen] a man so white.
> (Arthur Conan Doyle, "The Blanched Soldier.")

Compare with 24.

24. **Hyperbaton**—pronounced with the stress on the second syllable (from the Greek for "going over"), a more radical form of inversion for emphasis.

What they expect, I don't know.	[I don't know what they expect.]
Clever you call yourself?	[You call yourself clever?]
Hail to thee, blithe spirit!	
Bird thou never wert.	[Thou never wert a bird.]
(Percy Bysshe Shelley, "To a Skylark.")	

25. **Chiasmus**—pronounced "ky-AS-mus" (from the Greek for "crossing"), a crossing-over or reversal of word order.

> Ask not what your country can do for you, but what you can do for your country. (JF Kennedy.)
>
> There is no way to peace—peace is the way. (Mahatma Gandhi.)
>
> Nobody knows nothing about nothing and nobody.
> Some people eat to live; others live to eat.

26. **Antithesis**—(from the Greek for "opposition"), opposing ideas in a balanced structure.

> Give me liberty or give me death. (Patrick Henry.)
>
> For many are called but few are chosen. (Matthew 22:14.)
>
> They laugh best who laugh last. (Proverb.)

27. **Epanalepsis**—pronounced with the stress on the penultimate syllable (from the Greek for "to take up again"), the repetition of a word or a phrase.

> Break, break, break
> On thy cold gray stones, O Sea! (Alfred Lord Tennyson.)
>
> We shall fight on the beaches, we shall fight on the landing grounds, we shall fight in the fields and in the streets, we shall fight in the hills, we shall never surrender. (Winston Churchill.)

28. **Parallelism**—two parallel (similarly structured), word groups that have different words slotted into the same positions.

> The bigger they are, the harder they fall.
> Who steals my purse steals trash. (William Shakespeare, *Othello*.)
> What you see is what you get.

29. **Litotes**—pronounced "lee-TOE-tis" (from the Greek for "meagerness"), stating something by denying its contrary.

It's not a bad book.	[It's a good book.]
You're not wrong.	[You're right.]
I can't agree.	[I disagree.]

30. **Zeugma**—pronounced "ZOO-gma" or "ZYOO-gma" (from the Greek for "yoking"), a verb followed by two other words, either of which is a suitable follow-on, but in different senses.

> She might stain her honor or her brocade.
> (Alexander Pope, *The Rape of the Lock*.)
>
> He lost his wallet but not his cool.
>
> I caught the ball and the coach's attention.

FINITE AND NONFINITE—two forms, each with some subforms, that verbs can take. The forms are illustrated below.

FINITE FORMS	NONFINITE FORMS
eat, eats, ate	to eat, eating, eaten
give, gives, gave	to give, giving, given
am, is, are, was, were	to be, being, been

Finite means "bound." The finite forms are bound—while the nonfinite forms are not bound—by any one or more of the following three variables. If any of the variables changes, the finite verb (underlined) follows suit. (For the arrow ⇨ read "becomes.")

1. THE NUMBER OF THE SUBJECT NOUN OR PRONOUN:
   A child <u>sits</u>.   ⇨   Children <u>sit</u>.

2. THE PERSON OF THE SUBJECT PRONOUN:
   I <u>am</u>.   ⇨   You <u>are</u>.

3. THE TENSE—PRESENT OR PAST—OF THE VERB:
   I <u>can</u>.   ⇨   I <u>could</u>.

We look at the three variables below.

1. **The number of the subject noun or pronoun.** Finite verbs may change their form depending on whether their subjects are singular or plural; nonfinite verbs do not change their forms.

SINGULAR (*I*)	⇨	PLURAL (*WE*)
I <u>am</u> **reading**. <small>FINITE NONFINITE</small>		We <u>are</u> **reading**. <small>FINITE NONFINITE</small>

When *I* changes to *we*, the finite verb changes from *am* to a*re*, but the nonfinite verb *reading* remains unchanged.

PLURAL (*THEY*)	⇨	SINGULAR (*SHE*)
They <u>want</u> **to know** the answer. <small>FINITE NONFINITE</small>		She <u>wants</u> **to know** the answer. <small>FINITE NONFINITE</small>

When *they* changes to *she*, *want* changes to *wants*, but *to know* remains unchanged.

2. **Finite verbs may also change their form depending on the person of the subject pronouns.**

FIRST PERSON (*I*)	⇨	SECOND PERSON (*YOU*)
I <u>was</u> **reading** a book. <small>FINITE NONFINITE</small>		You <u>were</u> **reading** a book. <small>FINITE NONFINITE</small>

When *I* changes to *you*, *was* changes to *were*, but *reading* remains unchanged.

THIRD PERSON (*HE*)	⇨	FIRST PERSON (*I*)
He <u>has</u> **finished** the job. <small>FINITE NONFINITE</small>		I <u>have</u> **finished** the job. <small>FINITE NONFINITE</small>

When *he* changes to *I*, *has* changes to *have*, but *finished* remains unchanged.

3. **The third and surest way to tell whether a verb is finite or nonfinite is the tense-change method.** Change the text from the present tense to the past tense, or from the past tense to the present tense. Any verb that changes its form when you change the tense is finite; any verb that doesn't change its form is nonfinite.

In the box below, the original text is in the upper lines, the tense-changed text in the shaded lines. The verbs that show a change of form are finite; the verbs that don't, are nonfinite.

When you <u>sit</u> back and <u>admire</u> the sunset, <u>pay</u> homage to the fluffy cumulus clouds that <u>will</u> probably <u>be</u> <u>arrayed</u> along the horizon.

[When you <u>sat</u> back and <u>admired</u> the sunset, <u>pay</u> homage to the fluffy
           FINITE   FINITE   NONFINITE

cumulus clouds that <u>would</u> probably <u>be</u>   <u>arrayed</u> along the horizon.]
              FINITE   NONFINITE NONFINITE

For if biologists Bill Hamilton and Tim Lenton <u>are</u> right, these clouds <u>are</u> the home-<u>made</u> rafts of bacteria and algae <u>voyaging</u> across the world.

[For if biologists Bill Hamilton and Tim Lenton <u>were</u> right, these clouds
                                              FINITE

<u>were</u> the home-<u>made</u> rafts of bacteria and algae <u>voyaging</u> across the
FINITE   FINITE   NONFINITE

world.]

Scientists <u>have</u> known for some time that microbes <u>are</u> important in cloud formation.

[Scientists <u>had</u> known for some time that microbes <u>were</u> important in
         FINITE   FINITE

cloud formation.]

Cloud samples <u>have</u> often <u>been</u> <u>shown</u> <u>to harbor</u> microbes. But Dr Hamilton and Mr. Lenton <u>argue</u> that some microbes actually <u>evolved</u> <u>to seed</u> clouds in order <u>to aid</u> their own dispersal.

[Cloud samples <u>had</u> often <u>been</u> <u>shown</u> <u>to harbor</u> microbes. But Dr
              FINITE   NONFINITE NONFINITE NONFINITE

Hamilton and Mr. Lenton <u>argued</u> that some microbes actually <u>evolve</u>
                  FINITE   FINITE

<u>to seed</u> clouds in order <u>to aid</u> their own dispersal.]
NONFINITE   FINITE

(*The Economist*, March 28, 1998.)

4. **One more method of distinguishing between finite and nonfinite forms.**

Finite forms go with subjects.

You can say: *I go, she goes, he went.*

Nonfinite forms don't go with subjects.

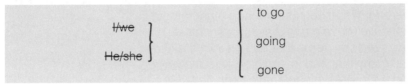

In standard English, you can't say *I to go*, *he going*, *she gone*.

See STANDARD AND NONSTANDARD ENGLISH.

The above method (4) has its loopholes, but it's easy and it does work in most cases.

5. **Why is it important to know which verbs are finite and which are not?**

    Because the finiteness or otherwise of verbs determines phrase and clause structures which, in turn, determine sentence structures. See CLAUSE and PHRASE.

FORMS OF THE VERB—the various forms that verbs can take, each form having one or more functions. The concept of verbs having various forms is similar to that of nouns having various forms: *child–children–childhood* ... So too with verbs: *go–goes–going* ...

1. **What forms can verbs can take?**

    There are two groups of verb forms: finite and nonfinite. Each of these two groups has three subdivisions.

FINITE FORMS				
	PRESENT:	walk	see	take
	PRESENT –*S*:	walks	sees	takes
	–*ED* FORM:	walked	saw	took

    *   The present form goes with the subject *I, you, we, they* or a plural noun (*I walk; people walk*).

    *   The present –*s* form goes with the subject *he, she, it* or a singular noun (*she sees, a person sees*).

    *   The –*ed* form is the form used in the past simple tense: *I noted, I walked, I talked*. The past simple form of the verb is called "–*ed* form" even if it does not end with –*ed*. Examples: *saw* and *took*.

NONFINITE FORMS				
	INFINITIVE:	(to) walk	(to) see	(to) take
	–*ing* FORM:	walking	seeing	taking
	–*en* FORM:	walked	seen	taken

    *   The infinitive form sometimes has the word *to* in front of it (this is called "the marked infinitive") and it sometimes does not have *to* in front of it (this is called the "unmarked infinitive" or "base form").

    MARKED INFINITIVES:
    He wants <u>to go</u>.   She intends <u>to return</u>.   He hopes <u>to play</u>.

    UNMARKED INFINITIVES:
    He must (~~to~~) <u>go</u>.   She might (~~to~~) <u>return</u>.   He can (~~to~~) <u>play</u>.

- The *–ing* form always ends in *–ing*: *walking, talking, laughing*.

- The *–en* form is the verb form that you use (among other things) in a compound verb with *have* (*have <u>eaten</u>, have <u>woken</u>, have <u>taken</u>*). There are many *–en* form verbs that do end with the letters *–en*. But there are also many that end in *–ed* or in *–t* (*have <u>walked</u>, have <u>hoped</u>, have <u>played</u> … have <u>meant</u>, have <u>sent</u>, have <u>kept</u>…*). Whatever endings they have, all the verb forms underlined in this paragraph are called *–en* forms.

On how to distinguish between finite and nonfinite forms, see FINITE AND NONFINITE.

The *–ing* form is also called the "present participle;" the *–en* form is also called the "past participle." See PARTICIPLE.

2. **How do the various forms of the verb function?**

(a) FINITE VERBS always function as verbs. Finite verbs (FV), alone or in compounds (underlined) tell you what the subjects are up to.

> The gardener **planted** a rosebush.
>   SUBJECT   FV
>
> We   **have** <u>finished</u> the job.
> SUBJECT   FV
>
> They   **will** <u>be arriving</u> any minute.
> SUBJECT   FVV

(b) INFINITIVES have two functions.

(i)	AS VERBS:	You ought <u>to go</u>.
		I used <u>to play</u> soccer.
		I need <u>to talk</u> to you.
(ii)	AS NOUNS:	<u>To swim</u> **is** fun.
		<u>To drive</u> **has** its risks.
		<u>To wait</u> **makes** them angry.

Why do the last three infinitives (underlined) function as nouns? Because they are the subjects of the finite verbs (bold). And subjects are always—always—nouns or noun equivalents.

(c) *–ING* FORMS have three functions.

(i)	AS VERBS:	We were <u>talking</u>.
		They were <u>loafing</u>.
		We have been <u>playing</u>.
(ii)	AS ADJECTIVES:	A <u>smiling</u> **face** …
		An <u>interesting</u> **book** …
		A <u>hopping</u> **frog** …

- On line (i) above, each *–ing* form is part of a compound verb. The *–ing* form is therefore functionally a verb.

- On line (ii) above, each *–ing* form modifies a noun (bold). That makes the *–ing* form functionally an adjective.

(iii)   AS NOUNS: <u>Swimming</u> **is** fun.
<u>Driving</u> **has** its risks.
<u>Waiting</u> **makes** them angry.

- The –*ing* forms on line (iii) above function as nouns because they are the subjects of finite verbs (bold).

(d)   –*EN* FORMS have two functions.

(i)   AS VERBS: I have <u>eaten</u>.
They have <u>spoken</u>.
We were <u>seen</u>.

(ii)   AS ADJECTIVES: A <u>broken</u> **twig** ...
A <u>hidden</u> **clue** ...
A <u>stolen</u> **letter** ...

- On line (i) above, each –*en* form is part of a compound verb. The –*en* form is therefore functionally a verb.

- On line (ii) above, each –*en* form modifies a noun (bold). That makes the –*en* form functionally an adjective.

The following text illustrates the various verb forms.

It <u>would</u> <u>be</u> far easier <u>to tune</u> the climate models if scientists <u>were</u>
–ED FORM   INFINITIVE   INFINITIVE   *–ED* FORM

able <u>to look</u> through centuries of records. "But we just <u>don't</u> <u>have</u> hundreds
INFINITIVE   PRESENT INFINITIVE

of years of data," Leetmaa <u>explains</u>. "<u>Analyzing</u> the data in combination
PRESENT *–S*   *ING* FORM

with computer-simulated experiments <u>is</u> where we <u>are</u> <u>going</u>
PRESENT *–S*   PRESENT *–ING* FORM

<u>to make</u> progress."
INFINITIVE

(*National Geographic*, March 1999.)

FUTURE IN THE PAST TENSE—See TENSE AND ASPECT.

FUTURE TENSE—See TENSE AND ASPECT.

FUTURE TENSE: DOES IT EXIST IN ENGLISH?

The commonsense view is that it does, and traditional grammarians support this view. After all, we can say *They will arrive tomorrow*. But most modern grammarians (including Noam Chomsky and Michael Halliday) insist that there is no such tense: only a present and a past tense.

Their reasoning runs as follows. The past tense is an inflected (changed) form of the present tense, the usual inflection being the ending –*ed*. There is no ending for the future tense; therefore there is no future tense.

This view is expressed by David Crystal.

English has no future tense ending ... Rather, future time is expressed by a variety of other means. One of these—the use of *will* or *shall*—is often loosely referred to as the "future tense." But this usage changes the meaning of the word "tense" so that it no longer refers only to the use of verb endings (1995:224).

The opposite view is taken by Otto Jespersen (1860–1943), by all accounts, the greatest scholar of English before the advent of modern linguistics.

> A notable feature of the history of the English language is the building up of a rich system of tenses on the basis of the few possessed by Old English ... The verbs *shall* and *will* have in many contexts come to be auxiliaries serving to express pure futurity, [their] original meaning of volition and obligation being more or less effaced ...
> (1962 [1938]:192).

The legitimacy of the future as a tense is also supported by at least two modern scholars. One of these is Robert Burchfield, the editor of *The Oxford English Dictionary*.

> After the Norman Conquest, *shall* and *will* emerged as the normal auxiliaries for expressing futurity ... As time went on, *shall* continued to be the dominant form in England to express simple futurity but it never became firmly distinguishable from *will* elsewhere (1992:60).

Another modern scholar who defends the legitimacy of a future tense in English is Celia Millward.

> Old English verbs were inflected for only two tenses, present and preterite [past]. There was no future conjugation ... However, by late Old English, *sculan* [*shall*] and *willan* [*will*] often carried some sense of future time ... [And in the glossary, under the entry for *tense*:] English has ... future (1989:90, 367).

So the question of whether English has a future tense boils down to whether we should count only forms with endings (inflections) as "tenses" or whether the term "tense" can also encompass forms constructed with auxiliary verbs such as *shall* and *will*.

A comparison of English with Italian is interesting.

	ENGLISH		ITALIAN	
PRESENT:	I find	PRESENTE:	trovo
PAST:	I found	PASSATO:	trovai
FUTURE:	I will find	FUTURO:	troverò
FUTURE IN THE PAST:	I would find	FUTURO NEL PASSATO:	troverei

Are we to say, then, that Italian has four tenses because they are all inflected, and English only two because only two are inflected? I believe not. Or are we to say that "I found" is tensed in English because it has no auxiliary, but "I did not find" is not tensed because it has the auxiliary *did*? Surely not.

Having an ending is neither a necessary nor a sufficient condition for something to be called "tense." A tense may indeed be formed with an ending (as in Italian), but it can also be formed with an auxiliary (as in English). Which way it is formed is a mere historical accident. I therefore stand with Jespersen, Burchfield, Millward—and with common sense—in considering the future to be a fully-fledged English tense.

See TENSE AND ASPECT.

GENDER—from the Latin for "kind" or "type." A feature of some nouns and pronouns. The gender of a noun or a pronoun usually (but not always) relates to the sex or lack of sex of the person or thing expressed by the noun or pronoun.

English has four genders.

1. **Masculine gender** refers to males.

NOUNS	PRONOUNS
boy, father, nephew …	he, him, his, himself.

2. **Feminine gender** refers to females.

NOUNS	PRONOUNS
girl, mother, niece …	she, her, hers, herself.

3. **Common gender** refers to either males or females.

NOUNS	PRONOUNS
child, parent, cousin …	I, you, we, they, me, us, them, mine, yours, ours, theirs, myself, yourself … anybody, somebody … who.

4. **Neuter gender** refers to sexless things.

NOUNS	PRONOUNS
table, chair, book …	it, its, itself … anything, something … which.

When you are referring to a baby, you can choose either a pronoun that relates to the baby's natural gender or a pronoun in the neuter gender.

The baby is beautiful: look at her (or "him" or "it") smile.

For some inanimate things, it is possible to use a masculine or a feminine pronoun instead of a neuter pronoun.

The ship heaved as the waves broke over her (or "it").

GENITIVE—See CASE.

GENRE—from the French for "kind" or "type." Genre is a term in text grammar, relating to the classification of texts. There are two ways in which we can classify texts into genres.

1. **One classification** is by the medium that we use to communicate the text: visual (through sight) and auditory (through hearing). Each

of these has two subtypes, each of which has many members.

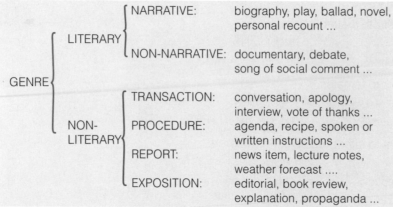

GENRE
- VISUAL
  - WRITING: report, letter, story, joke ...
  - OTHER: poster, mime, cartoon, traffic sign ...
- AUDITORY
  - SPEECH: conversation, song, story, joke ...
  - OTHER: whistle, groan, cheer, finger snap ...

Some of the members are specific to one genre or another: posters are visual and whistles are auditory. Others cut across the genres. For example, you can mime a story (visual) or you can tell it (auditory).

2. **The other classification** of texts into genres is literary (creating a pleasing effect) and non-literary (getting things done).

GENRE
- LITERARY
  - NARRATIVE: biography, play, ballad, novel, personal recount ...
  - NON-NARRATIVE: documentary, debate, song of social comment ...
- NON-LITERARY
  - TRANSACTION: conversation, apology, interview, vote of thanks ...
  - PROCEDURE: agenda, recipe, spoken or written instructions ...
  - REPORT: news item, lecture notes, weather forecast ....
  - EXPOSITION: editorial, book review, explanation, propaganda ...

3. **The above two ways of classifying genres overlap:** a text in a visual genre may be literary (a novel) or non-literary (a classified advertisement). Similarly, a text in a literary genre may be visual (a cartoon strip) or auditory (a radio play). The boundaries between the genres are not exact.

The following four texts are classified by both methods and their language features discussed.

Text A

The year's at the spring
And day's at the morn;
Morning's at seven,
The hillside's dew-pearled,
The lark's on the wing,
The snail's on the thorn;
God's in his heaven—
All's right with the world!

(Robert Browning, "Song.")

Text A is a poem in a literary non-narrative genre. It is visual if written down; auditory if read aloud.

LANGUAGE FEATURES. The text features short lines, each one starting with a capital letter. The top four lines rhyme with the bottom four: *spring–wing*, *morn–thorn*, and so on. The text has a metrical but irregular pattern of weakly accented syllables interspersed with strongly accented ones. There are two expressions in the text (*morn* and *dew-pearled*) that you would expect to find only in a poetic work. The text is very short, but it paints a beautiful word-picture that gives the reader or listener a lovely feeling.

Text B

RICHMOND Bedsit, spacious, sep. kitchen/meals with new lino. New carpet. Great loc. Refs nec. No pets. $210pw. 2 yr lease. Bond nec. Ph 9000 0009. Available NOW!!!

(From a Melbourne daily.)

Text B is in a non-literary visual genre. As a classified advertisement it is a kind of report.

LANGUAGE FEATURES. This text has a job to do: to get the right tenant for a small residence. It is written with some abbreviated words in incomplete sentences with skimpy and, at the end, unconventional punctuation. The last word is a "screamer," written in capital letters. The repetition of *nec* (for *necessary*) aims to keep unsuitable candidates from applying.

Text C

While I was walking home thinking my mother would kill me if she ever found out, I realized that a car was slowly following me. If it had been a motorbike it wouldn't have frightened me because I would have known it was Jacob.

(Melina Marchetta, *Looking for Alibrandi*.)

Text C is in a literary visual genre. It is a short narrative paragraph from a novel.

LANGUAGE FEATURES. The text has conventional, well-formed sentences. The first person narrative allows the reader to enter into the character's mind and feelings. The feelings are not good: the character is already worried about how her mother will react when she comes home and, on top of the worry, there is possible fright. In just two short sentences, the writer manages to build up a sense of tension and foreboding.

Text D

"Anything good on tonight?"
"Dunno. Have a look!"
"Where?"
"Where do you think? The TV guide."
"Oh!"

Text D is in a non-literary transaction genre. It is a domestic conversation. Normally it is auditory; but here, visual.

LANGUAGE FEATURES. The text presents two people—probably at home, probably related—having a casual but not entirely friendly conversation. We can see the casualness of the conversation from the incomplete sentences and the informal *Dunno*. The first speaker sounds woolly-headed. The second speaker sounds a bit testy: notice the snappish exclamation mark at the end of the second line and the exasperated question in the second-last line.

GERUND—a nonfinite form of the verb, ending in –*ing* (*walking*, *talking*, *thinking*), and functioning as a noun. Because of the characteristic –*ing* ending, grammarians also call the gerund an "–*ing* form."

The word "gerund" comes from a Latin word that means "perform." Although the gerund counts as a verb, it can also function (perform) as a noun. It can function, for example, as the subject (the doer) of a verb, or as the object (the done-to) of a verb (bold).

> Scrubbing **keeps** the floor clean. (Ric Throssell, *Jackpot*.)
> [*Scrubbing* is the subject of the verb *keeps*.]
>
> We **shouldn't need** any partitioning at all. (Ric Throssell, *Jackpot*.)
> [*Partitioning* is the object of the verb *need*.]

We can see that a gerund functions as a noun from the fact that a gerund shares a characteristic with other nouns. We can make it plural with the addition of the suffix –*s*.

> Not a day passed without one of the schoolgirls dropping in to bring her flowers and books and tell her all the happenings in the juvenile world of Avonlea ... I don't approve of such goings-on.
>
> (LM Montgomery, *Anne of Green Gables*.)

See –*ING* FORM.

GET—See LANGUAGE MYTH.

GOAL—See ACTOR, BENEFICIARY, GOAL.

GRAMMAR—a term used in two senses: (1) as the mechanism of language and (2) as the study of that mechanism.

1. **Grammar as the mechanism of language** is the internal organizing principle of language in general or of any given language in particular. It is the set of patterns that operate on the elementary sounds and symbols of language and organize them into coherent wholes. (See also the Introduction to this book.)

   Here is a sampling of some other views on grammar in this sense of the word.

   > The grammar of a language consists of the devices that signal structural meaning.
   > (Charles Carpenter Fries, *The Structure of English*.)
   >
   > Grammar deals with the structure of languages.
   > (Otto Jespersen, *Essentials of English Grammar*.)
   >
   > Grammar ... can be viewed as a device of some sort for producing the sentences of the language under analysis.
   > (Noam Chomsky, *Syntactic Structures*.)
   >
   > Grammar is the entire system of a language, including its syntax, morphology, semantics and phonology.
   > (Sylvia Chalker and Edmund Weiner, *The Oxford Dictionary of Grammar*.)

2. **Grammar as a study**—here is a sampling of some views on grammar in the second sense of the word.

> Grammar—... the art which teaches the relations of words to each other.
> (Samuel Johnson, *A Dictionary of the English Language*.)
>
> The grammarian's "rules" are generally synopses of the linguistic rules used by speakers, which [the grammarian] formulates on the basis of noticing normative regularities that can be subsumed under general rules ...
> (GP Baker and PMS Hacker, *Language, Sense and Nonsense*.)
>
> A descriptive grammar is, in the first instance, a systematic description of a language as found in a sample of speech or writing.
> (David Crystal, *A Dictionary of Linguistics and Phonetics*.)

The word "grammar" comes from the Greek for "letters," and is related to the word "glamour"—such is the enchantment of the alphabet and what you can do with it!

See LANGUAGE.

GRAMMAR UNITS—the units that grammar deals with. These units range from single morphemes at the small end of the scale to entire texts at the large end.

1. **We consider seven such units below.** The featured units are underlined and labeled. The bracketed items may contain similar units, but we ignore these for the present purpose.

   (a) **Morpheme**

   > (I will see you) short-ly.
   >   TWO MORPHEMES

   A morpheme is the smallest linguistic bit of meaning or of structure. In the example sentence above, *short–* is an example of a meaningful morpheme; *–ly* of a structural morpheme. The morpheme *–ly* has no independent meaning: it is a structural device for showing that the word *shortly* is an adverb. The two morphemes (*short + ly*) above, illustrate the fact that some morphemes (e.g. *short*) can function as independent words, while others (e.g. *–ly*) can function only if they are bound to other morphemes. The grammar term for the first kind is "free morpheme;" that for the second kind is "bound morpheme" or "affix." See AFFIX and MORPHEME.

   (b) **Word**

   > (I will see you) soon.
   >   A WORD

   A word—defined by Bloomfield as "the minimum of free form" (1933:178)—is the smallest linguistic bit of free-standing, independent meaning or function. In writing, you show the independence of a word by separating it with a space on either side; in speech, by the fact that you can utter it alone or with a pause before and after. People have an intuitive feeling when a word is a word. The whole of the example sentence above consists of five words: *I, will, see, you,* and *soon*. Most words are meaningful—*soon*, for example—but some words carry out primarily functional roles. The word *the* is an example of the latter kind of word. See CONTENT WORD AND FUNCTION WORD.

(c) Compound (also called "group")

> (I will see you) <u>as soon as</u> (I can).
> A COMPOUND

As soon as is a compound conjunction (or "conjunction group") standing in for the single conjunction *when*. See COMPOUND.

(d) Phrase

> (I will see you) <u>in a little while</u>.
> A PHRASE

A phrase is a word or a string of words that functions as a part (also called a "constituent") of a clause or a sentence. In the above example, the preposition phrase *in a little while* functions as a modifier of the verb *will see*. See PHRASE.

(e) Clause

> (I will see you) <u>but I can only do so in a little while</u>.
> A CLAUSE

A clause is a major part (a "constituent") of a sentence. Typically, it consists of a subject (*I*, in the example clause above) and a predicate (*can only do so in a little while*). See CLAUSE.

(f) Sentence

> (I will see you.) <u>It will just take me a little while, though</u>.
> A SENTENCE

A sentence is a coherent and, in context, fully independent unit of language. Usually, but not necessarily, it consists of a main clause (an "independent clause") or of two or more interrelated clauses. In writing, a sentence is marked off by a capital letter at the beginning and a full stop (or an exclamation mark or a question mark) at the end. In speech, a sentence is distinguished by a characteristic intonation pattern. See SENTENCE.

(g) Text

> "<u>Hello</u>."
> "<u>Hello, is that you</u>?"
> "<u>Yes, of course it's me</u>."
> "<u>Well, when will I be seeing you</u>?"
> "<u>Soon, I guess</u>."
> "<u>Okay, bye then</u>."
> "<u>Bye</u>."
> A TEXT

A text can be anything from a telephone conversation (as in the example text above) to an essay, story, poem, advertisement, speech or novel: in short, any sustained piece of language. Texts have their own subdivisions and conventions: turn-taking in a conversation, verses in a poem, paragraphs and chapters in a book.

- Items (a)–(c) above (morphemes, words and compounds) make up the "morphology" of grammar.
- Items (d)–(f) (phrases, clauses and sentences) make up the "syntax" of grammar.
- Item (g) above makes up "text grammar."

See MORPHOLOGY, SYNTAX and TEXT GRAMMAR.

To sum up: morphemes may make up words, which may combine into compounds, which can combine into phrases, which make up clauses, which make up sentences, which make up texts.

2. **What is the use of knowing about grammar units?**

It gives us freedom and flexibility of expression by allowing us, for example, to replace a bound morpheme with a word or vice versa, or a phrase with a word, or to join separate sentences into one sentence consisting of several clauses. (For the arrow ⇨ read "becomes.")

He is <u>not</u> very friendly.	⇨	He is pretty <u>un</u>friendly.	[A word ⇨ a bound morpheme.]
They came from <u>that place</u>.	⇨	They came from <u>there</u>.	[A phrase ⇨ a word.]
<u>I am thirsty but not hungry.</u>	⇨	<u>I am thirsty</u>. <u>I am not hungry</u>.	[One sentence ⇨ two sentences.]

HEAD—(also called "head word") the main (often the first) word in a phrase and, therefore, the word that characterizes the phrase.

... <u>for</u> a few minutes	[a <u>preposition</u> at the head of a preposition phrase]
... the <u>people</u> next door	[a <u>noun</u> at the head of a noun phrase]
... <u>goes</u> home in the evening	[a <u>verb</u> at the head of a verb phrase]
... <u>red</u> in the face	[an <u>adjective</u> at the head of an adjective phrase]
... <u>slightly</u> curved	[an <u>adverb</u> at the head of an adverb phrase].

See PHRASE IN MODERN GRAMMAR.

HYPERBATON—See FIGURE OF SPEECH.

HYPERBOLE—See FIGURE OF SPEECH.

HYPERCORRECTION—("overcorrection") using a wrong form in the belief that it is good English.

1. **Hypercorrection often occurs with the pronoun *I* when it should be *me*.**

The car for Mark Taylor and I entered a walled compound.
He approached Shane Warne and I at a reception.
(Mark Waugh in *Inside Edge*, November 1998.)

The first occurrence of *I* should be *me* because it is the object of the preposition *for*. The second occurrence should be *me* because it is the object of the verb *approached*. The intervention of the words

Mark Taylor and (also *Shane Warne and*) has no bearing on the sentences.

> The car for (~~Mark Taylor and~~) me entered a walled compound.
> He approached (~~Shane Warne and~~) me at a reception.

2. Hypercorrection also occurs with the misuse of the subjunctive *were* for the indicative *was*.

> If he were angry, he had a right to be.
> [Should read: If he was angry, he had a right to be.]

It is only if being angry is hypothetical—an unreal situation—that *were* is appropriate.

> If he <u>were</u> angry he would show it.
> [This means that he isn't showing anger; therefore he isn't angry.]

See SUBJUNCTIVE.

IF ... THEN ...—See LANGUAGE MYTH.

IMPERATIVE—from the Latin for "command." One of the three major moods. See MOOD.

1. What is the imperative?

The imperative is the mood of commands, orders or requests: <u>Go home</u>! <u>Don't forget</u>! Please <u>hand</u> me that. The term "imperative" relates both to the verb (underlined above) that expresses a command and the sentence in which the verb occurs.

The imperative contrasts with the indicative, which is the mood of statements.

> <u>The Queen said to the Knave</u>, "<u>Turn them over</u>!" <u>The Knave did so, very carefully, with one foot</u>.
>   INDICATIVE   IMPERATIVE   INDICATIVE
>
> "<u>Get up</u>!" <u>said the Queen</u>. <u>The three gardeners instantly jumped up</u>.
> IMPERATIVE   INDICATIVE   INDICATIVE
>
> "<u>Get to your places</u>!" <u>shouted the Queen</u>, <u>and people began running about in all directions</u>.
>   IMPERATIVE   INDICATIVE   INDICATIVE
>
> "<u>Don't look at me like that</u>!" <u>said the King</u>. "<u>A cat may look at a king</u>," <u>said Alice</u>.
>   IMPERATIVE   INDICATIVE   INDICATIVE   INDICATIVE
>
> (Lewis Carroll, *Alice in Wonderland*.)

2. The imperative and the unmarked infinitive.

The imperative is characterized by having an unmarked infinitive at its head. An unmarked infinitive is an infinitive (a *to*–verb) without the word *to*. The unmarked infinitives in the last set of examples above are *turn*, *get,* and *look*.

3. Do imperatives have (unstated) subjects?

Modern grammarians wage global war over the above question. The majority view is that the subject *you* is implicit in every imperative. Thus, *Go home!*, most grammarians would say, really means ~~You~~, *Go home!*—with the word *you* understood but not stated.

I believe that this view is mistaken, a view based on two grounds.

- GROUND 1: By definition, a "subject" is a noun (*Adam*) or a pronoun (*you*) that agrees with a verb (see AGREEMENT OF SUBJECT AND VERB). But clearly, the imperatives *Be good* and *Give me a hand* do not agree with a subject *you* or *Adam*. If they did, the sentences would have to read (*You*) *Are good!* and (*Adam*) *Gives me a hand*. But they don't read like that, so *you* can't be the subject of *be*, and *Adam* can't be subject of *give*.

- GROUND 2: Even if the word *you* or *Adam* does occur in an imperative, the word is:

    (i) separated from the verb with a comma

    (ii) movable from the start of the sentence to the end.

(For the arrow ⇨ read "becomes.")

You, be good!	⇨	Be good, you!
Adam, give me a hand.	⇨	Give me a hand, Adam.

So there is really no subject–verb bond between the pronoun *you* and the verb *be*, or between the noun *Adam* and the verb *give*.

If that is the case, what role do the words *you* and *Adam* play in the imperative sentences?

The answer is that they play the role of addressee. That is, I address the commands to *you* and to *Adam*; the commands are not about *you* and *Adam*. The grammar name for a noun or a pronoun that functions as a form of address is "vocative." And a vocative is different from a subject. See VOCATIVE and EXTRA.

The upshot of the argument is that imperatives are subjectless sentences.

I discussed the above matter in a private communication with Noam Chomsky. I believe he was half inclined to agree with me. With scholarly caution, he concluded: "I don't mean to suggest that everything is clear; far from it ..." (September 3, 1996).

INDICATIVE—See MOOD.

INFINITIVE—a form of the verb that may feature the word *to* before it. If it does feature the word *to*, the verb is called a "marked infinitive;" if it doesn't, it is called an "unmarked infinitive" or a "base form."

MARKED INFINITIVE:	to go	to run	to rest
	to sleep	to read ...	
UNMARKED INFINITIVE:	(to) go	(to) run	(to) rest
	(to) sleep	(to) read ...	

See FINITE AND NONFINITE.

1. When are infinitives marked and unmarked?

When you have two verbs in a row, the second one is often a marked infinitive.

A sharecropper on a nearby plantation <u>asked</u> <u>to live</u> and work on some of his land.

One incident finally <u>persuaded</u> him <u>to leave</u> Mississippi.

(*National Geographic*, April 1999.)

The infinitive can also appear without the word *to*—an unmarked infinitive. This happens if the previous verb is any one of the following anomalous finites. See ANOMALOUS FINITE.

will	can	must
would	could	do
shall	may	does
should	might	did

He <u>could</u>n't <u>move</u> off the plantation.

You <u>might</u> <u>think</u> that the exodus was welcomed.

We <u>did</u>n't <u>take</u> much.

(*National Geographic*, April 1999.)

Another two verbs—*dare* and *need*—are sometimes followed by a marked, and sometimes by an unmarked, infinitive.

MARKED INFINITIVE	UNMARKED INFINITIVE
I do not <u>dare</u> <u>to ask</u> for a raise.	I <u>dare</u> <u>say</u> you're right.
I do not <u>need</u> <u>to seek</u> their help.	You <u>need</u>n't <u>be</u> so cocky.

2. **What are the functions of the infinitive?**

   (a) The second of two verbs in a row—as we have already seen under item 1 above.

   (b) The infinitive as a noun. The infinitive can, like any other noun or noun phrase, take on the role of the subject or the object (underlined) of a verb (bold).

INFINITIVE AS SUBJECT	NOUN AS SUBJECT
<u>To exist</u> **is** not enough.	<u>Existence</u> **is** not enough.
<u>To endure</u> **was** difficult.	<u>Endurance</u> **was** difficult.

INFINITIVE AS OBJECT	NOUN PHRASE AS OBJECT
I **like** <u>to bathe</u>.	I **like** <u>a bath</u>.
I **began** <u>to sing</u>.	I **began** <u>the song</u>.

   (c) A third function of the infinitive in its unmarked form is at the head of a command.
   See IMPERATIVE.

<u>Go</u> home!
<u>Be</u> good!

3. **What is the dreaded split infinitive?**

   A split infinitive is a marked infinitive with a word or words (bold) inserted between the *to* element and the verb element.

<u>to</u> **suddenly** <u>go</u>	<u>to</u> **honestly and truly** <u>be</u>
<u>to</u> **unjustly** <u>take</u>	<u>to</u> **really and fully** <u>understand</u>.

Some language authorities say it is wrong to split an infinitive. Why? Because the two elements that make up the infinitive ("to" + verb) are so intimately related that you shouldn't separate them.

Other language authorities say there is nothing really wrong with splitting an infinitive. Why not? Because it happens to be what many good writers do from time to time.

Here are some example texts with split infinitives. The infinitives are underlined and the "splitters" are in bold.

> Trolleys and buses were bought and allowed <u>to</u> **just** <u>run</u> down until they folded.
> (Jessica Tuchman Mathews in *Bill Moyers: A World of Ideas*.)
>
> I wasn't trying to write a moral story, but <u>to</u> **simply** <u>look</u> at the social factors involved.
> (Elaine Pagels in *Bill Moyers: A·World of Ideas*.)
>
> Act in such a way as <u>to</u> **really** <u>control</u> decision making.
> (Noam Chomsky in *Bill Moyers: A World of Ideas*.)
>
> We're talking about whether kids have sufficient protein <u>to</u> **properly** <u>nourish</u> growing brains.
> (*National Geographic*, January 1999.)
>
> Mary Leakey preferred <u>to</u> **carefully** <u>evaluate</u> scientific evidence before reaching any conclusions.
> (*TIME*, April 10, 1999.)

There are many more examples of split infinitives by many more writers in many more texts. The fact that these writers choose <u>to</u> **occasionally** <u>split</u> their infinitives validates the practice for you and me—occasionally.

INFLECTION—See AFFIX.

–*ING* FORM—a nonfinite form of the verb ending in *–ing*: *walking*, *talking*, *dancing*. The *–ing* form has three functions.

- AS A VERB: I am <u>dancing</u>.
- AS AN ADJECTIVE: I saw a <u>dancing</u> dog.
- AS A NOUN: <u>Dancing</u> is fun.

In the first two functions, the *–ing* form is also called a "present participle;" in the last, a "gerund." See PARTICIPLE and GERUND.

INITIALISM—See ABBREVIATION.

INTERJECTION—from the Latin for "throwing in." A word class that contains a ragbag collection of expressions used for a variety of functions.

In writing, you often follow an interjection with an exclamation mark, but this and other punctuation marks are omitted below.

1. SOCIAL CALLS AND GREETINGS

ahoy	congratulations	hello	sorry
bon appetit	cool	hi	ta
bon voyage	farewell	hiya	ta-ta
bless you	good morning	how do you do	thank you
bye-bye	good afternoon	howdy	thanks
cheers	good evening	pardon	wakey-wakey
cheerio	good day	please	welcome
ciao	good night	so long	yoo-hoo …

2. EMOTIONAL OUTBURSTS AND COMMANDS

ah	drat	hooray	strewth
alas	fair dinkum	hush	tut-tut
bah	fair enough	oh	upsidaisy
bewdy	fair go	oh dear	well-well
blast	far out	oops	whew
boo	goodness	ouch	whoopee
bravo	goody	rack off	wow
bull	hallelujah	shoo	yippee
cool	heave-ho	shshsh	yuck
damn	heck	steady	yum …

3. WORK AND SPORTS CALLS

check	howzat (how's that)	objection
checkmate	play	overruled
fore	on	on a point of order
goal	off	timber…

4. ANIMAL SOUNDS

bow-wow	miaow	quack-quack	moo
tweet-tweet	purr	oink-oink	grrr …

5. BLASPHEMIES AND OBSCENITIES

jeez (Jesus)	gosh (God)	bloody oath	crap …

6. ASSENT AND DISSENT

yes	OK	no	sure thing
uh-huh	yeah	uh-uh	nope …

Many of the interjections listed above double as members of other word classes. It is the context that determines whether the expression is an interjection or something else.

Congratulations, you've had a promotion!
INTERJECTION

Thank you for your congratulations.
NOUN

Pass the salt, please.
INTERJECTION

I'll pass the salt, just to please you.
VERB

Interjections often occur in isolation.

Bye!	Thanks.	Blast!	OK.

Interjections can also occur within sentences. If they do, they have two features: (a) they are usually separated from the rest of the sentences with punctuation marks; (b) you can often shift them around in the sentences.

We see both these features in the text below.

"<u>Now</u>, tell me, Pat, what's that in the window?" [Or: "Tell me, <u>now</u>, Pat, what's in the window?"]
"<u>Sure</u>, it's an arm, your honor!" [Or: "It's an arm, your honor, <u>sure</u>!"]
"Who ever saw one that size? <u>Why</u>, it fills the whole window!"
"<u>Sure</u>, it does, your honor; but it's an arm for all that." [Or: "It does, <u>sure</u>, your honor, but it's an arm for all that."]
"<u>Well</u>, it's got no business there. Go and take it away!"

(Lewis Carroll, *Alice in Wonderland*.)

INTERROGATIVE—See MOOD.

INTRANSITIVE—See TRANSITIVITY.

INVERSION—See FIGURE OF SPEECH.

IRONY—See FIGURE OF SPEECH.

IRREGULAR ADJECTIVE—any adjective that forms its degrees of comparison in a way other than *long, longer, longest* (or *beautiful, more beautiful, most beautiful*). See DEGREES OF COMPARISON. Here are the main irregular adjectives.

POSITIVE	COMPARATIVE	SUPERLATIVE
good	better	best
bad	worse	worst
little	less	least
much	more	most
many	more	most
far	farther (or further)	farthest (or furthest)

IRREGULAR NOUN—any noun that forms its plural without an add-on –*s*. Here are the main irregular nouns.

SINGULAR	PLURAL	SINGULAR	PLURAL	SINGULAR	PLURAL
man	men	louse	lice	sheep	sheep
woman	women	mouse	mice	fish	fish
foot	feet	ox	oxen	swine	swine
goose	geese	child	children	salmon	salmon
tooth	teeth	deer	deer	cod	cod
crisis	crises	nebula	nebulae	species	species

Irregular nouns contrast with regular nouns, which have plural –*s* endings: *baby–babies*.

IRREGULAR VERB—any verb that forms its past and/or its past participle forms without an add-on –*ed*. Here are the main irregular verbs.

PRESENT	PAST	PAST PARTICIPLE
bear	bore	born
begin	began	begun
bend	bent	bent
bet	bet	bet
bite	bit	bitten
bleed	bled	bled
bring	brought	brought
cut	cut	cut
dream	dreamt/dreamed	dreamt/dreamed
have	had	had
hit	hit	hit
kneel	knelt	knelt
know	knew	known
learn	learnt/learned	learnt/learned
put	put	put
rise	rose	risen
shut	shut	shut
smell	smelt/smelled	smelt/smelled
spell	spelt/spelled	spelt/spelled
spoil	spoilt/spoiled	spoilt/spoiled

Irregular verbs (also called "strong verbs") contrast with regular ("weak") verbs, which take an *–ed* ending: *walk–walked*.

LANGUAGE—"the sounds that people make to tell each other what they are thinking." That was the definition my eight-year-old granddaughter gave me in 1996. It neatly encapsulates the four leading characteristics of language: namely, that it is primarily (though not necessarily only):

ORAL:	"It's the sounds …"
HUMAN:	"that people make …"
COMMUNICATIVE:	"to tell each other …"
COGNITIVE:	"what they are thinking."

Here are some other definitions of "language."

Language was at its beginning merely oral; all words were spoken before they were written.
(Samuel Johnson, *A Dictionary of the English Language*.)

Language is the whole set of linguistic habits that allow an individual to understand and to be understood.
(Ferdinand de Saussure, *Course in General Linguistics*.)

Language is a purely human and non-instinctive method of communicating ideas, emotions and desires by means of a system of voluntarily produced symbols. These symbols are, in the first instance, auditory and they are produced by the so-called "organs of speech."
(Edward Sapir, *Language*.)

Language is … a systematic and conventional means of human communication by vocal sounds.
(CM Millward, *A Biography of the English Language*.)

Language is a set (finite or infinite) of sentences, each finite in length and constructed out of a finite set of elements.
(Noam Chomsky, *Syntactic Structures*.)

"Language" comes from the Latin for "tongue," indicating the primacy of the spoken over the written word.

LANGUAGE MYTH—anything about language that you may have learned but that isn't valid.

How do we expose a language myth?

In the same way that we expose other myths: by showing that things are different in the real world. There was a myth, for example, that the world was flat. The circumnavigation of the earth (and space shots) exposed that myth. In language we can expose myths by showing that reputable writers and real-life writings defy the myths.

Below, we explore five such myths.

1. **Never start a sentence with a conjunction** (a word such as *and*, *but* or *because*).

   I found this myth expressed in Edward Down's *Mastering Grammar*: "Starting a sentence with a joining word is awkward and amateurish. Hide your joining word well inside your sentence" (1991:36). But Down ignores his own rule in many instances, among them the following.

   > <u>And</u> so the conversation continued ... (98)
   > <u>As</u> you mark their essays, ... (viii)
   > <u>When</u> you return their essays, ... (viii)
   > <u>If</u> nothing else, ... (ix).

   Here is a range of citations from reputable sources, showing that it is all right to start sentences with conjunctions (underlined).

   > <u>And</u> Laban said unto Jacob, "<u>Because</u> thou art my brother, shouldest thou therefore serve me for nought?"
   > (Genesis 29:15.)
   >
   > <u>But</u> wherefore do not you a mightier way
   > Make war upon this bloody tyrant Time?
   > (William Shakespeare, "Sonnet 16" the first two lines.)
   >
   > <u>Because</u> she has not seen enough of the evil attending such things, she goes and gets married.
   > (Charles Dickens, *David Copperfield*.)
   >
   > <u>Because</u> men, groping in the Arctic darkness, had found a yellow metal, thousands of men were rushing into the Northland.
   > (Jack London, *The Call of the Wild*.)
   >
   > <u>Because</u> of secrecy restrictions, Turing's role in this enterprise was not acknowledged until long after his death. <u>And</u> like the invention of the computer, the work done by the Bletchley Park crew was very much a team effort. <u>But</u> it is now known that Turing played a crucial role in designing a primitive, computer-like machine that could decipher Nazi codes at high speed.
   > (*Time*, March 23, 1999.)

2. **Never end a sentence (or a clause) with a preposition** (a word such as *in*, *on*, *by* or *for*).

   Here is a range of citations from reputable sources, showing that it is all right to end sentences with prepositions (underlined).

I will not leave thee, until I have done that which I have spoken to thee <u>of</u>.
(Genesis 28:15.)

The iron bit he crushes tween his teeth, Controlling what he was controlled <u>with</u>. (William
Shakespeare, *Venus and Adonis.*)

A mail journey from London in winter was an achievement to congratulate an adventurous traveler <u>upon</u>.
(Charles Dickens, *A Tale of Two Cities.*)

In my own teaching, I'm at my best when I have something that I feel passionate <u>about</u> but that I can find a way of presenting the play <u>in</u>.
(Sara Lawrence Lightfoot in *Bill Moyers: A World of Ideas.*)

What are you going to say or add or write that has not been said or written <u>about</u>?
(Vartan Gregorian in *Bill Moyers: A World of Ideas.*)

When this novel first appeared in book form a notion got about that I had been bolted away <u>with</u>.
(Joseph Conrad, *Lord Jim.*)

In her day it was a street of jazz and blues, men in suits, women dressed to kill or die <u>for</u>.
(*National Geographic*, April 1999.)

It was Salk's team that figured out how to grow polio in test tubes—suddenly giving vaccine hunters everywhere enough virus to work <u>with</u>.
(*TIME*, March 29, 1999.)

So a preposition is, after all, a word that you can end a sentence <u>with</u>.

3. Avoid the use of the word *get.*

A strange myth if ever there was one. The word *get* must be important: *The Oxford English Dictionary* devotes some thirty pages to it, giving some 300 meanings of the word. Here are some citations with *get.*

And Shechem spoke unto his father Hamor, saying, "<u>Get</u> me this damsel to wife."
(Genesis 34:4.)

<u>Get</u> thee to a nunnery!
(William Shakespeare, *Hamlet.*)

The passenger would then lower the window to <u>get</u> the reality of mist and rain.
(Charles Dickens, *A Tale of Two Cities.*)

Every president is also trying to make things happen, to <u>get</u> policy enacted.
(Sissela Bok in *Bill Moyers: A World of Ideas.*)

To play a leading part in the world the British have <u>got</u> to know what they are doing, and they have <u>got</u> to retain their vitality.
(George Orwell, *Collected Essays, Journalism and Letters*, vol. 3.)

It would have been all the better if she had <u>got</u> someone else to dress her.
(Lewis Carroll, *Through the Looking-Glass.*)

You <u>get</u> everything just as you like it when, guess what, it's time to upgrade.
(*New Scientist*, May 8, 1999.)

Americans <u>get</u> most of their complex carbohydrates from refined grains.
(*TIME*, May 10, 1999.)

All of Europe's banks face pressures to <u>get</u> bigger.
(*The Economist*, May 7, 1999.)

If the above reputable authors (and many more) can get away with it, so can you and I.

4. If you use *if*, then don't follow it up with *then*.

Why not, when virtually every good author does, from time to time?

> If thou wilt take the left hand, <u>then</u> I will go to the right; or <u>if</u> thou depart to the right hand, <u>then</u> I will go to the left.
> (Genesis 13:9.)
>
> <u>If</u> ten of thine ten times refigur'd thee,
> <u>Then</u> what could death do, if thou shouldst depart,
> Leaving thee living in posterity?
> (William Shakespeare, *Venus and Adonis*.)
>
> <u>If</u> his wife had implored the king for any tidings of him and all quite in vain, <u>then</u> the history of your father would have been the history of this unfortunate gentleman.
> (Charles Dickens, *A Tale of Two Cities*.)
>
> <u>If</u> you had to define humor in a single phrase, <u>then</u> you might define it as dignity sitting on a tin tack.
> (George Orwell, *Collected Essays, Journalism and Letters*, vol. 3.)
>
> <u>If</u> organic beings vary at all in the several parts of their organization; if there be at some age, season or year, a severe struggle for life, <u>then</u> it would be a most extraordinary fact if no variation ever had occurred useful to some being's own welfare.
> (Charles Darwin, *The Origin of Species*.)
>
> <u>If</u> humans and their descendants remain sufficiently motivated (that may be a big "if"), <u>then</u> technology will be bounded only by the laws of physics.
> (Paul Davies, *The Last Three Minutes*.)
>
> <u>If</u> you could introduce tests at, say, the age of three, <u>then</u> you could intervene early and reduce the long-term suffering of many people.
> (*New Scientist*, April 24, 1999.)
>
> <u>If</u> the questioner cannot determine by the responses to queries posed to them which is the human and which the computer, <u>then</u> the computer can be said to be 'thinking' as well as the human.
> (*Time*, March 29, 1999.)

Of course, you don't have to use *then* after *if*. The point is that you may, if you feel like it.

5. You can't say "very true."

Why not? Because *very* comes from the Latin "verus," which means "true," and it's nonsense to say "true true." A self-appointed expert in English told me that, so I checked the literature to see whether what he said had any truth in it.

> HAMLET: To be honest, as this world goes, is to be one man pick'd out of ten thousand.
> POLONIOUS: That's <u>very true</u> my lord.
> (William Shakespeare, *Hamlet*.)
>
> Simple they were, not savage; and their rifles,
> Though <u>very true</u>, were not yet used for trifles.
> (Lord Byron, *Don Juan*.)

> I said to Miss Mills that this was <u>very true</u>.
> (Charles Dickens, *David Copperfield*.)
>
> I crossed some white fantails, which breed <u>very true</u>, with some black barbs.
> (Charles Darwin, *The Origin of Species*.)
>
> "That is <u>very true</u>," replied Elizabeth, "and I could easily forgive his pride."
> (Jane Austen, *Pride and Prejudice*.)
>
> It was <u>very true</u>, that this kingdom was not in a flourishing state.
> (Thomas Paine, *The American Crisis*.)
>
> "<u>Very true</u>," said the Duchess: "flamingoes and mustard both bite."
> (Lewis Carroll, *Alice in Wonderland*.)
>
> This letter is from your <u>very true</u> friend.
> (Mark Twain, *Life on the Mississippi*.)
>
> "It is <u>very true</u>," Winterbourne pursued, "that Daisy and her mamma have not yet risen to that stage of culture."
> (Henry James, *Daisy Miller*.)

What is the error that this "expert" has fallen into? It is the false notion that the non-English meaning of a loan word keeps its original meaning when it comes into English. The fact is that, in English, *very* has not kept its original meaning but has come to mean "in a high degree."

6. **You can't use *since* in the sense of "because."**

Why not? Because some authority figure has declared that *since* means "from the time."

Is this true?

Only half true. It is true that *since* means "from the time:" *I have been waiting for your letter <u>since</u> January*. But *since* doesn't have only one meaning, any more than *box* has only one meaning—a "container." *Box* also means "fight with fists" and a "small evergreen tree" and a few other things.

So, while *since* does mean "from the time," it also means "because"—as the following texts show.

> I have not touched the pianoforte <u>since</u> [from the time] it was tuned. Her mother considered her to be safe in town <u>since</u> [because] his acquaintance must now be dropped by all who called themselves her friends.
> (Jane Austen, *Sense and Sensibility*.)
>
> Ever <u>since</u> [from the time] she's come back, she's been perfectly cheerful.
> <u>Since</u> [because] she liked plain things herself, it was all the more necessary to have jars and punchbowls and candlesticks in the company rooms for people who did appreciate them.
> (Willa Cather, *O Pioneers!*)
>
> Just over a year <u>since</u> [from the time] the business began in Barcelona, there are about 30 shops around Spain, with others in Portugal and one just opened in Milan.
> (*TIME*, April 5, 1999.)
>
> <u>Since</u> [because] customer retention costs a quarter of customer acquisition, the financial incentive to build customer loyalty should be very high on all makers' agendas.
> (*The Economist*, May 28, 1999.)

LEXICAL WORD—See CONTENT WORD AND FUNCTION WORD.

LITOTES—See FIGURE OF SPEECH.

MAIN CLAUSE—See CLAUSE TYPES.

MAIN VERB—See AUXILIARY VERB.

MARKED AND UNMARKED CLAUSE COMPLEX—terms in functional grammar that distinguish clause complexes (that is, sentences) in which the main clause stands first (unmarked) and those in which the main clause stands last (marked).

In traditional grammar, marked clause complexes are called "periodic sentences;" unmarked ones, "loose sentences." The main clauses below are underlined; the subordinate clauses are not.

> <u>They ate</u> when they were hungry. [UNMARKED CLAUSE COMPLEX OR "LOOSE SENTENCE"]
> MAIN CLAUSE   SUBORDINATE CLAUSE
>
> When they were hungry <u>they ate</u>. [MARKED CLAUSE COMPLEX OR "PERIODIC SENTENCE"]
> SUBORDINATE CLAUSE   MAIN CLAUSE

What is the difference between marked and unmarked clause complexes?

It is one of feel. The "normal" sequence of clauses is main clause first, then subordinate clause (unmarked). If you bring the subordinate clause to the beginning, you give it more prominence (marked). In everyday speech and writing, we usually switch between marked and unmarked clause complexes. This is exemplified in the text below. The main clauses are underlined; the subordinate clauses are not.

> Before vaccines are ready to combat tuberculosis worldwide, <u>tens of millions of people may die</u>. [MARKED]
> <u>Barry Bloom told scientists gathered in Chicago</u> that doctors won't have an effective immunisation ready for 30 to 40 years. [UNMARKED]
> By that time, we could see another 89 million deaths, <u>he says</u>. [MARKED]
> <u>Experts agree</u> that better drug treatments are needed. [UNMARKED]
> (*New Scientist*, May 9, 1998.)

See THEME AND RHEME.

MASCULINE—See GENDER.

MEIOSIS—See FIGURE OF SPEECH.

METAPHOR—See FIGURE OF SPEECH.

METONYMY—See FIGURE OF SPEECH.

MODALITY—from the Latin for "manner." The emotional manner or expressiveness of a text: whether it is calm or angry, polite or rude, pleading or commanding and so on.

There are two main ways in which a text can say something with different modalities. One is through the language of the text; the other is through non-language means such as tone of voice and body language—including smiles, gestures and so on.

Below, we discuss various ways of adding modality to written texts.

1. **In a play,** the playwright often indicates the intended modality (underlined) in brackets.

    > MRS. HIGGINS: You were surprised because she threw your slippers at you. I should have thrown the fire irons at you.
    >
    > HIGGINS: We said nothing except that we were tired and wanted to go to bed. Did we, Pick?
    >
    > PICKERING: (shrugging his shoulders) That was all.
    >
    > MRS. HIGGINS: (ironically) Quite sure?
    >
    > PICKERING: Absolutely. Really, that was all.
    >
    > (George Bernard Shaw, *Pygmalion*.)

2. **In a novel,** the author may indicate modality in other ways (underlined).

    > "Have some wine," said the March Hare in an encouraging tone.
    > "I don't see any wine," Alice remarked.
    > "There isn't any," said the March Hare.
    > "Then it wasn't very civil of you to offer it," said Alice angrily.
    > "Your hair wants cutting," said the Hatter.
    > "You should learn not to make personal remarks," Alice said with some severity.
    >
    > (Lewis Carroll, *Alice in Wonderland*.)

3. **In speaking (or in writing),** we can indicate modality by the use of vocabulary. There are several ways of doing this.

    (a) GENERAL VOCABULARY: *Pipe down!* versus *Keep quiet*
    (b) MODAL VOCABULARY: *kindly, please, excuse me*
    (c) MODAL VERBS: *must, could, might, would, should.*
         See MODAL VERB.

    Below, we see different modalities in sentences that serve the same purpose.

    > Belt up!
    > Keep quiet!
    > Pipe down, you idiot!
    > Must you make so much noise?
    > Dare I ask for a moment's silence?
    > Could you kindly tone it down a bit?
    > Might we have some shush, please?
    > Sorry, but would you mind keeping quiet?
    > I should like to ask for a bit of quiet as I am listening to the music.
    > Excuse me, please, I'm just listening to some music.

MODAL VERB—(also called "modal auxiliary") any of a twelve-member subset of the anomalous finites (see ANOMALOUS FINITE). The twelve modal verbs are:

can	shall	will	may	must	ought
could	should	would	might	dare	need.

Some grammars add the anomalous finite *used to*, as *in I used to live there*.

The modal verbs have three characteristics:

1. They don't take an *–s*, *–ing*, or *–en* ending.
2. They are verbs with an attitude (see below).
3. Some of them can be used in two senses—modally (with an attitude) or non-modally (expressing a matter of fact).

We explore the three characteristics below.

1. Modal verbs don't take an *–s, –ing,* or *–en* ending. This is unlike normal (non-modal) verbs, which do take these endings.

MODAL VERBS	NON-MODAL VERBS			
can	eat	eats	eating	eaten
must	do	does	doing	done

2. Modal verbs are verbs with an attitude—that is, they express permission, duty, doubt, probability, and so on, rather than matters of fact.

MODAL VERBS	NON-MODAL VERBS
They <u>should be</u> here any minute. [Expresses a hope or expectation.]	They <u>are</u> here now. [Expresses a matter of fact.]
They <u>shall not</u> pass. [Expresses my determination.]	They <u>passed</u> anyway. [Expresses what took place.]

3. Some modal verbs can be used in two senses—modally and non-modally.

NON-MODALLY: MATTER OF FACT	MODALLY: WITH AN ATTITUDE
I decided that I <u>would</u> go home. [I was actually heading for home.]	I <u>would</u> go home if I had a home to go to. [I am not going home because I haven't got a home.]
You <u>should</u> come at noon. [You have an actual obligation to come.]	If they <u>should</u> come, it would surprise me. [It is highly unlikely that they will come.]
You are so strong, you <u>can</u> smash a brick. [Expresses what you are in fact able to do.]	Here's a brick: you <u>can</u> smash it if you like. [Expresses what I permit you to do.]
When I was young I <u>could</u> rollerskate. [It was actually a fact in the past.]	I don't quite believe them: they <u>could</u> be wrong. [The matter is doubtful in the present.]
You <u>may</u> enter the room without knocking. [You actually have permission in the present.]	I have not made up my mind, but I <u>may</u> enter later. [There is some indecision about my future action.]
I said that they <u>might</u> do whatever they liked. [They actually had my permission in the past.]	It's getting late now, so I <u>might</u> do it tomorrow. [I am speculating about the future.]
The law says that I <u>must</u> pay taxes. [Paying taxes is an actual obligation.]	The door is open: I <u>must</u> have left it unlocked. [Leaving the door unlocked is a supposition.]
They <u>ought</u> to wait their turn. [They have an actual obligation to wait.]	I wrote to them weeks ago: they <u>ought</u> to write soon. [Not an obligation; just what I hope.]
She <u>needs</u> a hammer and nails. [With an *–s*, expresses a matter of fact.]	She <u>needn't</u> go just yet. [Without an *–s*, refers to her obligation or lack of it.]

If you include *used* to among the modal verbs, you also get the following contrasting pair.

They <u>used</u> books to teach themselves things. [That is, in fact, what they used.]	They <u>used</u> to live there when they were young. [A different meaning of *used*: reminiscing.]

Modal verbs are used both in subjunctive and in conditional sentences. See SUBJUNCTIVE and CONDITIONAL.

MODE—See CONTEXT.

MODIFY—from the Latin for "limiting." A term that describes the relation of an adjective, an adverb or a determiner (or phrases of the same type) to another word or word string. A modifier limits the meaning of the word (or string of words) to which it relates. Thus, *table* can mean any table in the world but, if you add *round* before *table*, you immediately limit the application of the word to tables of a certain shape.

These are <u>lovely</u> **children**. ADJECTIVE NOUN	[The adjective *lovely* modifies the noun *children*.]
They **are playing** <u>happily</u>. VERB ADVERB	[The adverb *happily* modifies the compound verb *are playing*.]
<u>Pat's</u> **friends** are loyal. DETERMINER NOUN	[The determiner *Pat's* modifies the noun *friends*.]

1. **If the modifier (underlined) stands before the related word or word string (bold),** it is called a "premodifier" or an "attributive modifier."

<u>Jerry Springer's</u> **appearance** had everything his viewers have come to love: <u>boorish</u> **behavior**, <u>mocking</u> **laughter**, and <u>lots of</u> **kicking**, **punching**, **hair-pulling** and **chair-throwing**. Except that <u>Mr. Springer's</u> **appearance**, on June 4th, was before the Police and Fire Committee of the Chicago City Council.

(*The Economist*, June 18, 1999.)

2. **If the modifier (underlined) stands after the related word or word string (bold),** it is called a "postmodifier" or a "predicative modifier."

The committee watched **videotapes** <u>of assorted Springer shows</u>, such as a segment entitled "**Klanfrontation!**" <u>in which hooded members of the Ku Klux Klan brawled with members of the Jewish Anti-Defamation League</u>. Mr. Springer urged officials to **take** his show <u>less seriously</u> and argued that there is nothing glamorous about the **people** <u>who appear on it</u> or their propensity to throttle each other.

(*The Economist*, June 18, 1999.)

3. **An adverbial modifier (underlined) can stand inside a compound verb (bold).**

I **had** <u>often</u> **petitioned** to be allowed to take the plate in my hand in order to examine it more closely, but **had** <u>always</u> <u>hitherto</u> **been deemed** unworthy of such a privilege.

(Charlotte Brontë, *Jane Eyre*.)

MOOD—a term that means "mode" or "manner" and that refers to the attitude of the speaker to what is spoken—the spin of the text. One can best illustrate this through a comparison of the following sentences.

Kim is happy.	[The speaker is conveying a fact.]
Kim, be happy!	[The speaker is issuing an order.]
If only Kim were happy.	[The speaker is expressing a wish.]

1. **Mood is expressed in two complementary ways.** One is the form of the verb (compare the verb forms *is*, *be* and *were* in the example sentences above); the other is the overall sentence structure (compare the differing structures of the example sentences above). Thus one can speak both of "the mood of a verb" and "the mood of a sentence."

2. **English has three moods.**

    INDICATIVE (from the Latin for "point out") expresses matters of fact: Kim <u>is</u> happy.

    IMPERATIVE (from the Latin for "command") expresses commands: Kim, <u>be</u> happy!

    SUBJUNCTIVE (from the Latin for "subjoin") expresses hopes and hypotheses: If only Kim <u>were</u> happy.

    Note that in the subjunctive you say *were* (not *was*) even with singular nouns or pronouns: *If only Kim <u>were</u>* ... [not: *If only Kim <u>was</u>* ...].

3. **Each of the three moods has several sub-moods.**

    INDICATIVE
    - POSITIVE (an affirmation):   I <u>like</u> reading.
    - EMPHATIC: I <u>do like</u> reading.
    - NEGATIVE (a denial):   I <u>don't like</u> reading.
    - INTERROGATIVE (a question):   <u>Do you like</u> reading?
    - NEGATIVE-INTERROGATIVE: <u>Don't you like</u> reading?

    IMPERATIVE
    - POSITIVE (a *do* command):   <u>Be</u> good!
    - EMPHATIC (a strong command):   <u>Do help</u> us, please!
    - NEGATIVE (a *don't* command):   <u>Don't be</u> selfish.

    SUBJUNCTIVE
    - THE FAILED PAST (past perfect):   I wish I <u>had saved</u> my money.
    - THE UNREAL PRESENT (past simple):   I wish it <u>were</u> the end of term.
    - THE DOUBTFUL FUTURE (future in the past simple):   If only they <u>would arrive</u> soon.

The indicative (for statements) is fairly straightforward. Well over ninety percent of normal speech is in the indicative. But the other moods also occur in texts.

"<u>If you knew Time as well as I do</u>," <u>said the Hatter</u>,
    SUBJUNCTIVE   INDICATIVE

"<u>you wouldn't talk about wasting it</u>. <u>It's him</u>."
    SUBJUNCTIVE   INDICATIVE

"<u>Have some wine</u>," <u>the March Hare said in an encouraging tone</u>.
    IMPERATIVE   INDICATIVE

(Lewis Carroll, *Alice in Wonderland*.)

See IMPERATIVE and SUBJUNCTIVE.

4. A note on terminology.

Some grammarians add another mood—the exclamative—illustrated by sentences such as the following.

> How immensely you must amuse them!
> What wonderfully blue eyes you have!
>
> (Oscar Wilde, *The Importance of Being Earnest.*)

I include sentences of this kind among the indicatives.

MORPHEME—from the Greek for "form" or "structure." The smallest linguistic bit of meaning or of structure.

(a)   Many morphemes make up independent words of one or more syllables.

> book   dinosaur   theater   hesitate

Such morphemes are called "free morphemes"—free in the sense that they can stand alone as words. Each of the above example words is made up of one free morpheme.

(b)   There are also words that are made up of more than one free morpheme.

> sideshow   downsize   tearoom   nevertheless

(c)   Other morphemes (underlined) can be used only when they are bound to a word. They are therefore called "bound morphemes." Bound morphemes are also called "affixes." A bound morpheme that appears at the beginning of a word is called a "prefix;" one that appears at the end of a word, a "suffix."

> book*ish*   dinosaur*s*   cinema*tic*   *un*hesita*ting*

Each of the above example words is made up of one free morpheme and one or more bound morphemes.

(d)   We distinguish among bound morphemes, not only according to their position, but also according to their function:

(i)   a "derivational affix" changes the meaning of a word (*happy* differs in meaning from *unhappy*; *media* from *multimedia*), or the word class of a word (the verb *diagnose* changes into the adjective *diagnostic*; the adjective *electric* into the noun *electricity*)

(ii)   an "inflectional affix" changes the grammar of a word (the singular *child* becomes the plural *children*; the positive *cool* becomes the comparative *cooler*).

For more information on derivational and inflectional affixes, see AFFIX.

The following text consists of 31 morphemes making up 23 words, one of them a hyphenated word.

A life-bear+ing comet arriv+ing at an Earth that had already acquir+ed its ocean+s and atmo(s)+sphere would effective+ly have seed+ed our planet with life.
(Fred Hoyle and Chandra Wickramasinghe, *Our Place in the Cosmos*.)

To sum up, morphemes are of the following kinds.

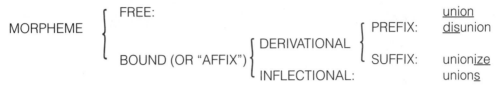

See ROOT AND STEM.

MORPHOLOGY—the "study of form." Morphology is the grammar of words and word forms. The following are some of the entries that deal with aspects of morphology.

MORPHEME	NOUN	PREPOSITION
ROOT AND STEM	PRONOUN	CONJUNCTION
AFFIX	ADJECTIVE	ADVERB
GRAMMAR UNITS	DETERMINER	INTERJECTION
WORD CLASSES	VERB	

MULTIPLE SENTENCE—See SENTENCE TYPES.

NEGATIVE—See MOOD.

NEUTER—See GENDER.

NOMINALIZATION—turning something that isn't a noun into a noun.
(For the arrow ⇨ read "becomes.")

VERB ⇨	NOUN	ADJECTIVE ⇨	NOUN
resolve	resolution	small	smallness
refer	reference	high	height

Here is a text with some non-nouns and, below it, the same passage with the nominalized words.

This century has been <u>amazing</u>, <u>inspiring</u> and <u>fascinating</u>.
          ADJECTIVE ADJECTIVE   ADJECTIVE

[This century has been one of <u>amazement</u>, <u>inspiration</u> and <u>fascination</u>.]
          NOUN   NOUN   NOUN

Sure, the 15th was pretty <u>wild</u>, with the Renaissance and the Spanish Inquisition.
          ADJECTIVE

[Sure, the 15th was pretty full of <u>wildness</u>, with the Renaissance and the Spanish Inquisition.]
          NOUN

And the 1st century <u>impacted</u> through Jesus having <u>lived</u> and <u>died</u> in it.
          VERB   VERB   VERB

[And the 1st century made its <u>impact</u> through Jesus' <u>life</u> and <u>death</u>.]
          NOUN   NOUN   NOUN

Socrates and Plato made the 5th century <u>important</u>.
          ADJECTIVE

[Socrates and Plato gave the 5th century <u>importance</u>.]
NOUN

But we who <u>live</u> in the 20th can probably <u>claim</u> that ours has been one of the top four or five of
VERB VERB

<u>recorded</u> history.
ADJECTIVE

[But we who have our <u>lives</u> in the 20th can probably make the <u>claim</u> that ours has been one of the top
NOUN NOUN

four or five in the <u>records</u> of history.]
NOUN

(Unbracketed text from *TIME*, April 13, 1998.)

NOMINATIVE—See CASE.

NONFINITE CLAUSE—in modern grammar, a clause that has one of the nonfinite verb forms.

1. INFINITIVE:		<u>To be or not to be</u>, that is the question.
2. –*ING* FORM {	(a) PRESENT PARTICIPLE:	<u>Being good</u>, I got a reward.
	(b) GERUND:	<u>Doing what I like</u> is what I enjoy.
3. –*EN* FORM:		They arrived home <u>tired but happy</u>.

See FORMS OF THE VERB.

In traditional grammar, (1.) would be called an "infinitive phrase;" (2. (a)) a "present participle phrase;" (2. (b)) a "gerund phrase;" (3.) a past "participle phrase." This is because, in traditional grammar, only word strings that contain finite verbs are counted as "clauses."

It is a feature of nonfinite clauses that, in many instances, you can change them into finite clauses. In the finite clauses below, the finite verbs are in bold. (For the arrow ⇨ read "becomes.")

NONFINITE CLAUSES (UNDERLINED) ⇨	FINITE CLAUSES (UNDERLINED)
<u>To be or not to be</u>, that is the question.	<u>Whether I **ought** to be or not</u>, that is the question.
<u>Being good</u>, I got a reward.	<u>Because I **was** good</u>, I got a reward.
<u>Playing chess</u> is what I enjoy.	I enjoy it <u>when I **play** chess</u>.
They arrived home <u>tired but happy</u>.	They arrived home <u>and they **were** tired but happy</u>.

Here are some textual examples that feature nonfinite clauses.

1. Infinitive clauses (with verbs preceded by to). See INFINITIVE.

<u>To make the results as legible as possible</u>, Argo Interactive has developed a system that removes unnecessary clutter from complicated Web pages. The software is designed <u>to run on an Internet service provider's proxy server</u>.

(*New Scientist*, May 1, 1999.)

2. *–ing* clauses.

(a) Present participle clauses (with verbs ending in *–ing* and functioning as adjectives). See PARTICIPLE.

> Scientists are exploring a newly discovered habitat <u>existing among the stones covering the seafloor</u>.
> <u>Rinsing the glass of his face mask</u>, Wahle pauses for a moment and looks back to the mainland.
> (*National Geographic*, 1999.)

(b) Gerund clauses (with verbs ending in *–ing* and functioning as nouns). See GERUND.

> These environments often provide researchers with <u>a better understanding of the intricate workings of life overall</u>. Wahle's experiments—<u>tethering newly emerged lobsters with a monofilament line to a stake on the seafloor</u>—have revealed just how vulnerable they are.
> (*National Geographic*, 1999.)

3. *–en* clauses (with verbs ending in *–en* or *–ed* or *–t* and functioning as adjectives). See PARTICIPLE.

> <u>Pioneered in Britain</u>, closed-circuit TV cameras now scan increasingly large swathes of urban landscapes in other countries too.
> <u>Given the easy availability of increasingly complex codes</u>, governments may just have to accept defeat.
> (*The Economist*, May 7, 1999.)

In traditional grammar all of the above nonfinite clauses would be counted as phrases.
See PHRASE and CLAUSE.

NONSTANDARD—See STANDARD AND NONSTANDARD ENGLISH.

NOUN—from the Latin for "name." One of the word classes.

1. How do you identify nouns?

(a) In traditional grammar, a noun is said to be a naming word—a word that gives the name of a person (*Alex*), a thing (*bush*), a place (*Washington*) and so on.

(b) Technically, a noun is a word to which you can add an *–s* suffix to make it plural. (For the arrow ⇨ read "becomes.")

SINGULAR	⇨	PLURAL
apple		apples
expectation		expectations
sighting		sightings

But there are also nouns that you make plural without an *–s*. See IRREGULAR NOUN.

(c) A noun is any word (other than a pronoun or a determiner) that fits into the blank space in the following sentence frame.

> (a)
> I am thinking about (an) _____. [mum whale evening resigning …]
> (the)   NOUN

The words in round brackets (*a*, *an* and *the*—called "articles") are optional: sometimes they stand before the nouns; sometimes they don't. Any of the words in square brackets are nouns because they fit into the frame—some with, some without, articles.

In the following text, the nouns are underlined; the articles are in bold.

> **The** first <u>thing</u> you noticed was **the** <u>face</u>, **a** dead-white <u>mask</u> of <u>anguish</u> with black <u>holes</u> for <u>eyes</u>, **a** curt <u>slash</u> of <u>red</u> for **a** <u>mouth</u> and <u>cheekbones</u> as high as **the** <u>sky</u>. Even if <u>Martha Graham</u> had done nothing else worth mentioning in her 96 <u>years</u>, she might be remembered for that <u>face</u>. But she also made <u>dances</u> to go with it—harsh, angular <u>fantasies</u> spun out of **the** strange <u>proportions</u> of her short-legged <u>body</u> and **the** <u>pain</u> and <u>loneliness</u> of her secret <u>heart</u>. If <u>Graham</u> ever gave <u>birth</u>, one <u>critic</u> quipped, it would be to **a** <u>cube</u>; instead, she became **the** <u>mother</u> of American <u>dance</u>.
> (*Time*, June 14, 1999.)

Martha Graham in the box above is a compound noun. See COMPOUND.

(d)   Some nouns originate as nouns (the first six in the box above); others derive from members of other word classes with the help of suffixes (underlined below).

ADJECTIVE ⇨	NOUN	VERB	⇨	NOUN	ADVERB	⇨	NOUN
solid	solid<u>ity</u>	enjoy		enjoy<u>ment</u>	well		well<u>ness</u>
competent	compet<u>ence</u>	attend		atten<u>tion</u>	together		together<u>ness</u>

The process of changing a non-noun into a noun is called "nominalization". See NOMINALIZATION.

All of the above features—from (a) to (d)—define what nouns are.

2. How do nouns function in sentences?

Nouns do several things in sentences, the main five of which—(a) to (e) below—are to express:

(a)   THE SUBJECT (the doer or actor) of a verb:
<u>Leigh</u> **bought** gifts for Gene.
<small>SUBJECT   VERB</small>

(b)   THE OBJECT (the done-to or goal) of a verb:
Leigh **bought** <u>gifts</u> for Gene.
<small>VERB   OBJECT</small>

(c)   THE OBJECT of (the word relating to) a preposition:
Leigh bought gifts **for**   <u>Gene</u>.
<small>PREPOSITION OBJECT</small>

The above three relationships of nouns to other words are illustrated in the following text.

<u>Jeffrey Woolf</u>   **of**   <u>London</u> **is patenting** a silent car <u>alarm</u>.
<small>NOUN   PREPOSITION NOUN   VERB   NOUN</small>
<small>SUBJECT OF *is patenting*   OBJECT OF *of*   OBJECT OF *is patenting*</small>

The <u>patent</u> **features** a <u>windshield</u> made **from** a special <u>material</u>.
  NOUN   VERB   NOUN   PREPOSITION   NOUN
SUBJECT OF *features*   OBJECT OF *features*   OBJECT OF *from*

The <u>material</u> **changes** when an electric <u>current</u> **hits** the <u>material</u>.
  NOUN   VERB   NOUN   VERB   NOUN
SUBJECT OF *changes*   SUBJECT OF *hits*   OBJECT OF *hits*

A <u>thief</u> trying **to hot-wire** the <u>car</u> **will trip** a <u>sensor</u>
 NOUN   VERB   NOUN   VERB   NOUN
SUBJECT OF *will trip*   OBJECT OF *to hot-wire*   OBJECT OF *will trip*

and **find** the <u>windshield</u> impossible to see through.
 VERB   NOUN
       OBJECT OF *find*

(*New Scientist*, May 31, 1997.)

(d)   THE VOCATIVE—a noun used as a form of address.

> "<u>Davy</u>, my <u>darling</u>, are you listening? Can you hear?"
> "Ye– ye– ye– yes, <u>Peggotty</u>!" I sobbed.
> (Charles Dickens, *David Copperfield.*)

See VOCATIVE.

(e)   THE COMPLEMENT of a verb—a noun (underlined) that completes a linking verb (bold).

> I **was** a posthumous <u>child</u>.
> (Charles Dickens, *David Copperfield.*)

See COMPLETION.

NOUN SUBCLASSES—there are two major subclasses of nouns. One of these has two subdivisions:

1. PROPER NOUNS: Debra   Mars   Sydney Opera House

2. COMMON NOUNS
   (a) COUNT: person   star   planet   building
   (b) NONCOUNT: milk   water   wool   steel

On line 1 above, *Sydney Opera House* is a compound proper noun. See COMPOUND.

We look at each of the subclasses below.

1. What are proper nouns?

Proper nouns are the names of people, geographic places, proprietary names and the like—words that would, in writing, normally start with capital letters.

2. What are common nouns?

Common nouns are all the rest—any noun that is not proper. A common noun can apply to any member of a broad class. So, for example, the common noun *person* can apply to *Jack, Jill, Adam, Eve* ...

The following text contains proper and common nouns.

<u>Emily Dickinson</u> was born in <u>Amherst</u>, <u>Massachusetts</u>, on <u>December</u> 10,1830, and died there on
  PROPER   PROPER   PROPER   PROPER

<u>May</u> 15, 1886. Her <u>father</u>, <u>Edward Dickinson</u>, was the leading <u>lawyer</u> of <u>Amherst</u>, and was <u>treasurer</u>
PROPER   COMMON   PROPER   COMMON   PROPER   COMMON

of the well-known <u>college</u> there.
                   COMMON

(Emily Dickinson, *Poems.*)

Common nouns are subdivided into the following.

(a) Count nouns (like *banana*) are those that you can count and that, consequently, have both singular and plural forms.

(b) Noncount nouns (like *steel*) are nouns that, usually, you can't count and that normally have only singular forms.

So we say: *One banana*, *two bananas*, *three bananas* … But not usually: *One steel*, *two steels*, *three steels*.

The following text contains count and noncount nouns.

The <u>subject</u> of this <u>essay</u> is not <u>liberty</u> of <u>will</u>, as opposed to the <u>doctrine</u> of <u>necessity</u>; but social
    COUNT   COUNT   NONCOUNT NONCOUNT   COUNT   NONCOUNT

<u>liberty</u>: the <u>nature</u> and <u>limits</u> of <u>power</u> which can be legitimately exercised by <u>society</u> over an <u>individual</u>.
NONCOUNT   COUNT   COUNT   NONCOUNT   NONCOUNT   COUNT

(John Stuart Mill, *On Liberty.*)

For a more comprehensive discussion, see COUNT NOUN AND NONCOUNT NOUN.

NOUN CLAUSE—a clause that does the job of noun. Typically a noun clause acts in one of the following capacities.

1. **The subject (underlined) of a verb (bold) in another clause (bracketed).**

    <u>Whether I can unlock the door</u> (**remains** to be seen).
    NOUN CLAUSE, SUBJECT OF *remains*   OTHER CLAUSE

    <u>Whatever it was</u>   (**detained** him).
    NOUN CLAUSE, SUBJECT OF *detained*   OTHER CLAUSE

    (Louisa May Alcott, *Little Women.*)

2. **The object (underlined) of a verb (bold) in another clause (bracketed).**

    (The girls **made**) <u>whatever they needed</u>.
       OTHER CLAUSE   NOUN CLAUSE, OBJECT OF *made*

    (Let's each **buy**) <u>what we want</u>.
       OTHER CLAUSE NOUN CLAUSE, OBJECT OF *buy*

    (Louisa May Alcott, *Little Women.*)

3. **The object (underlined) of a preposition (bold) in another clause (bracketed).**

    (I'm much obliged **to**) <u>whoever translated it for me</u>.
       OTHER CLAUSE   NOUN CLAUSE, OBJECT OF *to*

    (She fixed her eyes **above**) <u>what now seemed a sea of faces</u>.
       OTHER CLAUSE   NOUN CLAUSE, OBJECT OF *above*

    (Louisa May Alcott, *Little Women.*)

Apart from the way it functions, there is another way to identify a noun clause: you can always substitute the word *someone* or *something* for any noun clause. You can see this by making the substitutions in the above examples. The noun clauses and the substitute words below are underlined.

<u>Whether I can unlock the door</u> remains to be seen.	[<u>Something</u> remains to be seen.]
<u>Whatever it was</u> detained him.	[<u>Something</u> detained him.]
The girls made <u>whatever they needed</u>.	[The girls made <u>something</u>.]
Let's each buy <u>what we want</u>.	[Let's each buy <u>something</u>.]
I'm much obliged to <u>whoever translated it for me</u>.	[I'm much obliged to <u>someone</u>.]
She fixed her eyes above <u>what now seemed a sea of faces</u>.	[She fixed her eyes above <u>something</u>.]

See CLAUSE TYPES.

NOUN PHRASE—in modern grammar, any word (typically a noun or a pronoun) or any coherent string of words that has the function of a noun, and that has a noun (or a pronoun) as its head word. See HEAD.

Typically, a noun phrase acts as the subject or the object of a verb, or as the object of a preposition—the same functions fulfilled by a noun clause (see NOUN CLAUSE). Here are example texts with the noun phrases underlined and their functions indicated. The associated verbs and prepositions are in bold.

<u>Britain's building-society movement</u> **may have suffered** <u>a terminal blow</u>.
SUBJECT OF *may have suffered*   VERB   OBJECT OF *may have suffered*

But **in** <u>continental Europe</u>, <u>mutually owned banks</u> **remain in** <u>rude health</u>.
PREP   OBJECT OF *in*   SUBJECT OF *remain*   VERB PREP OBJECT OF *in*

<u>Banks</u>   **compete against**   <u>rivals</u> that are owned **by**   <u>the state</u> or **by** <u>their members</u>.
SUBJECT OF *compete* VERB   PREP OBJECT OF *against*   PREP   OBJECT OF *by*   PREP   OBJECT OF *by*

<u>Private banks</u> **say**   <u>mutuals</u>   **distort** <u>competition</u> and **prevent**   <u>them</u>   **earning** <u>a decent return</u>.
SUBJECT OF *say* VERB SUBJECT OF *distort* VERB   OBJECT OF *distort*   VERB OBJECT OF *prevent* VERB   OBJECT OF *earning*

<u>They</u>   **would like**   <u>all</u> to be forced to convert **into**   <u>banks</u>.
SUBJECT OF *would like*   VERB   OBJECT OF *would like*   PREP   OBJECT OF *into*

(*The Economist*, May 7, 1999.)

See PHRASE.

NULL ELEMENT—(also called "zero element") an element that is omitted from a language structure. A null element is there in spirit, but not actually expressed. There are two types of null elements:

1. those that are always omitted
2. those that may be omitted by choice.

1. Null elements that are always omitted.

(a) Most nouns have some way of marking plurality, but some nouns have a null plural marker. (For the arrow ➪ read "becomes.")

WITH AN –*S* PLURAL MARKER		WITH A NULL PLURAL MARKER	
SINGULAR ➪	PLURAL	SINGULAR ➪	PLURAL
page	pages	sheep	sheep
person	persons	deer	deer

(b)   Similarly, most verbs have an element to mark the past tense, but some verbs have a null tense marker. (For the arrow ⇨ read "becomes.")

WITH AN –*ED* PAST TENSE MARKER		WITH A NULL PAST TENSE MARKER	
PRESENT TENSE ⇨	PAST TENSE	PRESENT TENSE ⇨	PAST TENSE
laugh	laughed	hit	hit
cry	cried	put	put

2. **Elements that may be omitted by choice.** In the examples below, the null elements are crossed out and bracketed.

(a)   The nominal conjunction *that*. See CONJUNCTION.

> He said (~~that~~) it was getting warmer. She thought (~~that~~) the temperature was fine.

(b)   The relative pronoun *that*. See RELATIVE PRONOUN.

> This is the book (~~that~~) I want.

In the above two cases, both forms—with and without *that*—are equally valid as far as grammar is concerned. The following texts show that good writers switch at will between including and excluding nominal conjunctions and relative pronouns.

> THE NOMINAL CONJUNCTION *THAT*.
>
> I said in my last letter <u>that</u> antisemitism was not increasing, but now I think (~~that~~) it is.
> I am afraid (~~that~~) I answered rather roughly in the *Partisan Review* controversy.
> I am sorry <u>that</u> what I said rankled.
>
> (George Orwell, *Collected Essays, Journalism and Letters*, vol. 2.)
>
> THE RELATIVE PRONOUN *THAT*.
>
> Reading verse is not the sort of thing, being in a family of four boys, <u>that</u> you normally discuss.
> (Fred Hollows in Caroline Jones, *The Search for Meaning*.)
> The way (~~that~~) he handles the immediate problems will give some indication of whether he can regain credibility.
>
> (Laurie Oakes, *The Bulletin*, June 29, 1999.)

NUMBER—a grammar feature that relates to some determiners, nouns and pronouns, and to most present tense verbs. There are two numbers: singular (for one) and plural (for more than one). (For the arrow ⇨ read "becomes.")

SINGULAR	⇨	PLURAL
When <u>this</u> <u>baby</u> <u>cries</u> <u>it</u> <u>wants</u> <u>a</u> <u>bottle</u>. DET NOUN VERB PRON VERB DET NOUN		When <u>these</u> <u>babies</u> <u>cry</u> <u>they</u> <u>want</u> <u>bottles</u>. DET NOUN VERB PRON VERB NOUN

With the exception of *was–were*, verbs are not marked for number in the past tense.

A few present tense verbs are not marked for number: *it <u>can</u>, they <u>can</u>*; *it <u>must</u>, they <u>must</u>, it <u>may</u>, they <u>may</u>* ... The verbs *can, must, may* and a few others have no singular –*s* endings. See MODAL VERB. All other present tense verbs have singular –*s* endings: *it <u>seems</u>, they <u>seem</u>*.

The issue of number is important for subject–verb agreement and for antecedent–pronoun agreement. See AGREEMENT OF SUBJECT AND VERB and AGREEMENT OF ANTECEDENT AND PRONOUN.

OBJECT—(from the Latin for "thrown in") a word or a string of words thrown in after some verbs, and after all prepositions, to complete them. I deal with objects of verbs under COMPLETION, and with objects of prepositions under PREPOSITION. Below, I give some additional information on both kinds of objects.

1. What is the object of a verb?

The object of a verb is a noun (or a noun equivalent such as a pronoun) that expresses the goal (the done-to) of a transitive verb in the active voice. See TRANSITIVITY and VOICE.

> I <u>saw</u> <u>Esau</u> ...
>   VERB OBJECT

2. And of a preposition?

The object of a preposition is the necessary add-on (a noun or a noun equivalent) of a preposition.

> ... sitting <u>on</u> a <u>seesaw</u>.
>   PREPOSITION NOUN

3. Apart from nouns and pronouns, what else can serve as objects?

The following language items can serve as objects.

	VERB AND OBJECT	PREPOSITION AND OBJECT
• A NOUN:	They <u>cooked</u> <u>dinner</u>. VERB NOUN	They cooked <u>for</u> <u>Chris</u>. PREP NOUN
• A NOUN GROUP:	They <u>read</u> *King Lear*. VERB NOUN GROUP	They've heard <u>of</u> *King Lear*. PREP NOUN GROUP
• A GERUND:	They <u>like</u> <u>swimming</u>. VERB GERUND	They are fond <u>of</u> <u>swimming</u>. PREP GERUND
• A DETERMINER:	They <u>recognised</u> <u>that</u>. VERB DET	They looked <u>at</u> <u>that</u>. PREP DET
• A PRONOUN:	They <u>saw</u> <u>it</u> there. VERB PRONOUN	They've looked <u>at</u> <u>it</u> there PREP PRONOUN
• A NOUN PHRASE:	We <u>visited</u> <u>an open-air theater</u>. VERB NOUN PHRASE	We went <u>to</u> <u>an open-air theater</u>. PREP NOUN PHRASE
• A NOUN CLAUSE:	We <u>asked</u> <u>what was happening</u>. VERB NOUN CLAUSE	They heard <u>about</u> <u>what was happening</u>. PREP NOUN CLAUSE

Here is a text with objects (underlined) of verbs (V) and of prepositions (P).

> **By** <u>eavesdropping</u> **on** <u>neurons</u> **in** <u>the brains</u> **of** <u>cats,</u>
> P   GERUND, OBJECT OF *by*   P NOUN, OBJECT OF *on*   P NOUN PHRASE, OBJECT OF *in*   P NOUN, OBJECT OF *of*
>
> scientists **have made** <u>videos</u> **of** <u>what the cats actually see</u>.
>   V   NOUN, OBJECT OF *have made*   P   NOUN CLAUSE, OBJECT OF *of*

(*New Scientist*, October 2, 1999.)

4. Are there different types of objects?

Verbs (but not prepositions) can have different types of objects: direct objects and indirect objects.

I **mailed**	my friends	a parcel.		We **gave**	our parents	presents.
VERB	INDIRECT OBJECT	DIRECT OBJECT		VERB	INDIRECT OBJECT	DIRECT OBJECT

- The phrase *a parcel* is the direct object of *mailed* in the sense that the parcel is what I did the mailing to. I actually handled the parcel and mailed it.
- The phrase *my friends* is the indirect object of *mailed* in the sense that my friends were not the target of the action of mailing: I didn't put them in the mailbox—they were the recipients of what I mailed.

There are three technical ways to tell the difference between indirect and direct objects.

(a)   First, in any sentence that has both kinds of objects, the indirect object always stands before the direct object. The two sample sentences above illustrate this feature.

(b)   Second, in a sentence with both kinds of objects, the indirect object is omissible; the direct object isn't.

INDIRECT OBJECTS OMITTED	DIRECT OBJECTS OMITTED
I **mailed** ~~my friends~~ a parcel.	But not: I **mailed** my friends ~~a parcel~~.
VERB INDIRECT OBJECT DIRECT OBJECT	VERB INDIRECT OBJECT DIRECT OBJECT
We **gave** ~~our parents~~ presents.	But not: We **gave** our parents ~~presents~~.
VERB INDIRECT OBJECT DIRECT OBJECT	VERB INDIRECT OBJECT DIRECT OBJECT

The sentences in the left-hand column make sense; the sentences in the right-hand column don't.

(c)   Third, the sentences passivate differently, depending on whether you make the direct or the indirect object the subject of the passive sentence. I have marked the difference in underlined bold.

ACTIVE SENTENCE

I **mailed**	my friends	a parcel.
VERB	INDIRECT OBJECT	DIRECT OBJECT

PASSIVE SENTENCES

A parcel was mailed **to** my friends by me.
[The direct object becomes the subject—with *to*.]

My friends were mailed a parcel by me.
[The indirect object becomes the subject—without *to*.]

ACTIVE SENTENCE

We **gave**	our parents	presents.
VERB	INDIRECT OBJECT	DIRECT OBJECT

PASSIVE SENTENCES

Presents were given **to** our parents by us.
[The direct object becomes the subject—with *to*.]

Our parents were given presents by us.
[The indirect object becomes the subject—without *to*.]

OBJECTIVE—See CASE.

ONOMATOPOEIA—See FIGURE OF SPEECH.

OPEN AND CLOSED CLASSES—(also called "open and closed sets") terms that reflect the fact that newly-coined words, or new meanings of old words, are added to some word classes (nouns, adjectives, verbs and adverbs) but rarely if ever to other word classes (all the rest). Here are a few of the thousands of new words (or meanings) that came into English in the last half of the twentieth century.

byte	[noun, 1964]	microchip	[noun, 1974]
computerize	[verb, 1960]	privatize	[verb, 1969]
deconstruct	[verb, 1973]	sleazily	[adverb, 1959]
email	[noun and verb, 1982]	Thatcherite	[noun and adjective, 1976]
euro	[noun, 1990s]	videotext	[noun, 1980]
(*Oxford English Dictionary*.)			

See CONTENT WORD AND FUNCTION WORD.

OXYMORON—See FIGURE OF SPEECH.

PARADIGM—See SYNTAGM AND PARADIGM.

PARADOX—See FIGURE OF SPEECH.

PARALLELISM—See FIGURE OF SPEECH.

PARSE—from the Latin for "part." In traditional grammar, parsing is the process of taking apart and describing individual words in the setting of the sentence in which they occur. So, for example, we might parse a sentence as follows.

SENTENCE: I saw them.

I: pronoun, first person singular, common gender, subjective case, subject of the verb *saw*.
SAW: lexical verb, past tense, simple aspect, predicate verb of the pronoun *I*.
THEM: pronoun, third person, plural, common gender, objective case, object of the verb *saw*.

In modern terms, parsing has to do with morphology. See MORPHOLOGY and ACCIDENCE.

PARTICIPANT, PROCESS, CIRCUMSTANCE—three terms in functional grammar. They indicate what functions the parts of a clause carry out. The functional terms "participant," "process," "circumstance" are often (but not always) equivalent to the structural terms "subject" (and "object"), "verb," "verb modifier."

	We	saw	them	last night.
FUNCTION TERM:	PARTICIPANT	PROCESS	PARTICIPANT	CIRCUMSTANCE
STRUCTURE TERM:	SUBJECT	VERB	OBJECT	VERB MODIFIER

- THE PARTICIPANTS are the people or things (*we*, *them*) that take part in the process (the action) of the sentence. See ACTOR, BENEFICIARY, GOAL.
- THE PROCESS is the action, expressed by a verb (*saw*).
- THE CIRCUMSTANCE (*last night*) tells you the circumstance in which the process took place.

The functional terms are not substitutes for the structural terms. Rather, they are a different way of looking at the parts of a clause—indicating what functions the structures perform. Another name for "participants" is "arguments."

All three terms come from Latin:

- "participant" from the Latin for "one who takes part"
- "process" is allied to "proceeding" (hence, doing something)
- "circumstance" from the Latin for "surrounding condition"— literally, "standing around."

PARTICIPLE—from the Latin for "participating."

Participles are verb forms, but they participate both in the nature of verbs and of adjectives (as explained in parts 2 and 3 below).

1. What verb forms are participles?

Participles are words formed from verbs in either of two ways:

(a)   PRESENT PARTICIPLES, with the suffix *–ing*:

taking   wanting   keeping

You can always recognize a present participle from the fact that it has an *–ing* suffix.

(i)	**am** <u>running</u>	**were** <u>flying</u>	**is** <u>wagging</u>
(ii)	<u>running</u> water	a <u>flying</u> saucer	a <u>wagging</u> tail

(b)   PAST PARTICIPLES, with one of the suffixes *–en*, *–ed*, *–t*:

taken   wanted   kept.

You can always recognize a past participle from the fact that it is the form of the verb that you use after the auxiliary *have*.

They have { eaten, known, taken ...
walked, talked, laughed ...
kept, slept, felt ...

A past participle takes that form (the form after *have*) even if the word *have* is not before it.

(i)	**is** <u>broken</u>	**had** <u>surfaced</u>	**were** <u>spent</u>
(ii)	a <u>broken</u> twig	<u>surfaced</u> whales	a <u>spent</u> cartridge

Participles have two characteristics.

- They can always be used either as verbs or as adjectives. The examples under (a)(i) and (b)(i) above show participles used as verbs; the examples under (a)(ii) and (b)(ii) show them used as adjectives.

- When participles are used as verbs, they are always preceded by auxiliary verbs: in the examples above, the auxiliaries are in bold.

We now look at the two kinds of participle in greater detail.

2. **The present participle (also called "–*ing* form").**

   (a) When the present participle is used as a verb it is preceded by a form of the auxiliary verb *to be*. Together, the two elements—auxiliary + present participle—form a progressive aspect.
   See TENSE AND ASPECT.

   > Telltale features that have turned up in data from the Mars Global Surveyor <u>are</u> <u>forcing</u> scientists to rethink their ideas. "It <u>is</u> <u>going</u> to
   > AUX PRES PART   AUX PRES PART
   >
   > take more rigorous testing," Maria Zuber says.
   > (*New Scientist*, May 8, 1999.)

   (b) When the present participle is used as an adjective it modifies a noun or a noun equivalent such as a pronoun.

   > When Mars was young it had <u>shifting</u> tectonic <u>plates</u> on its surface, new
   >   PRES PART   NOUN
   >
   > data from the Mars Global Surveyor suggest. The Martian data reveal a pattern of <u>alternating</u> magnetic <u>polarizations</u> in the planet's crust.
   >   PRES PART   NOUN
   >
   > (*New Scientist*, May 8, 1999.)

Note: there is another use of the verb-form ending in –*ing*: namely, as a noun. In this function, the verb-form is called a "gerund" (not a "present participle"). The gerunds in the text below are underlined.

> Government at both levels has invested many of those dollars in research and <u>monitoring</u> to forge a better <u>understanding</u> of how all the pieces of
>   GERUND   GERUND
>
> the ecosystem fit together.
> (*National Geographic*, March 1999.)

See GERUND.

3. **The past participle (also called "–*en* form") has two uses; one of these has two subdivisions.**

   (a) AS A VERB, TO EXPRESS

      (i) THE PERFECT ASPECT: They have <u>gone</u>.

      (ii) THE PASSIVE VOICE: It was <u>done</u>.

   (b) AS AN ADJECTIVE: I took a <u>conducted</u> tour.

We look at each of these below.

(a) As a verb (underlined):

   (i) preceded by a form of the auxiliary verb *to have*, to express a perfect aspect (see TENSE AND ASPECT):

By polling day, national campaign headquarters will <u>have</u> <u>put</u> more
AUX   PAST PART

than $11 million through its advertising agency. And the advertising

<u>has</u> <u>had</u> an impact. Opinion poll results <u>have</u> <u>given</u> the Coalition
AUX PAST PART   AUX   PAST PART

a fright.   (Laurie Oakes. *The Bulletin*, September 29, 1998.)

   (ii)   preceded by a form of the auxiliary verb *to be*, to express
         a passive voice (see VOICE):

Labor has not <u>been</u> significantly <u>outspent</u> by the Liberal Party. He is
         AUX   PAST PART

clinging to what <u>is</u>   <u>left</u> of the "Australia needs tax reform" feeling.
            AUX   PAST PART

The Coalition might have <u>been</u> <u>expected</u> to open up new issues.
                 AUX   PAST PART

(Laurie Oakes. *The Bulletin*, September 29, 1998.)

  (b)   As an adjective (underlined), modifying a noun or a noun
        equivalent such as a pronoun.

The Steller sea lion, largest of all the <u>eared</u>   <u>seals</u> has been in serious
                            PAST PART   NOUN

decline in the northern Gulf of Alaska for 20 years. If you want to have
<u>marbled</u> <u>murrelets</u> you have to have old-growth trees for them to nest
PAST PART   NOUN

in. The <u>injured</u> <u>ecosystem</u> is on its way to recovery.
      PAST PART   NOUN

(*National Geographic*, March 1999.)

4. Participles as adjectives that become adverbs.

We have seen above (2 and 3) that both present and past participles
can function as adjectives. As with many other adjectives, it is
possible to derive adverbs from present and past participles with the
addition of the suffix –*ly*. (For the arrow ⇨ read "becomes.")

NORMAL ADJECTIVE	⇨	DERIVED ADVERB	PRESENT PARTICIPLE	⇨	DERIVED ADVERB	PAST PARTICIPLE	⇨	DERIVED ADVERB
slow		slowly	aching		achingly	reported		reportedly

Adverbs that are derived from participles function to modify verbs.
In this they are the same as other adverbs.

ADVERBS DERIVED FROM PRESENT PARTICIPLES

Elizabeth <u>laughingly</u> <u>answered</u>, "No, no; stay where you are."
         ADVERB   VERB

"I am not afraid of you," <u>said</u> he <u>smilingly</u>.
                       VERB   ADVERB

(Jane Austen, *Pride and Prejudice*.)

ADVERBS DERIVED FROM PAST PARTICIPLES

When he <u>met</u> me <u>unexpectedly</u> the encounter seemed welcome.
      VERB   ADVERB

Miss Miller <u>repeatedly</u> <u>exclaimed</u>, "Silence!"
         ADVERB   VERB

(Charlotte Brontë, *Jane Eyre*.)

See PARTICIPLE PHRASE.

PARTICIPLE PHRASE—a phrase that features a present or a past participle. See PARTICIPLE. Such a phrase functions as an adjective: that is, it modifies a noun (bold).

> PRESENT PARTICIPLE PHRASES (underlined)
>
> I knew that the solitary **roof** showing through bare branches was that of Frome's saw-mill.
> The **villagers**, being afoot, were the first to climb the slope.
> Hearing sleigh-bells, **Ethan** turned his head.
>
> (Edith Wharton, *Ethan Frome.*)
>
> PAST PARTICIPLE PHRASES (underlined)
>
> Lew huddled forward in his chair, a can of **beer** clenched in his fist
> Loaded **trolleys** stacked with the family's food were queued at the checkouts.
> His face was blank, all **expression** washed away.
>
> (Ric Throssell, *Jackpot.*)

See ABSOLUTE CONSTRUCTION.

PARTICLE—from the Latin for a "small part." A small word that does not fit easily into the standard word classes. There are three kinds of particles.

- THE NEGATIVE PARTICLE *not, as* in *I do not understand* (or *I don't understand*).
- THE INFINITIVE PARTICLE *to*, as in *to go, to sleep, to work, to play.*
- THE ADVERBIAL PARTICLE that combines with a verb to form a phrasal verb, as in *look out*.

See PHRASAL VERB.

PARTS OF SPEECH—See WORD CLASSES.

PASSIVE—See VOICE.

PAST PARTICIPLE—See PARTICIPLE.

PAST PARTICIPLE PHRASE—See PARTICIPLE PHRASE.

PAST TENSE—SEE TENSE AND ASPECT.

PATIENT—See ACTOR, BENEFICIARY, GOAL.

PERFECT ASPECT—See TENSE AND ASPECT.

PERSON—a grammar feature of personal pronouns and nouns. There are three persons: first, second, and third.

- THE FIRST PERSON expresses the person(s) speaking: *I, me, ours, ...*
- THE SECOND PERSON expresses the person(s) being spoken to: *you, yours, ...*

- THE THIRD PERSON expresses the person(s) or thing(s) being spoken about: *she*, *him*, *theirs* ... plus all the nouns, such as *Chris*, *Robin*, *tree*, *flowers* ...

In the present tense, the person of the subject may affect the form of the verb with which it is linked. Thus, the first person pronoun *I* is linked with the verb *am*; the second person pronoun *you*, with *are*; the third person pronoun *it*, with *is*.

But this is not always the case. A few verbs are unaffected by the person of their subjects: *I can*, *you can*, *he can*. See MODAL VERB.

PERSONIFICATION—See FIGURE OF SPEECH.

PHRASAL VERB—a word cluster that consists of a verb + one or two adverbial particles. See PARTICLE.

<u>Give</u>	<u>up</u> ...		<u>Go</u>	<u>on</u> ...	
VERB	PARTICLE		VERB	PARTICLE	
<u>Get</u>	<u>on</u>	<u>with</u> ...	<u>Get</u>	<u>out</u>	<u>of</u> ...
VERB	PARTICLE	PARTICLE	VERB	PARTICLE	PARTICLE

Phrasal verbs are also called "verb-particle constructions," "verb-adverb combinations" and, in the USA, "two-part verbs" or "three-part verbs"—depending on how many particles are attached to the verb.

We now look at two interesting features of phrasal verbs.

1. **They form a meaning distinct from that of the verb itself.** "Go" by itself means something like "walk," but note the range of meanings that "go" can carry if we add particles to it.

<u>go about</u> one's business	<u>go ahead with</u> one's plan
<u>go along with</u> the majority	<u>go on for</u> ever and ever
<u>go back on</u> one's word	<u>go down</u> fighting
<u>go after</u> a promotion	<u>go in for</u> painting
<u>go for</u> what one wants	<u>go against</u> the majority
<u>go far in</u> life	<u>go into</u> business

2. **If the phrasal verb has a noun object, you can often choose whether to put the object (bold) before or after the particle.**

<u>Blow</u>	**the balloon**	<u>up</u>.		<u>Blow</u>	<u>up</u>	**the balloon**.
VERB	OBJECT	PARTICLE		VERB	PARTICLE	OBJECT

Here are some texts, with the possible alternatives in brackets.

I'll <u>set</u> **your tea** <u>out</u> for you and I'll be home in time to milk the cows. [I'll <u>set</u> <u>out</u> **your tea** ...]
It's been my experience that you can nearly always enjoy things if you <u>make</u> <u>up</u> **your mind** firmly that you will. [... if you <u>make</u> **your mind** <u>up</u> firmly that you will.]
My mother was a teacher in the high school too, but when she married father she <u>gave</u> <u>up</u> **teaching**.
[... she <u>gave</u> **teaching** <u>up</u>.]
(The unbracketed texts are from LM Montgomery, *Anne of Green Gables*.)

PHRASE—from the Greek for "telling." A term used in two different senses in modern grammar and in traditional grammar. The entries below deal with each of these in turn.

PHRASE IN MODERN GRAMMAR—a word or a coherent string of words headed by the type-word and functioning as a unit in a sentence.

There are three points that need clarifying in the above definition.

1. **"A phrase is a word or a coherent string of words."** In modern grammar, the notion of phrase is very broad. A phrase (underlined) can consist of a word.

   <u>Robin</u> is a good friend.
   PHRASE

   Or it can consist of a coherent string of words.

   <u>My neighbor in the house to the left</u> is a good friend.
   PHRASE

2. **"A phrase is headed by the type-word."** "Is headed" does not necessarily mean "begins with" — "headed" means "contains as its most important element." See HEAD.

   (a) Thus, a noun phrase (underlined) is headed by a noun (bold).

   <u>My **neighbor** [NOUN] in the house to the left</u> is a good friend.
   NOUN PHRASE

   (b) An adjective phrase is headed by an adjective.

   That cake is <u>**good** [ADJECTIVE] to eat</u>.
   ADJECTIVE PHRASE

   (c) A verb phrase is headed by a verb.

   They <u>**liked** [VERB] your present very much</u>.
   VERB PHRASE

   (d) An adverb phrase is headed by an adverb.

   They came <u>too **late** [ADVERB] to do any good</u>.
   ADVERB PHRASE

   (e) A preposition phrase is headed by a preposition.

   The lamp swung <u>**above** [PREPOSITION] the table</u>.
   PREPOSITION PHRASE

   The five phrase types above are the ones recognized in modern grammar.

3. **"A phrase functions as a unit in a sentence."** As the previous examples show, phrases function as units ("constituents") of sentences. The underlined phrases don't make much sense on their own; they make sense as units within sentences.

   There are two other important features of phrases.

4. A phrase may have other phrases nested within it.

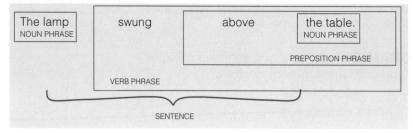

We can describe the above sentence as consisting of:

- two phrases—a noun phrase "The **lamp**" and a verb phrase "**swung** above the table,"
- the latter of which has a nested preposition phrase—"**above** the table,"
- which has a nested noun phrase—"the **table**."

5. Ultimately, we can resolve phrases into words.

The	lamp	swung	above	the	table.
DETERMINER	NOUN	VERB	PREPOSITION	DETERMINER	NOUN

For more detail on each phrase type, see separate entries for NOUN PHRASE, ADJECTIVE PHRASE, VERB PHRASE, ADVERB PHRASE, and PREPOSITION PHRASE.

PHRASE IN TRADITIONAL GRAMMAR—a coherent string of words that does not contain a finite verb. In this it contrasts with a clause, which is a coherent string of words that does contain a finite verb. A phrase forms part of a sentence and it does a job equivalent to the kind of word for which it is named.

- NOUN PHRASE: An old friend [= Alex] called me up.

NOUN PHRASE   NOUN

- ADJECTIVE PHRASE: A view, full of delight, [= delightful] met me.

ADJECTIVE PHRASE   ADJECTIVE

- PREPOSITION PHRASE: They stood in front of   [= before] the door.

PREPOSITION PHRASE   PREPOSITION

- PRESENT PARTICIPLE While whistling [= PHRASE:Whistling], I strolled home.

PRESENT PARTICIPLE PHRASE   PRESENT PARTICIPLE

- PAST PARTICIPLE PHRASE: They found the paper torn into bits   [= shredded].

PAST PARTICIPLE PHRASE   PAST PARTICIPLE

- INFINITIVE PHRASE: To go for a run [= To run] you need to be fit.

INFINITIVE PHRASE   INFINITIVE

- GERUND PHRASE: I thanked them for coming to my house [= visiting].

GERUND PHRASE   GERUND

- ADVERB PHRASE: They worked with a will [= willingly].

ADVERB PHRASE   ADVERB

The text below illustrates these kinds of phrases.

In a recent television broadcast, BBC commentator Brian Walden has argued that Nelson Mandela,
 ADVERB PHRASE   NOUN PHRASE

perhaps the most admired figure of our age, falls short of the giants of the past. Mandela himself
 ADJECTIVE PHRASE   NOUN PHRASE   NOUN PHRASE

argues that he was an ordinary man who had become a leader because of extraordinary circumstances.
                     NOUN PHRASE   NOUN PHRASE   NOUN PHRASE

Having run away from his guardian **to avoid** an arranged marriage, he joined a law firm
 PRESENT PARTICIPLE PHRASE   INFINITIVE PHRASE   NOUN PHRASE

in Johannesburg. The death of his father landed him **in** the care of a powerful relative. Mandela
 ADVERB PHRASE   NOUN PHRASE   PREPOSITION PHRASE   NOUN PHRASE

demonstrated that he didn't flinch from taking up arms, but his real qualities came to the fore
                                        GERUND PHRASE   NOUN PHRASE   ADVERB PHRASE

after his time as an activist—during his 27 years in prison and in the eight years since his release.
 ADVERB PHRASE   ADVERB PHRASE   ADVERB PHRASE

(*Time*, April 13, 1998.)

Note, in the above examples, that a present participle phrase contains a present participle; a past participle phrase, a past participle; an infinitive phrase, an infinitive verb; a preposition phrase, a preposition; a gerund phrase, a gerund—each in bold.

But an adverb phrase does not necessarily contain an adverb, nor an adjective phrase an adjective—as it does in the modern concept of these phrase types. In traditional grammar, whatever classes of words the phrase contains, it is enough that the phrase as a whole does the relevant job: an adjective phrase modifies a noun, and an adverb phrase modifies a verb.

It is in this respect that the traditional concept of "phrase" differs from the modern concept.

The two concepts of "phrase" also differ in that, in the modern concept, a "phrase" can be either a single word or a string of words while, in the traditional concept, a "phrase" can only be a string of words.

In both concepts, though, "phrases"—however defined—function as constituent parts of sentences; that is, bricks from which sentences are constructed, and not wholly independent units of language.

PLATITUDE—See FIGURE OF SPEECH.

PLURAL—See NUMBER.

POSITIVE—See DEGREES OF COMPARISON and MOOD.

POSSESSIVE—See CASE.

PREFIX—See AFFIX.

PREPOSITION—one of the word classes; a positional word such as *in*, *on*, *by*, *with*, *for* and the like.

1. What are prepositions?

(a)   A preposition is any word that fits into the blank space in the following sentence frame.

> I am moving _____ them. [with   from   to   among ...]
>   PREPOSITION

(b)   Prepositions (underlined) get their name from the fact that, normally, they are positioned before (that is, pre-positioned relative to) their objects (bold).

> ... <u>in</u>   **July**   ... <u>over</u>   **them**
> PREP OBJECT   PREP   OBJECT
>
> ... <u>with</u> **my best friend**   ... <u>for</u> **what they had done**
> PREP   OBJECT   PREP   OBJECT

- But you can also construct sentences in which prepositions (underlined) come after their objects (bold).

> **What**   are you afraid <u>of</u>? (George Bernard Shaw, *Man and Superman*.)
> OBJECT   PREP
>
> [<u>Of</u>   **what** are you afraid?]
> PREP OBJECT
>
> **What**   are you talking <u>about</u>?
> OBJECT   PREP
>
> [<u>About</u>   **what** are you talking?]
> PREP   OBJECT

- There are even structures in which the objects are understood but not stated.

> There's nothing more to worry <u>about</u>. (George Bernard Shaw, *Pygmalion*.)
>   PREP
>
> [There's nothing more <u>about</u>   **which** to worry.]
>   PREP   OBJECT
>
> That's the answer I was waiting <u>for</u>.
>   PREP
>
> [That's the answer <u>for</u>   **which** I was waiting.]
>   PREP OBJECT

Both of the above features—(a) and (b)—define what prepositions are.

2. How do prepositions relate to objects?

All prepositions have objects—though an object may be unstated, as the last two examples above show. And the prepositional objects are always nouns or noun equivalents. In the examples below, you can see the variety of object types that a preposition (PREP) can take.

> <u>For</u> <u>more than two years now</u>, I have lived <u>with</u> <u>constant reminders</u> <u>of</u> <u>danger</u>: armed soldiers guard
> PREP   NOUN PHRASE   PREP   NOUN PHRASE   PREP NOUN
>
> my house, bodyguards accompany me <u>in</u> <u>my Land Cruiser</u>, and others follow <u>in</u> <u>another vehicle</u> ...
>   PREP   NOUN PHRASE   PREP   NOUN PHRASE
>
> <u>In</u> <u>1989</u> Kenya's head <u>of</u> <u>state</u> surprised me <u>by</u> <u>appointing</u> me director <u>of</u> <u>the Kenyan Wildlife Service</u>
> PREP DET   PREP NOUN   PREP   GERUND   PREP   NOUN PHRASE
>
> I was aware <u>of</u> <u>what I was taking on</u>. I found <u>within</u> <u>myself</u> a certainty <u>about</u> <u>what I was about to learn</u>.
>   PREP   NOUN CLAUSE   PREP   PRONOUN   PREP   NOUN CLAUSE
>
> (Richard Leakey and Roger Lewin, *Origins Reconsidered*.)

See OBJECT.

PREPOSITION AT THE END OF A SENTENCE—See LANGUAGE MYTH.

PREPOSITION PHRASE—a phrase (underlined) with a preposition (bold) as its head word. See HEAD.

> ... **before** lunch   ... **after** doing the job   ... **in** a big hurry

1. What are the functions of preposition phrases?

In modern grammar, a preposition phrase can have either of two functions:

(a)   as an adjective, modifying a noun:

> Edward Windsor and his <u>girlfriend</u> <u>of five years</u> at last announced their
> NOUN   PREPOSITION PHRASE
>
> intention to marry.
> (*TIME*, January 18, 1999.)

(b)   as an adverb, modifying a verb:

> Prince Edward and Rhys-Jones <u>faced</u> the nation <u>with aplomb</u>.
> VERB   PREPOSITION PHRASE
>
> (*TIME*, January 18, 1999.)

We can see this dual role of preposition phrases from the two possible meanings that an ambiguous structure yields. The preposition phrase is underlined.

> I saw a child <u>with my binoculars</u>.

If we understand the preposition phrase to have an adjectival function it modifies the noun *child*, yielding the meaning:

> I saw a <u>child</u> <u>with my binoculars</u> [= who had my binoculars].
> NOUN   PREPOSITION PHRASE

If we understand the preposition phrase to have an adverbial function it modifies the verb *saw*, yielding the meaning:

> I <u>saw</u> a child <u>with my binoculars</u> [= when I looked through my binoculars].
> VERB   PREPOSITION PHRASE

See PHRASE IN TRADITIONAL GRAMMAR.

2. What are nested preposition phrases?

A special feature of preposition phrases is the nesting of phrases within phrases. As an example, consider the following sentence.

> There is cynicism after the failures of the first marriages of all three of Edward's siblings.
> (*TIME*, January 18, 1999.)

We can tease the sentence apart and show its individual preposition phrases (underlined), each with a preposition (bold) at its head.

There is cynicism
1. **after** the failures
2. **of** the first marriages
3. **of** all three
4. **of** Edward's siblings.

Preposition phrase 4 is nested within preposition phrase 3, which is nested within preposition phrase 2, which is nested within preposition phrase 1.

We can show the same thing with brackets:

There is cynicism {1. after the failures [2. of the marriages
(3. of all three <4. of Edward's siblings>)]}.

or graphically:

PRESENT PARTICIPLE—See PARTICIPLE.

PRESENT PARTICIPLE PHRASE—See PARTICIPLE PHRASE.

PRESENT TENSE—See TENSE AND ASPECT.

PROCESS—See PARTICIPANT, PROCESS, CIRCUMSTANCE.

PRO-FORM—See ANTECEDENT AND PRO-FORM.

PROGRESSIVE ASPECT—See TENSE AND ASPECT.

PROJECTION—from the Latin for "stretching out." A principle in Noam Chomsky's universal grammar. The notion that words have a built-in influence that stretches out to other items in a text.

For example, the adverb *dramatically* projects onto a verb: *They entered dramatically*. If you want to use the adjective *dramatic*, it projects onto a noun: *Their entry was dramatic*. Or you can look at the same projection the other way round: the verb *enter* projects onto the adverb *dramatically*; the noun *entry* projects onto the adjective *dramatic*.

In the same pair of sentences, there is a further projection onto other words: *They* in the first sentence; *Their* in the second. And the various changes project onto the sentence structures too. As Vivian Cook puts it: "The properties of lexical entries project onto the syntax of the sentence" (1988:11).

We can see a simple case of projection in the following example.

It was a clever political ploy.
(Laurie Oakes, *The Bulletin*, September 7, 1999.)

If we change *it* to *they*, or if we change *was* to *is*, or if we make both changes, we get the following projections.

> It was a clever political ploy.
> They were clever political ploys.
> It is a clever political ploy.
> They are clever political ploys.

We can also see projection at work in texts. If we were writing a piece about a princess, the noun *princess* would project onto subsequent words—*she, her, hers, herself*—throughout the text. Any change, say, from *princess* to *prince,* drags other changes along with it.

Projection acts simultaneously on every item of a text. So we could have a text stretching from here to a galaxy a billion light years away. If we were to make a change to the text here, it would affect the end of the text at the same instant—faster than the speed of light.

In theory, every lexical item has some projecting force and, again in theory, we could describe a language completely by the sum total of all the projections of all its lexical items.

PRONOUN—from the Latin for "instead of a noun." One of the word classes.

1. What are pronouns?

Pronouns are multipurpose words that you can use instead of nouns. For example, for each of the nouns *tree*, *flower,* or *bush*, you can substitute the pronoun *it*; for each of the nouns *Iris*, *Daphne,* or *Sylvie* you can substitute the pronoun *she*.

Here is a passage from a novel. The narrator, Josephine, writes about herself and her friend, Jacob Coote. Instead of repeating the names, she uses pronouns (underlined).

> I wagged school on Friday and went to Manly with Jacob Coote. When I think of it now, wagging in a school uniform was pretty stupid, but I was so caught up with seeing him that I didn't care. He was waiting for me. Usually when I like a guy I get instantly turned off when he likes me back.
>
> (Melina Marchetta, *Looking for Alibrandi*.)

2. How do pronouns function in sentences?

Pronouns substitute for nouns in sentences, so they do the same job that nouns do: they express subjects and objects of verbs, and objects of prepositions. (For the arrow ⇨ read "becomes.")

SENTENCES WITH NOUNS	⇨	SENTENCES WITH PRONOUNS
<u>Bees</u> <u>gather</u> <u>pollen</u>. SUBJECT VERB OBJECT		<u>They</u> <u>gather</u> <u>it</u>. SUBJECT VERB OBJECT
<u>Adam</u> <u>was looking</u> <u>for</u> <u>Tia</u>. SUBJECT VERB PREPOSITION OBJECT		<u>He</u> <u>was looking</u> <u>for</u> <u>her</u>. SUBJECT VERB PREPOSITION OBJECT

Two other noun-like functions of pronouns: (a) the complement of a verb (see COMPLETION) and (b) the form of address (see VOCATIVE). (For the arrow ⇨ read "becomes.")

SENTENCES WITH NOUNS	⇨	SENTENCES WITH PRONOUNS

(a) This <u>is</u> a <u>flower</u>.
     VERB   COMPLEMENT
		(a) This <u>is</u> <u>it</u>.
		     VERB COMPLEMENT

(b) <u>George</u>, don't pick it.
   VOCATIVE
		(b) <u>You</u>, don't pick it.
		   VOCATIVE

PRONOUN SUBCLASSES—there are four subclasses of pronouns.

1. PERSONAL PRONOUNS: I, me, mine, myself ...
2. INDEFINITE PRONOUNS: somebody, anybody, nobody, everybody ...
3. INTERROGATIVE PRONOUNS: who? whom? whose? what? which?
4. RELATIVE PRONOUNS: who, whom, which, that, whose ...

We look at each of these below.

1. What are personal pronouns?

Personal pronouns refer to you, to me and to other people or things. The list below shows the forms of personal pronouns—plus a closely related set of words that are not pronouns but, rather, determiners (see DETERMINER).

SUBJECTIVE PRONOUNS	OBJECTIVE PRONOUNS	POSSESSIVE PRONOUNS	[POSSESSIVE DETERMINERS]	EMPHATIC-REFLEXIVE PRONOUNS
I	me	mine	[my]	myself
you	you	yours	[your]	yourself
he	him	his	[his]	himself
she	her	hers	[her]	herself
it	it	its	[its]	itself
we	us	ours	[our]	ourselves
you	you	yours	[your]	yourselves
they	them	theirs	[their]	themselves

- THE SUBJECTIVE (*they*), also called the "nominative," is the form of pronoun that you use as the subject (the doer) of a verb (underlined).

    _____ <u>will arrive</u> tonight. [I   you   he   she ...]
        SUBJECTIVE PRONOUN

- THE OBJECTIVE (*them*), also called the "accusative," is the form of pronoun that you use as the object (the done-to) of a verb (underlined).

    The gossips were discussing _____. [me you him her ...]
                    OBJECTIVE PRONOUN

- The objective is also the form of pronoun that you use as the object of a preposition (underlined).

    The gossips were talking <u>about</u> _____. [me you him her ...]
                OBJECTIVE PRONOUN

- THE POSSESSIVE (*theirs*), also called the "genitive," is the form of pronoun that you use to show possession.

> That book is _____. [mine   yours   his   hers ...]
> POSSESSIVE PRONOUN

- THE POSSESSIVE determiners (*their*) are closely related to the possessive pronouns (*theirs*). The difference between the two is that possessive determiners appear with following nouns (underlined)—***my*** *friend*—while possessive pronouns appear without following nouns—*a* *friend* *of* **mine**. Compare the following sentence frames.

> That is _____ book. [my   your   his   her ...]
> POSSESSIVE DETERMINER   NOUN
>
> That book is _____. [mine   yours   his   hers ...]
> NOUN   POSSESSIVE PRONOUN

- THE EMPHATIC-REFLEXIVE (*themselves*) has two uses:

> EMPHATIC: I will do the job myself.   [Also: he ... himself, she ... herself, and so on.]
>
> REFLEXIVE: I wash myself.   [Also: he ... himself, she ... herself, and so on.]

In the reflexive (above), the subject and the object of the verb *wash* are one and the same person.

Here is a text that uses each of the pronoun subclasses.

> How would he like it himself?
>   SUBJECTIVE   EMPHATIC
>
> I   am   myself a student of Indian dialects.
> SUBJECTIVE EMPHATIC
>
> Poor girl, hard enough for her to live without being worried.
>   OBJECTIVE
>
> I did not wish to hurt her delicacy or yours.
> SUBJECTIVE   POSSESSIVE DET   POSSESSIVE PRON
>
> No man can teach himself what English sounds like.
>   REFLEXIVE
>
> (George Bernard Shaw, *Pygmalion*.)

2. What are indefinite pronouns?

The indefinite pronouns are *some–*, *any–*, *no–*, *every–*, combined with *–body*, *–one*, *–thing*:

somebody	anybody	nobody	everybody
someone	anyone	no one	everyone
something	anything	nothing	everything.

The indefinite pronouns in the sentences below are underlined.

> Everyone who sees her will say, "There is a discreet girl."
> To do everything in an orderly manner is a most important precept.
> She was ready to marry anybody that her mother was pleased to recommend.
> Everyone shapes the good to his own fancy.
> (Mary Wollstonecraft, *Vindication of the Rights of Woman*.)

3. What are interrogative pronouns?

Interrogative (question) pronouns are those that you use in questions and that prompt noun or pronoun replies. There are five interrogative pronouns:

who? whom? whose? what? which?

What? and *Which?* present no problem:

QUESTION	ANSWER
<u>What</u> do you want?	Chocolate.
<u>Which</u> do you prefer?	Milk chocolate.

Who? Whom? and *Whose?* can be a bit of a mystery.

• Use *Who?* in a question if the answer is a subjective pronoun (*he, she, they* ...).

QUESTION	ANSWER
<u>Who</u> spilled the soup?	<u>They</u> did.
<u>Who</u> wants more soup?	<u>They</u> do.

• Use *Whom?* in a question if the answer is an objective pronoun (*him, her, them* ...).

QUESTION	ANSWER
<u>Whom</u> did you call?	I called <u>him</u>.
<u>Whom</u> is he waiting for?	He is waiting for <u>her</u>.

• Use *Whose?* in a question if the answer is a possessive pronoun (*his, hers, theirs* ...).

QUESTION	ANSWER
<u>Whose</u> is this diamond?	It's <u>mine</u>.
<u>Whose</u> is that imitation?	It's <u>theirs</u>.

An illustrative text.

<u>Whom</u> are you talking about?	[I'm talking about <u>them</u>.]
<u>Whose</u> glove is this?	[It's <u>hers</u>.]
<u>Who</u> are Miss Worsley's parents?	[<u>They</u> are.]
(Oscar Wilde, *A Woman of No Importance*.)	

4. What are relative pronouns?

Relative pronouns (*who, whom, which, that* ...) stand at the head of adjective clauses (also called "relative clauses") that modify a noun or a pronoun. The most common relative pronouns are:

who whom whose which that when where.

• *Who* and *whom* relate to people: *The person <u>who</u>* ... *The person <u>whom</u>* ... You can tell when *who* is appropriate, and when *whom* is appropriate by changing the adjective clause into a free-standing sentence.

If the free-standing sentence contains *he, she,* or *they*—use *who.* (For the arrow ⇨ read "becomes.")

> People <u>who</u> get more to start with are probably better off. [⇨ <u>They</u> get more to start with.]
>
> (*New Scientist*, July 17, 1999.)

If the free standing sentence contains *him, her,* or *them*—use *whom.*

> There are many solitary pupils, for <u>whom</u> Internet chat sites are the easiest way to communicate.
> [⇨ Internet chat sites are the easiest way for <u>them</u> to communicate.]
>
> (*Time*, May 10, 1999.)

- *Whose* relates to people or to things: *The person <u>whose</u> ... The thing <u>whose</u> ...* You can tell when to use *whose* by changing the adjective clause into a free-standing sentence. If the sentence contains *his, her, its,* or *their,* use *whose* in the adjective clause.

> Stravinsky was a musical revolutionary <u>whose</u> own evolution never stopped.
> [⇨ <u>His</u> own evolution never stopped.]
>
> (*Time*, June 14, 1999.)

- *Which* and *that* relate to things: *The thing <u>which</u> ... The thing <u>that</u> ...* There is an intuitive way to decide which of the two you should use: if in doubt, always to try *that* first. If *that* sounds good, use it; if it doesn't, use *which.*

> Dams—with all the attitudes <u>that/~~which~~</u> back them up—are going out of fashion.
> The extent <u>~~to that~~/to which</u> wildlife and people can coexist has long been a worry to conservationists.
>
> (*The Economist*, June 18, 1999.)

For more information on the distinction between *which* and *that* (and the use of *that* for people) see RELATIVE PRONOUN.

- *When* relates to times; *where,* to places: *The time <u>when</u> ... The place <u>where</u> ...*

> Warm air pushes upwards during the summer months <u>when</u> the atmosphere is exposed to long hours of sunlight.
>
> (*New Scientist*, May 1, 1999.)

> Orders are placed direct with the factory <u>where</u> the model is manufactured.
>
> (*The Economist*, May 28, 1999.)

Here is a text that illustrates the use of all of the foregoing relative pronouns.

> I came by a house <u>where</u> a shepherd lived.
> There were some of the light shells <u>that</u> are called buckies.
> In three of the windows, <u>which</u> were very high up, the light of a fire began to glimmer.
> Day and night were alike in that ill-smelling cavern of the ship's bowels <u>where</u> I lay.

> He took a pull at the beer, <u>which</u> probably reminded him of hospitable duties.
> There come other whiles <u>when</u> you show yourself a spark.
> You should get to Cramond, <u>which</u> is near Edinburgh.
> It was a word <u>that</u> seemed to surprise them.
> (Robert Louis Stevenson, *Kidnapped.*)

PUN—See FIGURE OF SPEECH.

QUANTIFIER—See DETERMINER.

QUESTION TAG—See ANOMALOUS FINITE.

QUESTION TYPES—grammar distinguishes among several types of questions, depending on two factors:

(a) the form (structure) of the question itself
(b) the type of answer you expect from the question.

The three types of questions we consider below are the following:

1. *YES–NO* QUESTION: Are you happy?

2. *WH*-QUESTION: Who asked that dumb question?

3. ALTERNATIVE QUESTION: Are you asking me or someone else?

We look at each of these below.

1. *Yes–no* question.

This is a question that begins with the auxiliary *do*, *does*, *did* or any of the other anomalous finites. (See ANOMALOUS FINITE.) It is a question to which we normally expect the answer "Yes" or "No." The anomalous finites are underlined.

> <u>Does</u>n't that do you good?
> <u>May</u> I make a suggestion?
> <u>Do</u> you know what that is?
> <u>Will</u> you throw away even your hypocrisy?
> <u>Have</u> you proposed to her?
> <u>Do</u> you suppose I would read such a book?
> (George Bernard Shaw, *Man and Superman.*)

Tag questions (See ANOMALOUS FINITE) are a subtype of *yes–no* questions. The tags are underlined.

> You put it into his head, <u>didn't you</u>?
> Eyes don't trouble you any more, <u>do they</u>?
> You live near us, <u>don't you</u>?
> (Louisa May Alcott, *Little Women.*)

2. *Wh*-question (also called "*wh*–interrogative").

This is any question that begins with one of the *wh*–words and to which we normally expect an answer giving the relevant information. The *wh*–words are listed below:

who? whom? what? which? whose? when? where? why? how?

The *wh*–words are underlined.

> <u>What</u> does he mean?
> <u>Why</u> do you make that your special vanity?
> <u>Whom</u> are you talking about?
> <u>Who</u> are the people the world takes seriously?
> <u>Where</u> do you get your gowns?
> <u>How</u> do you do, Lady Windermere?
> (Oscar Wilde, *Lady Windermere's Fan.*)
>
> <u>Which</u> of us should tell them?
> <u>When</u> was the engagement actually settled?
> (Oscar Wilde, *The Importance of Being Earnest.*)
>
> <u>Whose</u> glove is this?
> (Oscar Wilde, *A Woman of No Importance.*)

3. Alternative question.

This is a question to which we expect any one of two or more alternative answers. An alternative question can also include one of the *wh*–words.

> Are you or Mrs. Barry crazy?
> Did you really say it, or did I only imagine that you did?
> "I'd like to look at some sugar." "White or brown?" queried Miss Harris patiently.
> Which would you rather be if you had the choice—divinely beautiful or dazzlingly clever or angelically good?
> (LM Montgomery, *Anne of Green Gables.*)

REFERENCE—from the Latin for "carrying." One of the methods of cohesion. See COHESION. One word, often a pronoun, refers (carries the meaning) to a different word in the same text, often a noun. There are three kinds of reference.

1. Anaphoric, in which the referring word (underlined) refers to an earlier word (bold).

> When **the dog** woke up <u>it</u> barked.
> [*It* refers back to *the dog.*]

2. Cataphoric, in which the referring word (underlined) refers to a later word (bold).

> When <u>it</u> woke up, **the dog** barked.
> [*It* refers forward to *the dog.*]

3. Exophoric (also called "deictic"), in which the referring word (underlined) refers to someone or something outside of the text.

> <u>I</u> want to give <u>you</u> <u>this</u>.
> [*I, you* and *this* do not refer to other words in the text.]

Together, the word referred to and the word that is doing the referring make up a reference chain. *Dog + it; it + dog* are two reference chains illustrated above.

Anomalous finites can also be used in reference chains. See ANOMALOUS FINITE.

> I'm **going home**, and I guess you <u>are</u> too.
> [*Are* refers back to *going home.*]

REGISTER—from the Latin for "list." A feature of text grammar, relating to the level of formality of language. On a scale of 1 to 10, you would find the register in a conversation among friends toward the lower end of the scale; the language of a legal document toward the upper end.

Here is how you might label the following texts, all of which have more or less the same meaning.

Oh, would that I knew what was transpiring here.	[10]	STILTED
I would like to know what is happening here.	[8]	FORMAL
What on earth is going on here?	[4]	INFORMAL
What's up, doc?	[2]	SLANG
What the hell are you up to?	[1]	RUDE

You achieve different registers mainly through vocabulary and sentence structure. You will see these features in the text below. The bracketed numbers indicate the register on a scale of 10.

"Josephine?" [9]

"Huh?" [2]

"I think you mean 'I beg your pardon?' don't you, dear?" [9]

"I beg your pardon, Sister." [9]

"What are you doing? You're reading, aren't you, young lady?" [6—a slightly challenging question]

"Um … yeah." [2]

(Melina Marchetta, *Looking for Alibrandi*.)

RELATIVE CLAUSE—See ADJECTIVE CLAUSE.

RELATIVE PRONOUN—a small subclass of the pronouns. The main relative pronouns are:

where   when   who   whom   whose   which   that.

They are called relative pronouns because they relate to a previously occurring noun called an "antecedent" (bold).

This is the **place**   where I was born.
         ANTE   REL PRON

I'll meet you at a **time**   when we are both free.
             ANTE   REL PRON

This is the **person**   who told me the story.
          ANTE   REL PRON

This is the **person**   whom I told you about.
          ANTE   REL PRON

This is the **person**   whose ladder I borrowed.
          ANTE   REL PRON

They live in **Hobart**,   which is the capital of Tasmania.
           ANTE   REL PRON

I want a **book**   that will interest me.
        ANTE   REL PRON

We look at each of the relative pronouns below.

1. ***Where* and *when***—*where* relates to places; *when* to times.

> Mutual funds are seen to serve the interests of the **communities** <u>where</u> they are based. (*The Economist*, May 7, 1999.)
>
> Between the long lines of ash-pits went the **alley** <u>where</u> the children played. (James Joyce, *Portrait of he Artist as a Young Man*.)

> Astronomical websites frequently publish **times** <u>when</u> major satellites are visible, including the shuttle and Mir. (*New Scientist*, May 8, 1999.)
>
> Remember the good old **days** <u>when</u> you could eat all the pasta you wanted and still feel virtuous?(*TIME*, May 10, 1999.)

- The relative pronoun *where* differs from the interrogative adverb *where*: <u>Where</u> *are you going?*
  See ADVERB.

- The relative pronoun *when* differs from the adverbial conjunction *when*: *We ate <u>when</u> we were hungry.* See CONJUNCTION.

2. ***Who, whom,* and *whose*** relate to people. You can tell which of these relative pronouns to use by changing the clause in which it occurs into a free-standing sentence.

   (a) If the free-standing sentence contains *he, she* or *they*—use *who.* (For the arrow ⇨ read "becomes.")

   > He had none of the appearance of a man <u>who</u> sailed before the mast. [⇨ <u>He</u> sailed before the mast.] (Robert Louis Stevenson, *Treasure Island*.) Irene Walker is a handsome woman of 63 <u>who</u> grew up a sharecropper's daughter. [⇨ <u>She</u> grew up a sharecropper's daughter.]
   >
   > (*National Geographic*, April 1999.)

   (b) If the free-standing sentence contains *him, her* or *them*—use *whom.*

   > A man stepped in on <u>whom</u> I had never set my eyes before. [⇨ I had never set my eyes on <u>him</u> before.]
   >
   > (Robert Louis Stevenson, *Treasure Island*.)
   >
   > Be careful not only when you drive but also with <u>whom</u> you drive. [⇨ You drive with <u>them</u>.]
   >
   > (*TIME*, April 5, 1999.)

   (c) If the free-standing sentence contains *his, her* or *their*—use *whose.*

   > I am walking beside my father <u>whose</u> name is Simon Dedalus. [⇨ <u>His</u> name is Simon Dedalus.]
   >
   > (James Joyce, *Portrait of the Artist as a Young Man*.)
   >
   > I had a man under my eyes <u>whose</u> life was forfeit. [⇨ <u>His</u> life was forfeit.]
   >
   > (Robert Louis Stevenson, *Kidnapped*.)

   You can also use *whose* for things—in which case it equates with *its* or *their*.

> He was aware of some desecration of the vestry, <u>whose</u> silence was now routed by loud talk. [⇨ <u>Its</u> silence was now routed by loud talk.]
>
> (James Joyce, *Portrait of the Artist as a Young Man*.)
>
> This is sovereign territory, <u>whose</u> borders are in principle inviolable. [⇨ <u>Its</u> borders are in principle inviolable.]
>
> (*The Economist*, April 5, 1999.)

3. ***Which** and **that** relate to things*—*The book <u>which</u> ... The book <u>that</u> ...*

   There are two methods by which you can tell which relative pronoun to use in any given situation: (a) an easier intuitive way and (b) a harder grammar way.

   (a) The intuitive method is always to try *that* first. If *that* sounds good, use it; if it doesn't, use *which*.

   > One of the greatest pleasures <s>that</s>/which I have in life is by virtue of my financial position.
   > I collect jade, <s>that</s>/which I think is a very tactile material.
   >
   > (Rene Rivkin in Caroline Jones, *The Search for Meaning Collection*.)
   >
   > It was a hard day's run over the great Chilcoot Divide, <s>that</s>/which stands between the salt water and the fresh.
   >
   > (Jack London, *The Call of the Wild*.)

   (b) The grammar method is to figure out whether the clause headed by *that* or *which* is defining or nondefining. If it is defining, use *that*; if it is nondefining, use *which*.

   • A defining clause—with *that*—is one that tells you which one, or what kind of, thing you are talking about.

   The sentence *I want to read a poem* leaves open the question: which poem (or what kind of poem) you want to read. To complete the sentence, we add the defining clause *that will interest me*. So we get:

   > I want to read a poem <u>that</u> will interest me.

   In the expanded sentence (boxed above), the clause *that will interest me*, defines the kind of poem *I want to read*. Putting it another way: the clause *that will interest me* answers the question, "What kind of poem do you want to read?"

   • A nondefining clause—with *which*—is one that amplifies the noun by giving some additional information about it, though the identity of the noun is already known.

   The sentence *I want to read Wordsworth's "Daffodils"* does not need any clause to define the work: we already know which poem I want to read. But we can amplify the noun "Daffodils" by adding a nondefining clause to it. So we get:

   > I want to read Wordsworth's "Daffodils," which is said to be one of his best poems.

   In the expanded sentence (boxed above), the clause *which is said*

to be one of his best poems does not define the poem "Daffodils"—
it merely adds more information about the already identified poem.

- If the relative pronoun follows a preposition—a word such as *in, on, by, for*—you will need to use *which* in any case, whether the clause is defining or nondefining. But even then, you can often convert *which* into *that* by shifting the preposition (bold) to the end of the clause.

> They secretly envied the numerical rigor **to** which they could not possibly aspire. (*The Economist*, July 2, 1999.)
> [... the numerical rigor that they could not possibly aspire **to**.]
>
> The color you see depends on the angle **at** which light hits the reflecting surface. (*New Scientist*, June 26, 1999.)
> [... the angle that light hits the reflecting surface **at**.]
>
> The speed **at** which the ball spins represents heart rate.
> (*New Scientist*, May 8, 1999.)
> [The speed that the ball spins **at** ...]
>
> On that day, Goddard sank into a sulk **from** which he never fully emerged. (*TIME*, March 29, 1999.)
> [... a sulk that he never fully emerged **from**.]

If the relative clause is defining, you can also use *that* for people.

> He's a child that's a deep thinker.
> (Princess Diana speaking on TV about Prince William, 1995.)
>
> I see a safe city, a hopeful city, full of young people that should have a peaceful and prosperous future.
> (President Bill Clinton. Quoted in *TIME*, December 11, 1995.)

A note on terminology: alternative names for "defining" and "nondefining" are "restrictive" and "nonrestrictive."

4. **There are two other points of interest about relative pronouns.**

   (a) You can often omit a relative pronoun altogether. (For the arrow ⇨ read "becomes.")

RELATIVE PRONOUN INCLUDED	⇨	RELATIVE PRONOUN OMITTED
That's the book that I want to read.		That's the book I want to read.
That's the person with whom I work.		That's the person I work with.

See NULL ELEMENT.

   (b) The *who–whom* distinction and the *which–that* distinction are not ironclad. You can ignore them in conversational or informal contexts.

> There'll be a risk, no matter who we get.
> (LM Montgomery, *Anne of Green Gables*.)
> [Formally: ... no matter whom we get.]
>
> What fun! Who are they from? (Louisa May Alcott, *Little Women*.)
> [Formally: From whom are they?]
>
> Those are the very things which the minister was trying to hide.
> (Reader's letter in a newspaper.)
> [Formally: ... that the minister was trying to hide.]

See STANDARD AND NONSTANDARD ENGLISH.

RHEME—See THEME AND RHEME.

ROOT AND STEM—terms that refer to the forms of words.

1. **The root of a word is the most basic form of that word.** It is the bare word from which other words may be derived with affixes, but which is itself not derived. See AFFIX. So, for example:

logic	is the root of *logical, illogical, logically, illogically*
beauty	is the root of *beautify, beautiful, beautifully*
be	is the root of *am, is, are, was, were, being, been*
hide	is the root of *hides, hid, hiding, unhidden.*

   The root of a verb is also called an "unmarked infinitive" or a "base form." See FORMS OF THE VERB.

2. **The stem of a word is the uninflected part of an inflected word.** That is, if you have an inflected word, its stem is the word minus its inflection.

   A stem can consist of either:

   (a) a root alone (bold), excluding the inflection (bracketed):

wait(ing)	**wait**(s)	**fast**(er)	**fast**(est)

   or

   (b) a root (bold) + a derivational affix (underlined), excluding the inflection (bracketed):

re**turn**(ing)	bi**cycle**(s)	**act**or(s')	un**beat**(en)

   All the unbracketed words under (a) and (b) above are stems of inflected words. For an explanation of the terms "derivational affix" and "inflection" See AFFIX.

3. **Roots and affixes, stems and inflections, can combine in various ways to form words.** In each of the following examples, the root is in **bold**, the derivational inflection (DER) underlined and the inflection (INFL) **bold and underlined**.

   table
   ROOT

   table + **cloth**
   ROOT   ROOT

   happi + ly
   ROOT   DER

   post + **lunch** + **time**
   DER   ROOT   ROOT

   un + **change** + able
   DER   ROOT   DER

   non + **foot** + **ball** + er
   DER   ROOT   ROOT   DER

   look + **ed**   [Stem: look–]
   ROOT   INFL

   over + **com** + **ing**   [Stem: overcome–]
   ROOT   ROOT   INFL

   wed(d) + ing + **s**   [Stem: wed–]
   ROOT   INFL   INFL

land– + **ing** + **strip** + **s** ROOT INFL ROOT INFL	[Stem: land– ... strip–]
un + **chain** + **ed** DER ROOT INFL	[Stem: unchain–]
basket + **ball** + **er** + **s** ROOT ROOT DER INFL	[Stem: basketballer–]
un + **expect** + **ed** + **ly** DER ROOT INFL DER	[Stem: unexpect– ... ly]
re + **turn** + **ing** + **s** DER ROOT INFL INFL	[Stem: return–]

In the above examples, the verbal roots (*change, look, come, wed, land, chain, expect* and *turn*) can also be called "unmarked infinitives" or "base forms."

SARCASM—See FIGURE OF SPEECH.

SENTENCE—(from the Latin for "opinion") a coherent and, in context, a fully independent syntactic unit of language.

In Bloomfield's definition, a sentence is "an independent form, not included in any larger (complex) linguistic form ..." (1984 [1933]:170). And this from Jespersen: "A sentence is a (relatively) complete and independent unit of communication ... the completeness and independence being shown by its standing alone or its capability of standing alone, ie of being uttered by itself" (1933:106).

In speech, a sentence is distinguished by a characteristic intonation pattern ("tune"). In writing, a sentence is marked off with a capital letter at its beginning; a terminal stop (a full stop, a question mark or an exclamation mark) at its end.

1. What does a sentence consist of?

A sentence can consist of a single word:

> Stop!

Or it can consist of an indefinite number of words:

> For our annual vacation, we went to the coast where we rented a cabin and had a good time swimming and roaming around and playing cards, which we all enjoyed, as well as just resting and relaxing, because we'd had a hard year's work behind us, not to mention having moved house just before the start of the vacation, as we'd had to vacate our previous house when the lease was up after we had been living there for eight years, ever since we ... (and so on and so forth).

Each underlined segment in the following text is a sentence. Note the varying punctuation.

> MACBETH: <u>I have done the deed</u>. <u>Didst thou not hear a noise</u>?
> LADY MACBETH: <u>I heard the owl scream and the crickets cry</u>. <u>Did not you speak</u>?
> MACBETH: <u>When</u>?
> LADY MACBETH: <u>Now</u>.

> MACBETH: <u>As I descended</u>?
> LADY MACBETH: <u>Ay</u>.
> MACBETH: <u>Hark</u>! <u>Who lies in the second chamber</u>?
> LADY MACBETH: <u>Donalbain</u>.
>
> (Shakespeare, *Macbeth*.)

In syntactic terms, sentences consist of one or more clauses, each clause normally featuring a subject and a predicate (see CLAUSE). Some of the sentences in the above text are complete sentences; others, elliptical sentences. The latter lack stated subjects and/or predicates—the lacking elements being understood from the context. See SENTENCE TYPES.

2. Extras and clauses.

Besides clauses, sentences may (but need not necessarily) also feature extras—that is, sentence elements that are neither subjects nor predicates. The following text features extras (underlined). Note that they are not essential to the sentence structures and may be left out.

> <u>Oh</u>, you were trying to say something constructive?
> INTERJECTION
>
> "<u>Guys</u>, let's get out of here."
> VOCATIVE
>
> "<u>But</u> you have to be there for them," I said angrily.
> CONJUNCTION
>
> <u>Thankfully</u>, I don't have to go through it every morning.
> ADVERB
>
> (Melina Marchetta, *Looking for Alibrandi*.)

The text illustrates four possible types of extras:

• AN INTERJECTION:	Oh
• A NOUN USED as a form of address:	Guys
• A CONJUNCTION:	But
• AN ADVERB that modifies the rest of the sentence:	Thankfully

In syntactic terms, then, we could say that a sentence consists of an optional extra plus one or more clauses. In symbolic notation, we can put it as follows (for the arrow ➜ read "consists of").

Sentence ➜ (extra) + clause/s.   [The brackets round "extra" show that the extra is optional.]

We can display the same thing in a tree diagram. Each extra and each clause is separately underlined.

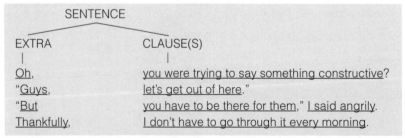

For more on extras (and alternative terminology) see EXTRA. For more on clauses see CLAUSE.

SENTENCE PARTS—the constituent parts of a sentence.

1. What are the parts of a simple sentence?

A simple sentence has two parts, the second of which we can divide into two.

(a) AN EXTRA (often optional), which is peripheral to the sentence itself. See SENTENCE.

(b) A CLAUSE, which is the informational part of the sentence, and which divides into two parts:

• A SUBJECT, which usually stands first, and which answers the question: "Who (or what) is the topic of the sentence?"

• A PREDICATE (from the Latin for "proclaim"), which usually stands after the subject, and which answers the question: "What does the sentence tell us about the subject?"

We can show these parts of a sentence under a tree diagram.

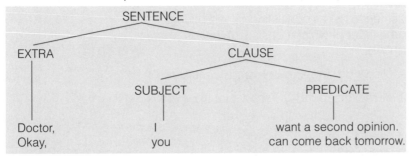

The "tree diagram" is so called, even though it is upside-down.

2. What are the parts of a multiple sentence?

In a multiple sentence (see SENTENCE TYPES), we can analyse the parts in the same way, clause by clause.

First, we separate the text into sentences, and we separate the clauses from each other with slashes.

An airline passenger came to the customs control with two suitcases.	[SIMPLE SENTENCE]
"What have you got in that small suitcase?"/the customs officer asked him.	[MULTIPLE SENTENCE]
"It is a rock, Ma'am,"/he answered.	[MULTIPLE SENTENCE]
"I do a nightclub act/in which I crack the rock on my head."	[MULTIPLE SENTENCE]
"What have you got in the large suitcase, then?"	[SIMPLE SENTENCE]
"Aspirins."	[ELLIPTICAL SENTENCE]

Then we stack the clauses under the tree diagram. In the box below, I have underlined the main noun or pronoun in each subject, and the verb in each predicate.

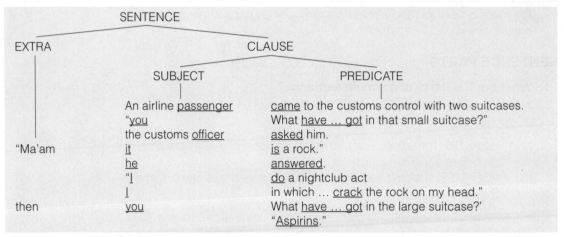

- Because a noun (or a pronoun) is the head—the grammatically important part—of the subject, the subject is also called a "noun phrase" (or NP for short).

- Because a verb is the head of the predicate, the predicate is also called a "verb phrase" (or VP for short).

So we can describe a sentence (S) as consisting of an optional extra (X) plus a clause, the latter of which consists of a noun phrase (NP) plus a verb phrase (VP).

We can express this as follows (for the arrow → read "consists of"):

S → (X) + Clause   [The brackets round "X" show that the extra is optional.]
Clause → NP + VP.

3. **What are the parts of a subject?**

  (a) Typically, a subject consists of a noun or a noun equivalent. (The predicates are in brackets.)

SUBJECT	(PREDICATE)
Cats NOUN	(purr).
They PRONOUN	(purr).
David Hume COMPOUND NOUN	(was a Scottish philosopher and historian).
The philosopher David Hume NOUN PHRASE	(was also a historian).

You can even have a clause—a noun clause—as the subject of the predicate.

Whoever wrote this NOUN CLAUSE	(was very wise).

The noun clause, *Whoever wrote this*, has its own subject (*Whoever*) and predicate (*wrote this*).

(b) The noun or noun equivalent part can be expanded by the addition of modifiers—usually determiners, adjectives or adjective phrases.

In the following text, the extras are in bold, the noun (or equivalent) parts of the subjects are underlined; the rest of the subjects (not underlined) are modifiers.

EXTRA	SUBJECT	(PREDICATE)
	The morning <u>charities and ceremonies</u>	(took so much time)
that	the <u>rest</u> of the day	(was devoted to preparations for the festivities.)
	Being still young, the <u>girls</u>	(put their wits to work)
and		(made whatever they needed.)
	Some of their <u>productions</u>	(were very clever—gorgeous robes of old cotton.)
	The <u>furniture</u>	(was used to being turned topsy-turvy,)
and	the big <u>chamber</u>	(was the scene of many innocent revels.)

(Louisa May Alcott, *Little Women*.)

4. What are the parts of a predicate?

(a) The predicate consists of at least a verb. The verb may be associated with optional modifiers of various kinds.

> PREDICATE
>
> ... <u>went</u>   home.
>   VERB   ADVERB
>
> ... <u>went</u>   to see a friend.
>   VERB   INFINITIVE PHRASE
>
> ... <u>went</u>   round a corner.
>   VERB   PREPOSITION PHRASE

A verb alone, or a verb plus its modifier, is called a "verbal." See VERBAL. Each line in the box above, taken together, is the verbal constituent of a predicate.

(b) The predicate may also have a completion—that is: (i) an object or (ii) a complement or (iii) both an object and a complement. See COMPLETION.

A completion—unlike a verb modifier—is not optional: it is an obligatory addition to a verb (underlined). The two kinds of completions (bold) are illustrated below.

> (i) OBJECT COMPLETIONS
>
> Love at first sight <u>saves</u> **an awful lot of time**.
>   VERB   OBJECT
>
> You can <u>avoid</u> **the Christmas rush** by drinking now.
>   VERB   OBJECT
>
> (ii) COMPLEMENT COMPLETIONS
>
> They <u>feel</u> **happy** only when they <u>are</u> **miserable**.
>   VERB COMPLEMENT   VERB COMPLEMENT
>
> Classical music <u>is</u> **music composed by dead foreigners**.
>   VERB   COMPLEMENT
>
> (iii) OBJECT + COMPLEMENT COMPLETIONS
>
> They <u>made</u> **me**   **sing**.
>   VERB OBJECT COMPLEMENT

Note that, if we omitted the completions, the sentences would be incomplete.

Here is the expanded tree diagram with an example text. The head words are underlined; the modifiers are not.

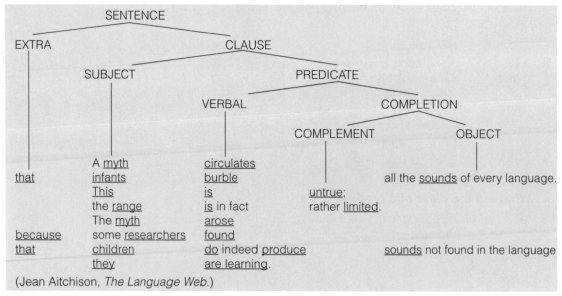

(Jean Aitchison, *The Language Web*.)

5. What kinds of objects are there?

There are two kinds of objects—indirect and direct objects. See OBJECT. So we add another fork to the branched diagram, and this completes the tally of sentence parts.

In the examples below, the heads are underlined; their modifiers are not.

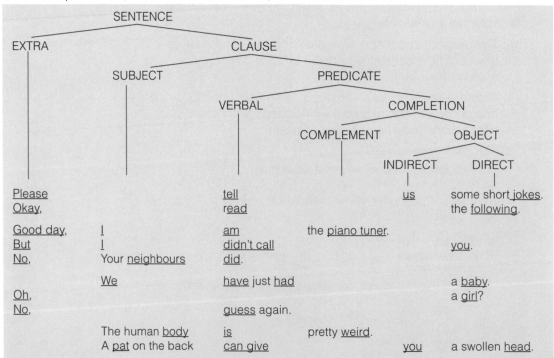

The above scheme represents the ten parts of a sentence. Each part can have a head (underlined) and, possibly but not necessarily, a modifier (not underlined).

6. A word of caution.

The neat tree diagram on the previous page suggests that sentence parts come in a fixed order. They don't always. Word order in English can be very fluid. The branches of the diagram can become entangled in all sorts of interesting ways.

So, for example, the usual sequence of words in a sentence may be:

<u>We</u> <u>don't need</u> <u>this</u>.
SUBJECT   VERBAL   OBJECT

But there is nothing wrong with:

<u>This</u>   <u>we</u>   <u>don't need</u>.
OBJECT SUBJECT   VERBAL

Frequently, too, the modifiers of verbs get separated from their verbs. So, we can have the following "normal" word order.

<u>My sister and I</u>   <u>often</u>   <u>entertain</u> <u>other family members and friends</u>.
   SUBJECT   VERB MODIFIER   VERB   OBJECT

But just look at where else the verb modifier (*often*) can go, yielding different nuances of the same meaning or different meanings altogether.

<u>Often</u>, my sister and I entertain other family members and friends.
My sister, <u>often</u>, and I entertain other family members and friends.
My sister and I <u>often</u> entertain other family members and friends.
My sister and I entertain—<u>often</u>—other family members and friends.
My sister and I entertain other family members, <u>often</u>, and friends.
My sister and I entertain other family members and, <u>often</u>, friends.
My sister and I entertain other family members and friends <u>often</u>.

And that's just for *often*: other sentence parts can also move around! This mobility of the parts of a sentence may appear daunting, but you can also regard it as a form of language liberation.
See THEME AND RHEME.

7. A hint of greater complexity.

In the diagrams above, we have considered single words or short phrases as making up the parts of clauses. But the parts of clauses can, and often do, consist of other clauses. See CLAUSE TYPES. These other clauses are themselves capable of analysis.

For example, we can analyse the sentence *Some succeeded* as follows.

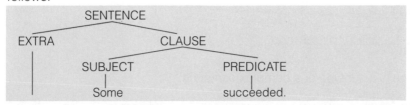

But if we substitute the clause *Whoever tried* for the word *Some*, we get the following analysis.

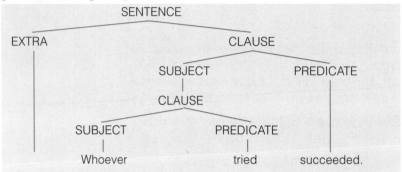

See clauses, their interrelationships, and sentence types.

SENTENCE TYPES—a classification of sentences, depending on how many and what types of clauses a sentence consists of. See clause.

Following, we consider the following sentence types.

1. SIMPLE: Food is an essential part of a balanced diet.
2. MULTIPLE
    (a) COMPOUND: Doctors bury their mistakes and lawyers hang them.
    (b) COMPLEX: Children wear sweaters when their mothers feel cold.
    (c) COMPOUND-COMPLEX: He is a careful driver, so he looks before he hits anything.
3. ELLIPTICAL: Any good, these jokes?

1. A simple sentence consists of a single (a main) clause.

> Careful drivers watch the car behind the car in front of them.
> MAIN CLAUSE

2. A multiple sentence (in functional grammar, a "clause complex") consists of more than one clause. There are three subtypes of multiple sentences.

(a) A compound sentence ("compound," from the Latin for "put together") consists of a main clause plus one or more coordinate clauses.

> The fortune-tellers held their annual general meeting
> MAIN CLAUSE
>
> and read the minutes of next year's meeting.
> COORDINATE CLAUSE

(b) A complex sentence ("complex," from the Latin for "twine together") consists of a main clause plus one or more subordinate clauses.

> I am changing to a new dentist
> MAIN CLAUSE
>
> because the old one is getting on my nerves.
> SUBORDINATE (ADVERB) CLAUSE

A cleft ("split") sentence is a subtype of a complex sentence.

See dummy pronouns *it* and *there*.

(c)   A compound-complex sentence (also called a "mixed sentence") consists of a main clause plus one or more coordinate clauses plus one or more subordinate clauses.

> I do not care to speak ill of any man but I believe
>   MAIN CLAUSE   COORDINATE CLAUSE
>
> that gentleman is an attorney.
>   SUBORDINATE (NOUN) CLAUSE
>
> (Samuel Johnson)

3. **An elliptical sentence** ("elliptical," from the Greek for "defective") is an incomplete sentence: one that has one or more essential elements understood but not explicitly stated—as in the third sentence in the text below.

> I had a parrot once that laid square eggs.   MULTIPLE SENTENCE
>   MAIN CLAUSE   SUBORDINATE (ADJECTIVE) CLAUSE
>
> Did it speak?   SIMPLE SENTENCE
>   MAIN CLAUSE
>
> Sometimes—"Ouch !" [It sometimes said "Ouch!"]   ELLIPTICAL SENTENCE
>   ELLIPTICAL CLAUSE

4. **The three major sentence types are illustrated in the text below.**

> THE WONDER-CHILD
>
> Little Jackie had not spoken since he was born six years before.   MULTIPLE SENTENCE
>   MAIN CLAUSE   SUBORDINATE (ADVERB) CLAUSE
>
> One day he piped up.   SIMPLE SENTENCE
>   MAIN CLAUSE
>
> "Mom, I am sorry to say that the toast is burnt."   MULTIPLE SENTENCE
>   MAIN CLAUSE   SUBORDINATE (NOUN) CLAUSE
>
> "What—you can speak?"   SIMPLE SENTENCE
>   MAIN CLAUSE
>
> "Of course."   ELLIPTICAL SENTENCE
> MAIN CLAUSE
>
> "Then why haven't you spoken for the past six years?"   SIMPLE SENTENCE
>   MAIN CLAUSE
>
> "Well, everything has been all right till now."   SIMPLE SENTENCE
>   MAIN CLAUSE

Jespersen (1933:105–6) adds a fourth type—an amorphous ("formless") sentence, such as *Tut tut!* or *Shshsh!* Worth noting, but not syntactically significant.

SIMILE—See FIGURE OF SPEECH.

SIMPLE ASPECT—See TENSE AND ASPECT.

SIMPLE SENTENCE—See SENTENCE TYPES.

SINGULAR—See NUMBER.

SPLIT INFINITIVE—See INFINITIVE.

STANDARD AND NONSTANDARD ENGLISH—two ways of speaking (or writing). We begin with examples.

STANDARD (FORMAL)	NONSTANDARD (INFORMAL)
It is I.	It's me.
Whom do you want to see?	Who do you want to see?
Tia and I went to town.	Tia and me went to town.

1. **Standard English** is the common form of English—as distinct from various regional or slang forms of the language. Standard English is the form of speech considered by most people to be "correct" and "grammatical." It is the form of language used on formal occasions: in speeches, or in documents and official letters.

2. **Nonstandard English** is the form of speech that people use when they let their hair down, or it may represent regional or subcultural varieties of the language. Though it is often looked down on, there is in fact nothing wrong with nonstandard speech in its own context or among people who use it as their form of communication.

   Here are texts by two authors—one British and one American—who make effective literary use of nonstandard English.

   > ALFRED DOOLITTLE: I ask you, what am I? I'm one of the undeserving poor: that's what I am. Think of what that means to a man. It means that he's up against middle class morality all the time. If there's anything going, and I put in for a bit of it, it's always the same story: "You're undeserving; so you can't have it." But my needs is as great as the most deserving widow's that ever got money out of six different charities in one week for the death of the same husband.
   > (George Bernard Shaw, *Pygmalion.*)

   > You don't know about me, without you have read a book by the name of *The Adventures of Tom Sawyer*, but that ain't no matter. That book was made by Mr. Mark Twain, and he told the truth, mainly. There was things which he stretched, but mainly he told the truth. That is nothing. I never seen anybody but lied, one time or another, without it was Aunt Polly, or the widow, or maybe Mary.
   > (Mark Twain, *Huckleberry Finn.*)

STEM—See ROOT AND STEM.

STRONG VERB—See IRREGULAR VERB.

SUBJECT—See SENTENCE PARTS.

SUBJECTIVE—See CASE.

SUBJUNCTIVE—a way of expressing a wish (*I wish I were better at maths*) or a hypothesis (*I would be able to travel the world if I had a lot of money*). The term "subjunctive" comes from the Latin for "subjoined." The subjunctive is so called because it often occurs in subjoined (that is, "subordinate") clauses. See CONDITIONAL.

1. **How does the subjunctive differ from other forms of expression?**

   The subjunctive contrasts with the indicative (which expresses matters of fact) and with the imperative (which expresses commands).

INDICATIVE (A FACT)	IMPERATIVE (A COMMAND)	SUBJUNCTIVE (A WISH)
Kim is going home.	Kim, go home.	If only Kim would go home.

The terms "indicative," "imperative," and "subjunctive" relate both to the verbs and to the sentences in which the verbs occur. See MOOD.

Here are some typical subjunctive sentences. Each subjunctive verb is underlined, and each sentence as a whole is also subjunctive.

1. I wish I <u>were</u> a bird.
2. He drove as if he <u>were</u> mad.
3. If only they <u>would</u> come.
4. I move that the meeting <u>be</u> adjourned.

2. What is special about the subjunctive?

The most characteristic feature of a subjunctive sentence is the form of the verb. In sentences 1 and 2 above, the verb *were* appears with singular subjects: *I <u>were</u>, he <u>were</u>*. In indicative sentences it would be: *I <u>was</u>, he <u>was</u>*. In sentences 3 and 4, the indicative equivalents would read *they <u>will</u> come* (rather than *<u>would</u> come*) and *the meeting <u>is</u> adjourned* (rather than *<u>be</u> adjourned*).

Compared to the indicative, there is always some special language twist in the subjunctive, as we shall see below.

3. How do you use the subjunctive?

We distinguish three uses of the subjunctive:

(a)   IN STOCK EXPRESSIONS: Heaven help us!
(b)   TO EXPRESS A DESIRE OR INTENTION: I suggest it be left alone.
(c)   TO EXPRESS A HYPOTHESIS ABOUT
    (i)   THE FUTURE: I wish they would reconsider.
    (ii)   THE PRESENT: If only I were better at maths.
    (iii) THE PAST: It's as if it had never happened.

We look at each of these below.

(a)   You use the subjunctive in stock expressions that indicate wishful thinking, rather than matters of fact. Next to each subjunctive sentence below, you can see how the sentence would look in the indicative. Note the twist in the subjunctive that makes it different from the indicative. The pairs of sentences, side by side, have different meanings.

SUBJUNCTIVE	(INDICATIVE)
Be that as it may.	(That may be so.)
God bless us.	(God blesses us.)
May the best player win.	(The best player wins.)
May it please the court ...	(It pleases the court ...)
Come the revolution!	(The revolution comes.)
Your kingdom come.	(Your kingdom comes.)
Lest we forget ...	(Let us not forget ...)
Should auld acquaintance be forgot ...	(If old acquaintance is forgotten...)
So be it.	(It is so.)
Suffice it to say ...	(It is sufficient to say ...)
... as it were.	(... as it was.)

(b) Next, there are subjunctive sentences that express a desire or an intention. Such sentences usually begin with an introductory *I move that* or *I recommend that* or some such expression. Following the introduction comes the informational part of the sentence, featuring an unmarked infinitive. (An unmarked infinitive is a *to*–verb without the *to*–: (~~to~~) *go*, (~~to~~) *be*, (~~to~~) *have*, ...).

SUBJUNCTIVE	(INDICATIVE)
I move that the meeting <u>be</u> adjourned.	(... <u>is</u> adjourned.)
I recommend that she <u>be</u> heard in silence.	(... <u>is</u> heard.)
I suggest that he <u>resume</u> his seat.	(... <u>resumes</u> his seat.)
I ask that he <u>leave</u> the chamber.	(... <u>leaves</u> the chamber.)

Here the special twist is the use of *be*, *resume* and *leave* instead of *is*, *resumes* and *leaves*.

(c) Then there are sentences in the subjunctive that express a wish or a hypothesis about:
   (i)   the future
   (ii) the present
   (iii) the past.

These subjunctives often feature a formulaic introduction such as *I wish* or *if only* or *just suppose*, or some other expression that indicates the hypothetical nature of the sentence.

(i) The future hypothetical uses a verb form (underlined below) such as *would go*, *would be* or the like (called "future in the past simple tense"). The future hypothetical implies that I am uncertain about whether what I say will actually take place in the future. In the examples below, you will find the implications in square brackets.

"Oh dear," cried Alice, "I do wish they <u>would put</u> their heads down." [= But it's doubtful that they will.]
"I wish they <u>would get</u> the trial done," Alice thought. [= But that seems unlikely to happen.]
(Lewis Carroll, *Alice in Wonderland*.)

The special twist is the use of the future in the past tense to express the future.

(ii) The present hypothetical uses a verb form (underlined below) such as *went*, *were* or the like (called "past simple tense"). A special feature of the present hypothetical is the use of the verb *were* with both singular and plural subjects: *I wish I <u>were</u> ...*; *I wish we <u>were</u> ...* The present hypothetical implies that what I say is not actually the case in the present. In the examples below, you will find the implications in square brackets.

<u>I wish she were</u> safe home. [= But she's not safe home.]
(Charlotte Brontë, *Villette*.)

Oh, <u>if only I thought</u> I had a chance! [= In fact, I don't actually think so.]
(George Bernard Shaw, *Man and Superman*.)

The special twist is the use of the past tense to express the present.

(iii)   The past hypothetical uses a verb form (underlined below) such as *had gone*, *had been* or the like (called "past perfect tense"). The past hypothetical implies that what I am saying was not in fact the case in the past. In the examples below, you will find the implications in square brackets.

> It seems <u>as if we had only just left</u>. [= Actually, we left some time ago.] (Oscar Wilde, *A Woman of No Importance*.)
>
> Lord Henry found Dorian Gray burying his face in the lilac blossoms, drinking in their perfume <u>as if it had been wine</u>. [= But it wasn't wine.] (Oscar Wilde, *The Picture of Dorian Gray*.)

The special twist is the use of the past perfect tense to express the past.

SUBORDINATE CLAUSE—See CLAUSE TYPES.

SUFFIX—See AFFIX.

SUPERLATIVE—See DEGREES OF COMPARISON.

SYNECDOCHE—See FIGURE OF SPEECH.

SYNTAGM AND PARADIGM—two terms in structural linguistics. In functional linguistics, they are called "chain and choice." "Syntagm" comes from the Greek for "arranging together;" "paradigm," from the Greek for a "pattern."

1. **A syntagm** (pronounced "SIN-tam") is any coherent string of words, such as a compound, a phrase, a clause or a sentence. In Saussure's terms: "Words arranged in sequence on the chain of speaking ... The syntagm is always composed of two or more words" (1916:123). Each of the following is a syntagm.

have gone	once upon a time
when you are ready	I like bushwalking

Some of the above syntagms have syntagms within them: the syntagm *once upon a time* contains within it the syntagm *a time*. Both syntagms—*once upon a time* and *a time*—are coherent sequences.

2. **A paradigm** (pronounced "PA -ra-dime") is a set of possible substitutions for any word or syntagm. A paradigm, in Saussure's words, "is the point of convergence of an indefinite number of coordinate terms" (1916:126).

By way of example, let us take the sentence: *I have two apples*. For *I have*, we can substitute *I saw* or *Charlie ate* and so on. For *apples* we can substitute *bananas* or *pears* and so on. And for *two* we can substitute any number except *one*. In this way we can construct the following table of syntagms and paradigms.

	PARADIGM 1	PARADIGM 2	PARADIGM 3
SYNTAGM 1	I have	two	apples.
SYNTAGM 2	I saw	three	bananas.
SYNTAGM 3	You have	eighteen	pears.
SYNTAGM 4	Charlie ate	five	plates of soup.
SYNTAGM 5	We want	sixty	delicious potatoes.

We can recombine (permutate) this table of syntagms and paradigms into any of 125 possible sentences: *I saw eighteen plates of soup; We want three pears; Charlie ate sixty bananas; You have three delicious potatoes ...*

The connection between paradigm and syntagm was nicely expressed by Jakobson and Halle in 1956: "A given significative unit may be replaced by other signs of the same code [paradigm], while its contextual meaning is determined by its connection with other signs within the same system [syntagm]."

Theoretically, it should be possible to base the grammar of any language on the collaborative opposition of the two notions, syntagm and paradigm. Whether this can actually be done remains to be seen.

SYNTAX—the grammar of strings of words. The following are some of the entries that deal with aspects of syntax.

PHRASE	GRAMMAR UNITS	THEME AND RHEME
CLAUSE	NONFINITE CLAUSE	SYNTAGM AND PARADIGM
SENTENCE	CLEFT SENTENCE	PARTICIPANT, PROCESS, CIRCUMSTANCE
SENTENCE PARTS	QUESTION TYPES	ACTOR, BENEFICIARY, GOAL
SENTENCE TYPES	CLAUSE COMPLEX	

"Syntax" comes from the Greek for "arranging together"—the arrangement of words.

TAG QUESTION—See QUESTION TYPES and ANOMALOUS FINITE.

TENOR—See CONTEXT.

TENSE AND ASPECT—a feature of verbs. Tense indicates the time (such as present or past) of whatever is expressed by the verb; aspect does the fine tuning to the tense. Both words come from the Latin: "tense" from "time;" "aspect" from having another "look at."

1. How many tenses are there?

Most modern linguists argue that English has, properly, only two tenses: present and past. They argue on historical grounds that verbs with *will* or *shall* are present tense forms that have their past tense counterparts with *would* and *should*.

A few linguists agree with the commonsense view that, today, English has a separate future tense—forms with *shall* or *will*. I agree with the latter view and, in company with some other linguists, add a fourth tense—the future in the past, with *should* or *would*. See FUTURE TENSE: DOES IT EXIST IN ENGLISH?

Here is the table of tenses.

PRESENT	PAST	FUTURE	FUTURE IN THE PAST
I go	I went	I will go	I would go

What is this weirdly named tense "future in the past"?

It is the tense that we use to indicate that, at some time in the past, something was yet to happen in the future.

> I decided that I would take a vacation.

When I made the decision—at some time in the past—my vacation was still in the future.

2. **How many aspects are there?**

Each of the four abovementioned tenses has four variants, called "aspects:"

- SIMPLE

- PROGRESSIVE (also called "continuous") characterized by having a verb ending in –*ing*

- PERFECT, characterized by having an auxiliary verb *have, has* or *had*

- PERFECT PROGRESSIVE, with both the perfect and the progressive characteristics.

Four tenses, each having four aspects, gives us the following sixteen tense-aspects.

	PRESENT	PAST	FUTURE	FUTURE IN THE PAST
SIMPLE	I go	I went	I will go	I would go
PROGRESSIVE	I am going	I was going	I will be going	I would be going
PERFECT	I have gone	I had gone	I will have gone	I would have gone
PERFECT PROGRESSIVE	I have been going	I had been going	I will have been going	I would have been going

3. **A word of caution.**

While it is true that "present tense" verbs are usually about the present time, and "past tense" verbs are usually about a time in the past, this is not always the case.

We can, for example, use a present tense verb to refer to the future: *The bus leaves at dawn tomorrow.* Or we can use a past tense verb to refer to the present: *I wish I knew the answer.*

For a full treatment of the tense-aspects see Stern, 1997a.

TEXT GRAMMAR—(also called "discourse analysis") the grammar features of whole texts. The term "text grammar" contrasts with "morphology" (the grammar of words), and with "syntax" (the grammar of sentences). See GRAMMAR UNITS.

For entries on six features of text grammar see the following.

COHESION   MODALITY   CONTEXT
REGISTER   GENRE   TURN-TAKING

THEME AND RHEME—"theme" comes from the Greek for "setting down;" "rheme" from the Greek for "that which is said."

Theme and rheme are terms in functional grammar to indicate the beginning (theme) of a clause or a sentence and the rest (rheme) of the clause or sentence. The theme also goes under the name of "given;" the rheme, of "new" or "information."

The idea behind this division is that the beginning of a sentence is more prominent; the end of a sentence less prominent. So, by thematizing—that is, by bringing to the beginning—various parts of a sentence, we can draw the listener's (or the reader's) attention to those parts.

The operation of making something other than the actor of a sentence its theme is called "thematization." A thematized sentence is also called a "marked sentence;" an unthematized sentence, an "unmarked sentence."

See ACTOR, BENEFICIARY, GOAL.

The following sentence is unmarked ("unthematized"): the actor (underlined) is in the theme position.

THEME	RHEME
They	told the children a story at bedtime.

But we can also thematize various parts of the above sentence by bringing those parts to the theme position and, thereby, making them more prominent. The following sentences are all thematized (or "marked"). The actors (underlined) are banished from the theme position.

THEME	RHEME
Telling	the children a story at bedtime is what they did.
The children	were told a story by them at bedtime.
A story	was told to the children by them at bedtime.
At bedtime	they told the children a story.

When we talk or write, we usually switch between marked and unmarked clauses and sentences. If everything we said were unthematized, it would be boring; if it were all thematized, it would be too gushy. Here is a typically varied text, with some of the clauses and sentences marked and some of them unmarked. The actor in each clause or sentence is underlined.

THEME	RHEME	
Sonny	came home from school one day with his report card.	[UNMARKED]
To her dismay,	his mother saw	[MARKED]
that he	had failed in all but one subject.	[UNMARKED]
That subject	was singing.	[UNMARKED]
She	looked at him disapprovingly:	[UNMARKED]
"With marks like that	you still feel like singing?"	[MARKED]

See MARKED AND UNMARKED CLAUSE COMPLEX.

TRANSITION WORD—See EXTRA.

TRANSITIVITY—from the Latin for "going across." A concept that relates to whether a verb is or is not followed by an object or a complement; that is, whether the action of the verb stops with the verb or goes across to something else—an object or a complement.

1. **A transitive verb** (abbreviated to TV) takes an object.

   They <u>borrowed</u> <u>my garden hose</u>.
      TV   OBJECT

   [Other transitive verbs are: *take, hit, burgle.*]

2. **An intransitive verb** (IV) does not take an object.

   They <u>snore</u>.
        IV

   [Other intransitive verbs are: *sneeze, sit, apologize.*]

3. **A transitive-intransitive verb** (TIV) sometimes does, and sometimes doesn't, take an object.

   They <u>ate</u>. They <u>ate</u> <u>peas</u>.
        TIV   TIV   OBJECT

   [Other transitive-intransitive verbs are: *drink, write, understand.*]

   In the sentence, *They ate*, the verb *ate* functions intransitively; in *They ate peas*, transitively.

4. **A ditransitive verb** (DV) takes two objects—one direct and one indirect.

   They <u>sent</u> <u>their friends</u> <u>an email message</u>.
        DV   INDIRECT OBJECT   DIRECT OBJECT

   [Other ditransitive verbs are: *tell, give, lend.*]

5. **A linking verb—also called a "copula"—**(LV) takes a complement.

   They <u>are</u> <u>my friends</u>.
        LV   COMPLEMENT

   [Other linking verbs are: *become, remain, seem.*]

6. **A transitive-linking verb** (TLV) takes both an object and a complement.

   They <u>made</u> <u>me</u>   <u>chairperson</u>.
        TLV OBJECT   COMPLEMENT

   [Other transitive-linking verbs are: *appoint, order, command.*]

   For a more detailed treatment of 1–6 above, see OBJECT and COMPLETION.

TURN-TAKING—a term in text grammar and a feature of transactional texts such as conversations, or of dialogues in novels or plays. The term means what it says: people taking turns when they are speaking. The following text illustrates turn-taking.

> "Dad,"
> "Yes?"
> "There's going to be a meeting of the Parents and Teachers Association at school tomorrow."
> "All right."
> "Just a small one, though, Dad."
> "How small?"
> "Just you, me and the principal."

VERB—from the Latin for "word." One of the word classes. The verb really is *the* word. It is the engine of the sentence: the part of the sentence that determines the structure of the sentence (whether it does or doesn't have a completion); the mood of the sentence (whether it expresses a command or a wish); the tense of the sentence (whether it is about the past or the future); and many other sentence features.

Traditionally, a verb was defined as a "doing word." But there is a bit more to it than that.

1. What are verbs?

Verbs make up a word class, most of whose members:

(a) have to do with doing:

> take   went   jumping   talks   ran
>
> though a few verbs have nothing to do with doing: *is, must, may, shall, will ...*

(b) can take a number of forms, including the infinitive (with *to*) and the *–ing* form:

> to swim–swimming   to read–reading   to be–being   to take–taking
>
> though a few verbs cannot take these forms: *can, must, may, ought, shall ...*

(c) can appear either singly or in compounds—that is, a string of verbs that combine into one meaning:

> SINGLE VERBS
> know   learns   discover   understood
> COMPOUND VERBS
> have known   is learning   will discover   may have understood

(d) combine with nouns or pronouns (underlined) to tell us who is doing what:

> <u>We</u> **laughed**.   <u>Jack and Jill</u> **swam**.
> <u>They</u> **need** <u>a plumber</u>.   <u>Adam</u> **gave** <u>Tia</u> <u>a present</u>.

(e) either start off as verbs:

> walk   talk   sleep   wake

or derive from members of other word classes with a suffix:

SUFFIX	DERIVED VERBS		
–en	lengthen	shorten	widen
–ify	electrify	glorify	purify
–ize	realize	theorize	apologize

or with a prefix:

PREFIX	DERIVED VERBS		
en–	engulf	enclose	enable
em–	embalm	embark	embitter

(f)   fit into the blank spaces in any of the following sentence frames:

We _____. VERB	[laugh swam read waited ...]
We _____ them. VERB	[like saw found took ...]
We _____ happy. VERB	[are felt seem became ...]

All of the above features—from (a) to (f)—define what verbs are.

In the text below, each verb is separately underlined.

> Once upon a time, biology <u>was</u> simple. Its practitioners <u>cultivated</u> things in Petri dishes and flowerpots, or <u>studied</u> them through field glasses. They <u>might</u> <u>count</u> them, <u>measure</u> their lengths, or even <u>weigh</u> them. But the numbers rarely <u>taxed</u> their mathematical skills beyond a level that they <u>would</u> <u>have</u> <u>learned</u> at school.
> (*The Economist*, July 2, 1999.)

There are two compound verbs in the text above: *might count* and *would have learned*.

See COMPOUND.

2. How do verbs function in sentences?

The main job that verbs (underlined) do is to express the actions or states of being that are taking place in the sentences in which the verbs occur. In technical terms: verbs predicate.

ACTIONS:	She <u>scored</u> a goal.	Everybody <u>was cheering</u>.	The team <u>had won</u> the cup.
STATES OF BEING:	He <u>was</u> tired.	She <u>became</u> the captain.	We <u>have been</u> successful.

But, depending on the form that they take (see below), verbs—as well as doing verb-like jobs—can also do noun-like or adjective-like jobs. That is, they can take the forms of verbs, but have the functions of nouns or adjectives.

> Biological data <u>are flooding</u> in at an <u>unprecedented</u> rate. As a result, many of the challenges in
> COMPOUND VERB   ADJECTIVE
>
> biology <u>have become</u> challenges in <u>computing</u>. America's National Institutes of Health—the body
> COMPOUND VERB   NOUN
>
> responsible for <u>disbursing</u> the lion's share of federal money for biomedical research—<u>issued</u> a
> NOUN   VERB
>
> report that <u>talked</u> of "the <u>alarming</u> gap between the need for computation in biology and the skills and
> VERB   ADJECTIVE
>
> resources available <u>to meet</u> that need" and <u>recommended</u> <u>spending</u> up to $160m on <u>rectifying</u>
> VERB   VERB   NOUN   NOUN
>
> matters through a network of <u>biocomputing</u> centers across the country. (*The Economist*, July 2, 1999.)
> NOUN

3. What other features do verbs have?

(a) Verbs have number. That is, they may be singular to go with singular subjects (*She walks. He talks*). Or they may be plural to go with plural subjects (*They walk. They talk*). This is a feature of verbs in the present tense. In the past tense, with one exception (see below) there is no number distinction for verbs (*She walked, They walked; He talked, They talked*).

The only verb that does have a singular–plural distinction in the past tense is *was* and *were* (*I was happy. We were happy*). For more information on the close tie between singulars and plurals in verbs and their subjects—and on some tricky variations—see AGREEMENT OF SUBJECT AND VERB.

(b) Verbs have person. That is, they can have different forms in the first person (the person(s) speaking), in the second person (the person(s) spoken to) and in the third person (the person(s) spoken about).

FIRST PERSON	SECOND PERSON	THIRD PERSON
I am, we are	you are	he is, she is, it is, they are
I walk	you walk	he walks, they walk

The "person" of the verb is the same as (that is, it agrees with) the person of the subject of the verb. Thus, *I* goes with *am*, *it* goes with *is*, and so on.

(c) Verbs can have various forms (*go, going, gone*) which, in turn, can have various functions. For a fuller treatment of the forms of the verb and their functions see FORMS OF THE VERB.

(d) Verbs come in a variety of tenses and aspects: present tense, past tense; simple aspect, perfect aspect, and others. For the range of tense-aspects, see TENSE AND ASPECT.

(e) Some verbs are unusual in that they don't inflect with *–s* (*must*) in the present tense. This is in contrast with the majority of verbs that do inflect with *–s* (*talk–talks*). For an account of these unusual verbs see MODAL VERB.

(f) Most verbs have their past tense ending in *–ed* (*walked, talked*); but some verbs change to the past tense without an *–ed* ending (*give–gave, take–took*). For a list of the latter kind of verbs, see IRREGULAR VERB.

(g) Some verbs are unusual in that they fulfill only a grammar function (*Do you understand?*). This is in contrast with the majority of verbs that have a definite meaning (*Do you understand?*). For an account of these function verbs, see AUXILIARY VERB.

(h) Some verbs are incomplete unless there is something after them (*I borrowed ...*); others make complete sense even if there is nothing after them (*I laughed*). For an account of the difference between these kinds of verbs, see TRANSITIVITY.

(i) Some verbs have the actor (the doer) standing in front of them (*We* [= ACTOR] *ate chocolate*); others have the goal (the done-to) standing in front of them (*The chocolate* [= GOAL] *was eaten by us*). For the difference in structure between these two ways of saying much the same thing, see VOICE.

(j) The way you use verbs can indicate your attitude to what you are saying. So, for example, we can use verbs to make statements (*I am going home*) or to deny something (*We are not stopping you*) or to issue commands (*Go home now*). To see the variety of attitudes you can get across with the use of verbs, see MOOD.

VERB PHRASE—a term used in modern grammar for "predicate." See SENTENCE PARTS.

VERBAL—a term with different meanings in different grammars. In this book "verbal" is a constituent part of a sentence (as distinct from "verb," which is a word class). See SENTENCE PARTS.

1. What part of a sentence is a verbal?

Givón (1993, vol. 1:124) calls the verb, or the combination of verb + its modifier, "a verbal frame". I adopt the term from Givón and shorten it to "verbal." By "verbal" I mean either:

• a verb + its modifier or modifiers:

They <u>studied</u> <u>together</u>. VERB + MODIFIER	[studied + together = VERBAL]
They <u>always</u> <u>complained</u> <u>needlessly</u>. MODIFIER + VERB + MODIFIER	[always + complained +needlessly = VERBAL]
They <u>slept</u> <u>soundly</u> <u>yesterday</u>. VERB + MODIFIER + MODIFIER	[slept + soundly + yesterday = VERBAL]

or

• if the verb has no modifier, the verb alone:

My next door neighbour's dog <u>barks</u>. VERB	[barks = VERBAL]
We all <u>sang</u>. VERB	[sang = VERBAL]

2. What features does a verbal have?

(a) The modifier part of a verbal is optional; that is, you can always omit it. We can see this from the fact that, in the example sentences two boxes up, the modifiers can be omitted and the sentences are still all right.

> They <u>studied</u> ~~together~~.
> They ~~always~~ <u>complained</u> ~~needlessly~~.
> They <u>slept</u> ~~well~~ ~~yesterday~~.

(b) The position of the modifier part of a verbal is variable.

The modifier part may stand:

- before a verb:

> They <u>slowly</u> <u>opened</u> the door.
>   MODIFIER   VERB

- within a compound verb:

> They <u>have</u> <u>almost</u> <u>finished</u> the job.   [*Have finished* is a compound verb.
>   VERB MODIFIER   VERB   SEE COMPOUND.]

- after a verb:

> They <u>sang</u> <u>merrily</u>.
>   VERB MODIFIER

All the underlined segments in the three boxes above are verbals, each consisting of a verb + a modifier.

(c)   The modifier part of a verbal is often separated from the verb part by other parts ("constituents") of the sentence, most notably by the completion (bold) of the verb.
    SEE COMPLETION:

> An osteopath <u>works</u> **his fingers** <u>to your bone</u>.   [works + to your bone = VERBAL]
>   VERB   COMPLETION   MODIFIER
>
> Banks <u>lend</u> **money** <u>to the rich</u>.   [lend + to the rich = VERBAL]
>   VERB COMPLETION   MODIFIER
>
> I <u>learned</u> **ice-skating** <u>in ten sittings</u>.   [learned + in ten sittings = VERBAL]
>   VERB   COMPLETION   MODIFIER

The separation of the parts of a verbal by a completion is due to the operation of the "principle of adjacency," which requires the completion of a verb (in English) to be nearer to the verb than its modifier. This principle also goes under the name of "Behaghel's Law," after Otto Behaghel (1854–1936), who studied adjacency as it relates to German.

VERY TRUE—See LANGUAGE MYTH.

VOCATIVE—from the Latin for "calling." A noun (underlined) used to call or address someone.

> <u>My dear</u>, you must indeed go and see Mr. Bingley ... You mistake me, <u>my dear</u>.
> (Jane Austen, *Pride and Prejudice*.)
>
> You know, <u>Mr. Ramsden</u>, I don't care about money.
> (George Bernard Shaw, *Man and Superman*.)
>
> MR. BEAZLEY—<u>Mr. Speaker</u>, I raise a point of order.
> (*Hansard*, March 10, 1998.)

The pronoun *you* (underlined) can also act as a vocative.

> <u>You</u> there, what's going on?
> What's going on, <u>you</u> there?
> What's going on there, <u>you</u>?

The six sentences in the two boxes above illustrate two special features of the vocative:

- the vocative is separated from the rest of the sentence with punctuation

- the vocative can move to various positions in the sentence.

We see both features again below.

> NOUN VOCATIVE
>
> <u>Children</u>, I wish that you wouldn't make such a racket.
> I wish, <u>children</u>, that you wouldn't make such a racket.
> I wish that you wouldn't make such a racket, <u>children</u>.
>
> *YOU* VOCATIVE
>
> <u>You</u>—where do you think you're going?
> Where do you think you're going, <u>you</u>?

The vocative is often used in the imperative. SEE IMPERATIVE.

VOICE—a feature of verbs.

1. **There are two voices in English:**

   (a) The active voice (from the Latin for "doing") has the actor (also called "agent" or "doer") of the verb before the verb.

   > <u>The child</u> <u>washed</u> <u>the dog</u>.
   >   ACTOR   VERB   GOAL

   (b) The passive voice (from the Latin for "suffering") has the goal (also called "patient" or "done-to" of the verb before the verb.

   > <u>The dog</u> <u>was washed</u> <u>by the child</u>.
   >   GOAL   VERB   ACTOR

   A more technical way of expressing the active–passive distinction is to say that, in the active, the agent fills the subject role; in the passive, the goal fills the subject role. Another perspective from Otto Jespersen: the change from active to passive, or the other way round, represents a "shift in the point of view" (1933:120).

   - It is a feature of the passive that you can omit the actor:

   > <u>The dog</u> <u>was washed</u> (~~by the child~~).   [Without the actor the
   >   GOAL   VERB   ACTOR   passive sentence is all right.]

   - But you can't omit the actor from the active:

   > (~~The child~~) <u>Washed</u> <u>the dog</u>.   [Without the actor the active
   >   ACTOR   VERB   GOAL   sentence is not all right.]

2. **Each of the sixteen tense-aspects of the verb has an active and a passive voice.** These are shown in the table of tense-aspects below. In each pair of sentences, the upper one features an active verb; the lower one, a passive verb. Four of the passive tense-aspects are virtually never used and I have therefore crossed them out.

	PRESENT	PAST	FUTURE	FUTURE IN THE PAST
SIMPLE	I eat it it is eaten	I ate it it was eaten	I will eat it it will be eaten	I would eat it it would be eaten
PROGRESSIVE	I am eating it it is being eaten	I was eating it it was being eaten	I will be eating it it will be being eaten	I would be eating it it would be being eaten
PERFECT	I have eaten it it has been eaten	I had eaten it it had been eaten	I will have eaten it it will have been eaten	I would have eaten it it would have been eaten
PERFECT PROGRESSIVE	I have been eating it ~~it has been being eaten~~	I had been eating it ~~it had been being eaten~~	I will have been eating it ~~it will have been being eaten~~	I would have been eating it ~~it would have been being eaten~~

3. How do you recognize a passive verb?

A passive verb always consists of:

(a)   at least one of the eight possible forms of the verb *to be*: namely, *am, is, are, was, were, be, being, been*; and

(b)   an *–en* form of the verb (also called a "past participle") typically ending in *–en* or *–ed* or *–t*.

You can see (a) and (b) in the above table and also in the example texts below.

> I <u>was</u> <u>sent</u> to Lowood to get an education.
> I <u>was</u> <u>shaken</u> from head to foot with acute distress.
> I must watch feverishly while the change <u>was being</u> <u>effected</u>.
> I <u>was</u> <u>taken</u> from Bessie's neck, to which I clung with kisses.
> Christmas and the New Year had <u>been</u> <u>celebrated</u> at Gateshead.
> I see you <u>are being</u> <u>metamorphosed</u> into a lion.
> (Charlotte Brontë, *Jane Eyre*.)

WEAK VERB—See IRREGULAR VERB.

***WH*-QUESTION**—See QUESTION TYPES.

WORD CLASSES—(also called "parts of speech") the categories that grammarians sort words into: "nouns," "adjectives," "pronouns," and so on.

We can be reasonably confident that members of the same word class will have broadly similar characteristics and that they will function in broadly similar ways. To give two examples:

- loosely speaking, nouns are words that can take a plural *–s* ending (*apple–apples* ...)

- also loosely speaking, adjectives are words whose function it is to modify nouns (<u>*green*</u> <u>*apples*</u>).
  ADJECTIVE   NOUN

How many such word classes there are, and how we arrive at the number, is still a matter of contention. The Roman scholar Marcus

Varro (116–27 BC) listed four word classes; the American linguist Charles Carpenter Fries (1952) listed twenty-odd. Most dictionaries and traditional grammar books recognize the following eight:

nouns   adjectives   prepositions   adverbs

pronouns   verbs   conjunctions   interjections.

To these eight, modern grammarians have added one or more additional—and differing—classes. But one class that all grammarians now agree should be added is the class of determiners.

Here is an anonymous nursery rhyme with its definitions of the eight traditional parts of speech.

A **noun's** the name of anything;
As *school* or *garden, hoop* or *swing.*

Adjectives tell the kind of noun;
As *great, small, pretty, white* or *brown.*

Instead of nouns the **pronouns** stand:
Me and *mine, you* and *yours, she, he*—and

Verbs tell of something being done:
You r*ead, count, sing, laugh, jump* or *run.*

How things are done the **adverbs** tell;
As *slowly, quickly, not* or *well.*

Conjunctions join the words together;
As men *and* women, wind *or* weather.

The **prepositions** stand before
A noun, as *in* or *through* a door.

The **interjections** show surprise,
As *Oh! How pretty! Ah! How nice!*

To this ditty we add a definition for **determiners**: words that stand before nouns, or that replace nouns, and that tell you how determinate (how definite) the nouns (underlined) are. Examples: *this* or *that* book; I have *ten* books and you have *six.*

Wayne Beswick offers the following (almost) rhyming couplet.

And **determiners** like *that* or *this*
Show that I have *ten* books and you have *six.*

How do we identify what word class a given word belongs to?

We can identify the class of a word through any one or a combination of six ways:

1. EXAMPLE MEMBERS OF THE WORD CLASSES
2. DEFINITIONS OF THE WORD CLASSES
3. SENTENCE FRAMES
4. ASSOCIATED WORDS
5. DERIVATIONAL AFFIXES
6. INFLECTIONAL AFFIXES.

We look at each of these ways below.

1. Example members of the word classes.

Once we know that *in, on, with, by,* and *under* are examples of prepositions, we can probably figure out that *over, through,* and *for* belong to the same word class.

2. Definitions of the word classes.

The nursery rhymes in the boxes above give elementary (and not very reliable) definitions of the traditional word classes. You will find somewhat less elementary (and possibly more reliable) definitions under the separate entries for each word class.

3. Sentence frames.

This, as far as I know, is an invention of Charles Carpenter Fries (1952). We can construct a sentence frame such as the following and say that any word that fits into the blank space is a determiner.

_____ horse galloped along.   [a   the   one   our   Pat's ...]
DETERMINER

The square-bracketed words fit into the frame and they are, therefore, determiners.

We can also create sentence frames for other word classes.

4. Associated words.

Adjectives, and also adverbs, are words that associate with expressions of intensity (bold).

... **rather** big	... **very** quickly
ADJECTIVE	ADVERB
... **extremely** useful	... **highly** probable
ADJECTIVE	ADJECTIVE

You can be sure that the underlined words, because of their association with the words in bold (called "intensifiers"), are either adjectives or adverbs, because they associate with intensifiers.

5. Derivational affixes.

The prefix *en–* and the suffix *–ify* are typical of verbs. Hence the following words that feature these affixes are likely to be verbs.

PREFIX *EN–*:	endanger	engrave	engulf
SUFFIX *–IFY*:	terrify	notify	rectify

Other derivational affixes identify members of other word classes. See AFFIX.

6. Inflectional affixes.

You can be sure that any word that forms its plural with the inflectional affix *–s* (or *–es*) is a noun. Thus, all of the following plural words are nouns.

gardens	trees	bushes	flowers	boxes

Other inflectional affixes identify members of other word classes. See AFFIX.

7. A word of caution.

To identify the class membership of a word, you often have to look at it in the environment of a sentence. Thus, for example, the affix *–s* may be misleading. A word with that affix may, in different contexts, be a noun or a verb.

There are flowers in my garden.	This bush flowers in spring.
PLURAL NOUN	SINGULAR VERB

Even without affixes, words get their class membership from their environment.

I <u>like</u> chocolate.
VERB

There is nobody quite <u>like</u> you.
PREPOSITION

We now look at a text that contains members of the nine word classes dealt with above.

Speak	roughly	to	your	little	boy,
VERB	ADVERB	PREP	DET	ADJ	NOUN

And	beat	him	when	he	sneezes;
CONJ	VERB	PRON	CONJ	PRON	VERB

He	only	does	it	to	annoy,
PRON	ADV	VERB	PRON	ADV	VERB

Because	he	knows	it	teases.
CONJ	PRON	VERB	PRON	VERB

CHORUS
NOUN

"Wow,	wow,	wow!"
INTERJ	INTERJ	INTERJ

(Lewis Carroll, *Alice in Wonderland.*)

See ADJECTIVE, ADVERB, CONJUNCTION, DETERMINER, INTERJECTION, NOUN, PREPOSITION, PRONOUN, VERB.

WORD FORMATION—See AFFIX.

YES-NO QUESTION—See QUESTION TYPES.

ZERO—See NULL ELEMENT.

ZEUGMA—See FIGURE OF SPEECH.

Bibliography

Beswick, Wayne A. 1996. *The Pleasure of Being: Culture, Dialogue and Genre*. Canberra: unpublished doctoral thesis.

Blake, NF. 1988. *Traditional English Grammar and Beyond*. London: Macmillan.

Bloomfield, Leonard. 1933. *Language*. New York: Holt, Reinhart and Winston.

Bolinger, Dwight. 1971. *The Phrasal Verb in English*. Cambridge, Mass: Harvard University Press.

Burchfield, Robert W. 1985. *The English Language*. Oxford: OUP.

Burchfield, Robert W. 1992. *Points of View*. Oxford: OUP.

Burchfield, Robert W (editor). 1996. *The New Fowler's Modern English Usage*. Oxford: OUP.

Butt, David; Fahey, Rhondda; Spinks, Sue; Yallop, Colin. 1995. *Using Functional Grammar: An Explorer's Guide*. Sydney: Macquarie University.

Chalker, Sylvia and Weiner, Edmund. 1994. *The Oxford Dictionary of English Grammar*. Oxford: Clarendon Press.

Chomsky, Noam. 1957. *Syntactic Structures*. The Hague: Mouton de Gruyter.

Chomsky, Noam. 1965. *Aspects of the Theory of Syntax*. Cambridge, Mass: MIT Press.

Chomsky, Noam. 1966. *Cartesian Linguistics: A Chapter in the History of Rationalist Thought*. New York: University Press of America.

Chomsky, Noam. 1993. *Lectures on Government and Binding: The Pisa Lectures*. Seventh edition. The Hague: Mouton de Gruyter.

Chomsky, Noam. 1997 [1995]. *The Minimalist Program*. Cambridge, Mass: MIT Press.

Close, RA. 1975. *A Reference Grammar for Students of English*. London: Longman.

Collerson, John. 1994. *English Grammar: a Functional Approach*. Newtown: Primary English Teaching Association.

Cook, VJ. 1988. *Chomsky's Universal Grammar: An Introduction*. Oxford: Blackwell.

Cook, VJ and Newson, Mark. 1996. *Chomsky's Universal Grammar: An Introduction*. Second edition. Oxford: Blackwell.

Crystal, David. 1995. *The Cambridge Encyclopedia of the English Language*. Cambridge: CUP.

Crystal, David. 1997. *A Dictionary of Linguistics and Phonetics*. Fourth edition. Oxford: Blackwell.

De Joia, Alex and Stenton, Adrian. 1980. *Terms in Systemic Linguistics: a Guide to Halliday*. London: Batsford.

Eggins, Suzanne. 1994. *An Introduction to Systemic Functional Linguistics*. London: Pinter.

Flexner, SB (editor in chief). 1987. *The Random House Dictionary of the English Language*. Second edition, unabridged. New York: Random House.

Fries, Charles Carpenter. 1952. *The Structure of English: an Introduction to the Construction of English Sentences*. New York: Harcourt, Brace and Company.

Galèas, Grazia Crocco. 1998. "Scalar Categorization." Internet: *The Web Journal of Modern Language Linguistics 3*.

Givón, Talmy. 1993. *English Grammar: A Function-Based Introduction*. In 2 volumes. Amsterdam: John Benjamins.

Greenbaum, Sidney. 1988. *Good English and the Grammarian*. London: Longman.

Greenbaum, Sidney. 1996. *The Oxford English Grammar*. Oxford: OUP.

Halliday, MAK. 1975. *Learning How to Mean: Explorations in the Development of Language*. London: Edward Arnold.

Halliday, MAK. 1994. *An Introduction to Functional Grammar*. Second edition. London: Edward Arnold.

Halliday, MAK and Hasan, R. 1976. *Cohesion in English*. London: Longman.

Halliday, MAK and Martin, JR (editors). 1981. *Readings in Systemic Linguistics*. London: Batsford.

Hawkes, Terence. 1983. *Structuralism and Semiotics*. London: Routledge.

Hornby, AS. 1954. *A Guide to Patterns and Usage in English*. Oxford: OUP.

Horrocks, Geoffrey. 1987. *Generative Grammar*. London: Longman.

Jakobson, Roman and Halle, Morris. 1956. *Fundamentals of Language*. 's-Gravenhage: Mouton.

Jespersen, Otto. 1924. *Philosophy of Grammar*. New York: Henry Holt.

Jespersen, Otto. 1933. *Essentials of English Grammar*. New York: Henry Holt.

Jespersen, Otto. 1962. *Growth and Structure of the English Language*. Ninth edition. Oxford: Blackwell.

Kennedy Chris. 1982. "Systemic Grammar and Its Use in Literary Analysis." *Language and Literature: an Introductory Reader in Stylistics*. Edited by Ronald Carter. London: Unwin Hyman.

Leech, Geoffrey and Svartvik, Jan. 1975. *A Communicative Grammar of English*. Harlow: Longman.

Lyons, John. 1981. *Language and Linguistics: An Introduction*. Cambridge: CUP.

Lyons, John. 1995. *Linguistic Semantics: An Introduction*. Cambridge: CUP.

Martin, James R. 1984. "Language, Register and Genre." *Children Writing*. Edited by F Christie. Geelong: Deakin University Press.

Martin, James R. 1992. *English Text: System and Structure*. Amsterdam: John Benjamins.

Martin, James R; Matthieson, Christian; Painter, Clare. 1997. *Working with Functional Grammar*. London: Edward Arnold.

McArthur, Tom (editor). 1992. *Oxford Companion to the English Language*. Oxford: OUP.

Millward, CM. 1988. *A Biography of the English Language*. New York: Holt, Rinehart and Winston.

Morley, GD. 1985. *Introduction to Systemic Grammar*. London: Macmillan.

Nunan, David. 1993. *Introducing Discourse Analysis*. London: Penguin.

Onions, CT. 1971. *Modern English Syntax*. Revised edition. London: Routledge and Kegan Paul.

Poynton, C. 1984. "Names as vocatives: forms and functions." *Nottingham Linguistics Circular* 13.

Quirk, Randolph; Greenbaum, Sidney; Leech, Geoffrey; Svartvik, Jan. 1985. *A Comprehensive Grammar of the English Language*. London: Longman.

Radford, Andrew. 1997. *Syntax: a Minimalist Introduction*. Cambridge: CUP.

Richards, Jack; Platt, John; Weber, Heidi. 1985. *Longman Dictionary of Applied Linguistics*. London: Longman.

Saussure, Ferdinand de. 1966. *Course in General Linguistics*. Edited by Charles Bally and Albert Sechehaye; translated by Wade Baskin. New York: McGraw-Hill.

Simpson, John A and Weiner, Edmund SC (editors). 1992. *Oxford English Dictionary*. Second edition. Oxford: OUP.

Skeat, Walter W. 1882. *A Concise Etymological Dictionary of the English Language.* Oxford: Clarendon Press.

Stern, George. 1994. *Choosing Your Mark: a Guide to Good Expression and Punctuation.* Canberra: Australian Government Publishing Service.

Stern, George. 1997a. *The English Tenses and Aspects.* Canberra: Australian National University.

Stern, George. 1997b. *Using Grammar in Your Prose.* Canberra: Australian Government Publishing Service.

Stern, George. 1998. *An Outline of English Grammar: with Practices and Key.* Canberra: Australian National University.

Stern, George; Bolitho, Robert; Lutton, Russell. 1993. *The Guide to Australian Usage and Punctuation.* Melbourne: Collins Dove.

Thomas, Owen. 1965. *Transformational Grammar and the Teacher of English.* New York: Holt, Rinehart and Winston.

Trask, Robert Lawrence. 1993. *A Dictionary of Grammatical Terms in Linguistics.* New York: Routledge.

Wardhaugh, Ronald. 1993. *Investigating Language: Central Problems in Linguistics.* Oxford: Blackwell.

Williams, Geoff. 1994. *Using Systemic Grammar in Teaching Young Learners: an Introduction.* Melbourne: Macmillan.